Love After
The Tale of Genji

Rewriting the World of the Shining Prince

Harvard East Asian Monographs 286

Love After The Tale of Genji

Rewriting the World of the Shining Prince

Charo B. D'Etcheverry

Published by the Harvard University Asia Center
and distributed by Harvard University Press
Cambridge (Massachusetts) and London, 2007

Printed in the United States of America

The Harvard University Asia Center publishes a monograph series and, in coordination with the Fairbank Center for East Asian Research, the Korea Institute, the Reischauer Institute of Japanese Studies, and other faculties and institutes, administers research projects designed to further scholarly understanding of China, Japan, Vietnam, Korea, and other Asian countries. The Center also sponsors projects addressing multidisciplinary and regional issues in Asia.

Library of Congress Cataloging-in-Publication Data

D'Etcheverry, Charo B.

Love after the Tale of Genji : rewriting the world of the shining prince / Charo B. D'Etcheverry.

p. cm. -- (Harvard east asian monographs ; 286)

Includes bibliographical references and index.

ISBN-13: 978-0-674-02507-3 (hardcover : alk. paper)

ISBN-10: 0-674-02507-5 (hardcover : alk. paper)

1. Japanese literature--Heian period, 794–1185--History and criticism. 2. Courts and courtiers in literature. 3. Rokujo Saiin no Senji, d. 1092. Sagoromo monogatari. 4. Sugawara no Takasue no Musume, b. 1008. Hamamatsu Chunagon monogatari. I. Title.

PL747.25.C7D48 2007

895.6'09358--dc22

2006038258

Index by the author

Printed on acid-free paper

Last figure below indicates year of this printing

17 16 15 14 13 12 11 10 09 08 07

For my parents,
John and Mary D'Etcheverry
and my late great-uncle,
John Melanson

Acknowledgments

A number of people and institutions have supported the research that became this book, both directly and through the less obvious means of example and friendship. This second list includes many teachers and colleagues, but especially Edwin Cranston, Doris Bargen, Robert Khan, Edith Sarra and the late Earl Miner. I am very happy to thank them here. I also enjoy a host of more specific debts. Atsuko Sakaki introduced me to *The Tale of the Hamamatsu Middle Counselor* in a graduate seminar at Harvard. Mitani Kuniaki and Mitamura Masako, who directed a Japan Foundation doctoral grant in 1997–98, read *The Tale of Sagoromo* and other texts with me in their classes in Yokohama. Mitani also pushed me to weigh late Heian's debt to *The Tale of Genji,* a task I took up—after completing a dissertation on the later tales' court setting with the wonderful Richard Okada at Princeton—during a postdoctoral fellowship at the Reischauer Institute of Japanese Studies in 2002–2003.

My colleagues at the University of Wisconsin-Madison, notably James O'Brien and William Nienhauser, Jr. commented on this work, while the UW's Graduate School Research Council provided summer funding for it. Chapter 2 is revised from an article originally published by *Monumenta Nipponica,* Sophia University, 2004. Kate Wildman Nakai first edited the material in the article, and the journal's referees gave good advice for improving it. Finally, William Hammell and the two anonymous manuscript referees at the Harvard University Asia Center suggested countless helpful revisions to the book manuscript. For the errors and idiosyncrasies that remain I apologize first to my husband, Jody Shaw, who will no doubt have to hear about them as I do and without the consolations of scholarly interest.

Contents

Reference Matter

Figures

Note on Conventions

Although this book will appeal mainly to scholars of Japanese literature, it is also written with a broader audience in mind. *The Tale of Genji*, which all three tales discussed here deliberately rewrite, attracts readers from all walks of life, and it seems plausible that some of these people would enjoy knowing what earlier fans had to say about it. I have therefore tried to make my analyses as accessible as possible without alienating specialists. Most of my concessions to the casual reader are quite common. When I refer to a Japanese term, for example, I first give the English translation, then the transliterated original; however, in the case of poems (usually quoted in their entirety) I reverse this order in deference to convention. Where possible I key my translations to published versions so that readers unversed in Japanese can consult the "original" if they wish; I also retain familiar details like Tyler's English versions of *Genji* chapter titles throughout. Finally, I have included simplified genealogical charts in each chapter, as well as basic plot summaries of the later tales and a glossary at the end of the book. I encourage all readers, casual and academic alike, to review these materials before perusing the study itself.

I break more significantly with precedent in limiting discussion of earlier critical work on these tales to analyses that treat their relationship to *Genji*, the particular subject of this study. This is a strategic decision, made for the sake of coherence as well as accessibility, defined here as keeping the book to a reasonable length. Generally, authors of introductory studies begin by reviewing earlier research in order to contextualize their own contributions. Since I am writing about multiple texts, however, and ones that have generally been treated independently when analyzed at length, a broad literature review would have been both unwieldy and needlessly chaotic. Instead, I chose to focus on the major common criticism of these tales: that they borrow from *Genji* without purpose or art. I felt that a study addressing this complaint, a stunning reversal of the premodern view that these texts were *Genji*'s best successors, had the greatest chance of both attracting readers and stimulating further work on the later texts. I find this approach appropriate to the subject, as it mirrors the tales' own selective engagements with *Genji*. It is in any case pragmatic, a stance that the authors of all three texts—and Murasaki herself—might appreciate.

Love After The Tale of Genji

Rewriting the World of the Shining Prince

INTRODUCTION
Lights Out in Heian

Once his light vanished, there could hardly be anyone dazzling enough among his heirs to take his place. Mentioning the retired emperor would be irreverent, and while the current third prince and the princess's young lord, who had grown up with him, were much admired and certainly impressive, they did not belong in the ranks of the truly brilliant. However, because of that storied relationship, their rather ordinary elegance and good looks occasioned even greater praise than Genji had enjoyed in his own youth.

—Murasaki Shikibu, *The Tale of Genji*

These lines, the introduction to "The Perfumed Prince" (Niou hyōbukyō or Niou miya) chapter of Murasaki Shikibu's *The Tale of Genji* (*Genji monogatari*, ca. 1000), are perhaps the most notorious in all of Japanese fiction. After 41 chapters and 60 fictional years, Murasaki suddenly and inexplicably abandons Hikaru Genji, the "shining" prince introduced as her hero at the start of the tale. No more contests at his Rokujō mansion, known for its quasi-imperial collection of women; Genji, like his Heian (794–1185) era audience, is polygamous, although unlike his peers he lives with his lovers. Normally only emperors avoided the Heian custom of visiting women in their homes. No more tributes from the true palace, which names Genji an "equivalent retired emperor" (*jun dajō tennō*) in honor of his impending fortieth birthday. The man responsible for this promotion, referred to above as "the retired emperor" but better known as Reizei, grants the distinction when he learns that the commoner is actually his father; that is why the narrator calls mentioning Reizei in her list of Genji's heirs "irreverent." In fact, Murasaki Shikibu pulls Genji from the story without even a funeral. The last time the reader sees the hero, in fictional terms, is eight years earlier, when he is mourning someone else.

Murasaki does not, however, end her tale here. Instead, as the excerpt reveals, she abruptly turns to Genji's heirs, particularly the "perfumed" prince Niou and his childhood playmate, the "fragrant" captain Kaoru.[1] As their scent-oriented nicknames suggest, Kaoru and Niou lack most or all of Genji's radiance, a common metaphor for imperial right in a culture that claimed descent from the Sun Goddess.[2] As a result, and as the excerpt stresses with its series of luminous metaphors ("light," "dazzling," "brilliant"), the tale grows darker with Genji's death. The last ten chapters are set in a town literally homophonous with gloom (Uji), where Kaoru, like Genji in his later years, frequently talks of abandoning the world and becoming a monk. Niou and his friend do inherit some things from Genji. Kaoru, born late in the hero's life and actually a rival's bastard, shares the same natural fragrance as Genji, a gift that nicely captures the boy's obsession with his parentage. In Heian poetry, as in reality, scent is the sense most closely linked with memory and thus with concern for the past.[3] Genji's grandson Niou, meanwhile, has the hero's skill in seduction and some share of his charisma. Etymologically, *niou* (which can also be written with the character for *kaoru*) means to blossom or to become red, like a budding flower in springtime. While Niou gets the nickname for his rich blends of incense, it thus suggests an additional sense of visual splendor and so a connection to Genji's radiance. The imperial connotation holds as well. At the close of the tale, Niou is well on his way to becoming crown prince, an appointment that Genji loses (along with his princely rank) at the narrative's start. Even the later characters' shortcomings prove useful, at least for Niou, who sneaks past some guards to steal Kaoru's mistress by copying his friend's scent. Despite his reputation for gallantry, Genji himself could not have managed this escapade. For better or worse, every character in the tale knows when he is dealing with the "shining prince,"[4] as a telling scene from the chapter "The Green Branch" (Sakaki) illustrates. In this passage, Genji—sneaking out of the rooms of his brother's lover and so carefully disguised to avoid detection—is nonetheless recognized through a thick morning mist since he "cuts a figure like no one else."[5] The contrast with Niou and Kaoru could hardly be greater. While these friends, apparently on the strength of their ties to Genji, enjoy greater recognition at their age than did the hero, they are also—quite unlike Genji—easily confused. Even the later characters' nicknames indicate their interchangeability, through the words' common olfactory meaning and shared representation in Chinese script. Moreover, Kaoru's name, too, once had visual significance. At root the verb *kaoru* denotes the trembling of a flame, fog, or smoke, perhaps the sharpest contrast of all to Genji's cloudless brilliance and another reminder of Uji's darkness.

Perhaps influenced by the opening of "The Perfumed Prince," most critics prefer Genji to his heirs as well. With their nostalgia for the past and strong interest in Buddhism, "Kaoru-type" (*Kaoru-gata*) protagonists enjoyed a brief vogue during the gloomy medieval era, when religious leaders claimed that the "Latter Days of the Law" (*mappō*) had arrived to usher in a final era of social and spiritual decay. Readers who failed to take holy orders and flee to the hills, the idealized response to this crisis, could identify with the Kaoru-type's similar vacillations. Even medieval commentators, however, judged Kaoru and Niou inferior to Genji, claiming that someone had forged this section of the tale after allegedly losing a chapter called "Vanished into the Clouds" (Kumogakure) that described Genji's death. Admirers also distinguish this section from the so-called "main chapters" (*seihen*) of the tale, calling the former a series of "supplementary chapters" (*zokuhen*) possibly written by Murasaki's daughter Daini no Sanmi (ca. 1000–82). In recent years, however, Genji's heirs have once again become popular. Although the distinction between the two sections of the tale persists, critics now consider the latter chapters, particularly those set in Uji, more compelling than the earlier part of the narrative. The prose here is so nuanced, they argue, and the perspectives so intricate, as to constitute both a high-water mark for the tale genre and its "dissolution" into something different.[6] Kaoru and Niou, meanwhile, have been rehabilitated as the split halves of Genji's psyche, "second readings" of a hero still tantalizingly opaque when he exits the text.[7]

As scholars reassess this section of *Genji*, not surprisingly, the authorship debates have quieted. Murasaki's reputation, particularly her standing as the world's first novelist, largely rests on her psychological portraits, and none are more delicate than those found in the Uji chapters. This reappraisal of the tale extends to the actual Uji. Today, the city boasts a *Genji* museum and an annual stamp rally based on the tale's final chapters; aficionados can even go there to buy *Genji* beer. Nonetheless, nostalgia for Genji himself continues to shape Japan's literary histories, particularly the evaluation of the "late" Heian tales that came after him. These texts, written in the century and a half after *Genji*, have long been the Kaoru and Niou of the old scholarly consensus: judged similar to their precursor but at best of lesser interest. *The Tale of Sagoromo* (*Sagoromo monogatari*, ca. 1070), the most famous of these texts, was once even assigned, like the Uji chapters, to Murasaki's daughter.

There is, however, a key difference between Genji's heirs and Murasaki's. While Niou and Kaoru now rank beside Genji, at least in their critical standing, late Heian fiction remains overshadowed by the earlier tale. In fact, the reputation of these texts, and that of the late Heian era as a whole, has actually declined over time in direct proportion to *Genji*'s success. *Sagoromo* and the other two texts discussed in this study—the roughly coeval *Nezame at Night* (*Yoru no nezame*) and *The Tale of the Hamamatsu Middle Counselor* (*Hamamatsu chūnagon monogatari*)—were once considered *Genji*'s best successors, and in some ways even superior to Murasaki's tale. Today, however, only specialists read them, and some of these scholars warn that studying late Heian is a professional misstep. Critics often explain the problem as a material one: in part because of the turmoil that ended the Heian period, these texts are available only in damaged or otherwise compromised manuscripts. As a result, translations and even modern Japanese versions can be scarce and their publication somewhat arbitrary. *Hamamatsu,* for example—the least studied and historically least celebrated of the three tales listed—is currently the only one fully published in English. Moreover, as a result of these textual problems, it can be difficult to build the kinds of thematic arguments that made *Genji* itself famous.

The inaccessibility of late Heian texts, however, clearly also reflects a misplaced affection for *Genji* and its hero. Once again, "The Perfumed Prince" is suggestive on this point. After introducing Genji's heirs, the narrator returns to the hero, noting that: "There was none under heaven who did not long for the late minister, and no time when they lacked fuel for their grief. It was as if all the world's lamps had been doused."[8] This passage paints Genji's death as a loss of epic proportions in all areas of life. The narrator begins by recycling the light motif familiar from earlier in the tale; with Genji dead, all the lights in the "world" (*yo*)—a common metaphor for the political realm—seem to have gone out. She then compares Genji's death to that of the historical Buddha, alluding to the following line from the *Lotus Sutra,* the Heian aristocracy's favorite Buddhist text: "that night the Buddha entered extinction, as the fire dies out when the firewood is exhausted."[9] Here Genji's death is treated as a spiritual catastrophe on par with the loss of the founder of Buddhism, a particularly striking claim on the supposed eve of the "Latter Days of the Law." What is most interesting about the "Perfumed Prince" statement, however, is its romantic diction. People are described as "longing" (*koi*) for Genji, the same verb used for separated lovers. This is also one of the first words Murasaki uses to describe characters' yearning for the dead Kiritsubo,[10] an emotion which many critics argue motivates Genji's actions for the rest of the text. Moreover, the word "world"—noted above for its political valence—can also be glossed as the more intimate sphere of romantic relationships. In short, Genji's death also leaves people emotionally and perhaps even erotically bereft. One can trace a similar series of reactions to the "death"—that is, the conclusion—of *The Tale of Genji* itself. As I discuss below, scholars have tended to act as if Heian cultural contributions essentially ended with *Genji*, both in the genre of tale fiction and the broader world of the court. As a result, those "longing" for the tale and era have chosen to revisit *Genji* by reading or creating a variety of user-friendly editions and translations, rather than read the fiction that came after it. Finally, and most destructively, some readers—modern critics in particular—have treated late Heian tales as mere substitutes for *Genji*, tracing Murasaki's shadow in their plots and characters without considering the thematic uses to which these allusions are put. All three responses resemble the reaction to Genji's disappearance in "The Perfumed Prince." By fixating on one loss, and allowing it to color their view of other subjects—in effect, acting as if "all the world's lamps had been doused"—these readers deny themselves the joy of discovering new favorites. Moreover, they do a disservice to the later texts. As Murasaki herself warned, any search for a substitute risks ruining both parties, particularly when the desired replacement, like Niou and Kaoru, emits a less obvious light than its precursor.

Saying Goodbye to Genji

As this introduction suggests, readers have always been fascinated with Genji, even during the Heian period. According to Murasaki's diary, Fujiwara Michinaga (966–1027), the era's leading politician, took time from his duties as chancellor (*kanpaku*) to steal a draft of the tale for one of his daughters, even though fiction was nominally considered beneath male interest. Courtiers were supposed to read and compose poetry, formal diaries, and histories, genres borrowed (and transformed) from China and thus retaining a certain Continental prestige. When men did write tales, as did a number of Murasaki's predecessors, they supposedly considered women and children their main audience. *Genji,* however, was clearly a special case from the beginning, since Murasaki also records in her diary that Emperor Ichijō (r. 986–1011), Michinaga's son-in-law, compared the tale to an official history, revealing that he was both familiar with her text and impressed enough to rank it with more prestigious subjects. *Genji* was even more popular, however, with its target audience: aristocratic women. Sugawara Takasue's daughter (b. 1008), better known as the Sarashina diarist, repeatedly describes herself neglecting her prayers to daydream about the hero, fantasizing that he will whisk her away to a mountain village for an annual visit. Once she obtains a copy of the tale, meanwhile, the diarist exults that "even the rank of empress"—supposedly the zenith of Heian female ambition—"is nothing compared to it."[11] The *Genji* beer mentioned earlier, as well as *Genji*-themed graphic novels, pop-music groups, and even a line of Mary Kay toiletries, testifies to a similar enthusiasm in the modern era. *Genji* today is practically a brand name, and as such has been attractive even to those who have never actually read it.

Genji's reception history, however, also has another thread, one that is particularly important for understanding late Heian fiction. As the excerpts from "The Perfumed Prince" illustrate, Murasaki deliberately encourages reflection on her hero, inviting readers to assess his life before following Niou and Kaoru to Uji. This technique appears as early as the tale's opening line, which speculates "during what kind of reign it might have been"[12] that the story is set. Unlike earlier examples of court fiction, which typically begin with a formulaic description of the main characters and their parentage, this question urges the reader to become involved in the story and perhaps even to seek historical models for it.[13] More directly, Murasaki uses her various narrators—positioned as court attendants of varying ranks and experience—to present competing views of the hero throughout the tale. For instance, at the end of the introductory "Paulownia Pavilion" (Kiritsubo) chapter, one narrator relates that Genji is known as the "shining lord" (*hikaru kimi*), a nickname coined by a Korean physiognomist to describe the hero's good looks and talents. The nickname, source of the "shining prince" sobriquet, recapitulates the chapter's many admiring descriptions of the hero, although it also hints at trouble. Since Genji is no longer a "lord" in the strict sense of the word, his imperial charisma and impulses are at best inappropriate. The physiognomist recognizes this when he later worries that "there is a contradiction"[14] between Genji's quality and his station, but the nickname is nonetheless meant as a compliment. The narrator of the subsequent "Broom Tree" (Hahakigi) chapter, by contrast, begins her episode with an assault on the hero's character and reputation.

> The Shining Genji, awe-inspiring in name only, had many flaws worth mentioning, but the person who shared these romantic indiscretions with the world, when Genji himself tried to hide them for fear of earning a name for frivolity, really didn't know when to stop. Still, given how greatly Genji feared gossip and tried to keep up appearances, there really wasn't anything very interesting to tell. How Minor Captain Katano would have laughed![15]

Unlike the narrator of the first chapter, this woman does not defer to Genji. She casts both his behavior and heroic stature into question, pointing out first the hypocrisy with which he hides his affairs and then noting that these affairs are so boring that Captain Katano, the amorous hero of a nonextant tale, would have found them ridiculous. Most tellingly, this narrator mocks Genji's nickname, deliberately reminding the reader that, far from being a "lord," the hero is a mere commoner, newly-minted or not. The most this woman offers in Genji's defense is the tacit admission that she, like whoever first spread these rumors, doesn't "know when to stop"—in short, that she is a gossip. The real fault, by implication, is with Genji himself, who is equally undisciplined in courtship. This pattern of praising the hero only to criticize him recurs throughout the tale, culminating in the final juxtaposition of Genji's public glory as quasi-retired emperor with two private tragedies: his betrayal by the Third Princess, his new wife; and the death of his dearest love, the heroine or female protagonist Murasaki. In short, the *Genji* author constantly asks readers to weigh competing views of her hero and evaluate him for themselves. This pattern lends special significance to the strange silence about Genji's death. Some critics who think that "Vanished into the Clouds" never existed argue that Murasaki wrote the title, normally composed by later copyists, to force audiences to imagine the subject themselves, thus providing them with a final chance to review Genji's life.

Later readers inherited this spirit of inquiry from *Genji* along with the Heian audience's enthusiasm for it. Fujiwara Shunzei (1114–1204), the leading poet of his day, declared that anyone who tried to write verse "without looking at *Genji*" was "lamentable,"[16] raising the question of what exactly the poet should find there when he did. Since classical Japanese includes no title markers, Shunzei may have meant that poets should "look at" the hero himself before writing, although few critics interpret the line so narrowly. Either way, some reflection on the tale was clearly recommended. To aid in such study, Shunzei's equally famous son Teika (1162–1241) recreated what he considered the original *Genji* from several muddled lines of manuscripts. The task, as many critics point out, ignored a tradition of readers creating their own versions of court tales, but it also once again reflects Murasaki's analytical imperative: by choosing one lineage of *Genji*, Teika inevitably also sanctioned its content, in effect offering a judgment on both hero and text. Other critics, inspired by these efforts and a changed social climate, took the task of interpreting *Genji* still more seriously. As the Heian court faded and samurai came to power in the twelfth and thirteenth centuries, some aristocrats turned to tutoring the ruling elite in court texts, a profession that required both mastery of the canon and the creation of learned studies to prove it. Poets and scholars thus began writing *Genji* commentaries, generally summaries of key subplots and explanations of garbled or dated poetic allusions. In time, these commentaries, which probably served initially as both reading aids and credentialing tools, gained independent prestige as formal guides to the tale. Some of these writers, the first *Genji* specialists, even offered "secret teachings" (*hiden*) about the text only transmitted to their worthiest (or perhaps wealthiest) students: for instance, clarifications of such "riddles" (*nazo*) as the timing of the first, unnarrated meeting between Genji and Reizei's mother.

Despite their esoteric side, medieval commentaries on *Genji* also reveal a thirst for broader discussions of the tale, epitomized by the popular legends they collected about why Murasaki wrote it in the first place. One famous story contends that Murasaki was on retreat at Ishiyama Temple when she looked out on the moon over nearby Lake Biwa and, flipping over her sutra, began writing about Genji's exile to the Suma coast. A related tradition describes Murasaki herself as a bodhisattva or enlightened being who has pledged to help others attain enlightenment. Murasaki, the legend argued, had written *Genji* as an "expedient means" (*hōben*) to teach readers one of the key insights of Buddhism: life is suffering, and so suffering can only be avoided by renouncing a worldly life. Not all of the legends about *Genji*'s composition are so favorable. One story, perhaps responding to the Ishiyama legend, sends Murasaki to hell for distracting her readers from their prayers and defacing her sutra. A later text, while sympathetic to Murasaki, symbolically balances her actions at Ishiyama by having a woman copy a sutra on the back of a *Genji* manuscript.[17] Despite their differing perspectives on Murasaki, all of these stories offer religious interpretations of *Genji*, providing a view of the tale distinct from the textual focus of the poets' commentaries. Nō playwrights, composing for a somber, well-educated warrior audience, drew on both traditions.[18] *A Memorial Service for Genji* (*Genji kuyō*, perhaps fourteenth century), for example, opens with Murasaki's ghost forced to wander the afterlife for not giving Genji a funeral service, acknowledging the controversy over the supposed missing chapter. In the second act, however, a priest defends her by explaining in detail how the various chapter titles teach Buddhist truth, greatly expanding the earlier "expedient means" argument. Even artists got into the game, as the illustration on the cover of this book suggests. Medieval painters and Edo-period (1600–1868) woodblock carvers produced dozens of prints depicting scenes and characters from *Genji*, often relying on special abbreviated guides to the tale for advice on which episodes to illustrate. This artist, however—Tosa Mitsunobu (ca. 1434–1525)—chose an atypical scene. Instead of depicting Genji's first meeting with lowborn lover Yūgao, usually symbolized by the eponymous white flowers she sends him, the artist paints the morning after the lovers' first night together, when Genji is awakened by the sounds of Yūgao's neighbors saying prayers and fulling silk. This cacophony drives Genji, used to quieter neighborhoods, to take Yūgao to the abandoned estate where she later meets her death. While the scene retains the religious overtones emphasized by the nō theater, it thus foregrounds the role that the lovers' social gap plays in Yūgao's fate.[19]

The most noteworthy response to *Genji*, however, at least for understanding the late Heian tales, came from other creative writers. The earliest credited effort goes to Shunzei's Daughter (ca. 1175–1250?), sometimes identified as his granddaughter. She devotes a third of *The Untitled Book* (*Mumyōzōshi*, ca. 1201), a fictionalized conversation of court tales, to discussing favorite passages and characters from *Genji*. Not surprisingly, given her parentage, Shunzei's Daughter retains a commentary-like format and explores an essentially aesthetic issue, what one critic calls "the relationship of religious devotion and literary pleasures."[20] Writers in other genres, however, took a more imaginative approach toward *Genji*, while retaining this exegetical impulse. Medieval authors created several sequels about Genji's final years as a monk, including a tale called *"Vanished into the Clouds" in Six Chapters* (*Kumogakure rokujō*, fourteenth century)—one chapter presumably not being enough to satisfy several centuries of curiosity on the subject. Even Edo humorists leavened their parodies of *Genji* with critical comments. Ryūtei Tanehiko (1783–1842), for example, pokes fun at the authorship controversy in the title of his *Fake Murasaki and Hick Genji (Nise Murasaki inaka Genji*, 1829), while Ihara Saikaku (1642–93) concludes *Life of an Amorous Man* (*Kōshoku ichidai otoko*, 1682) with a mock explanation for the hero's disappearance. At the end of the story, Saikaku's aging "Genji"—identified as such by the character's precocious love affairs and the text's 54-chapter structure, identical to Murasaki's tale—sets sail for a final voyage to the legendary Isle of Women, complete with an endless supply of aphrodisiacs. Here, as in *Genji*, the reader never sees the hero's last years and death, although Saikaku implies something quite different than Genji's supposed end as a monk.

These popular interpretations of *Genji* continue into our own day, alongside and largely innocent of a veritable industry in scholarship on the text. Some books, like *The Tale of Genji: Women Who Don't Sleep* (*Genji monogatari: nemuranai himetachi*, 2000) and *A Psychological Reading of Men and Women in The Tale of Genji* (*Shinrigaku de yomitoku Genji monogatari no otoko to onna*, 1999),[21] resemble an updated version of Shunzei's daughter's work. Like the women in *The Untitled Book*, these authors, usually not specialists in *Genji*, select and discuss favorite characters for an enthusiastic audience. Performances based on the tale, like the female Takarazuka revue's *I Dreamed a Shallow Dream* (*Asaki yume mishi*) or the St. Louis Opera's *The Tale of Genji*, both of which premiered in 2000, can also be read in this way. They inevitably abridge the text according to the company's sense of what is thematically important. A recent Japanese film, starring a Takarazuka actress in the role of Genji, even introduces a glimpse of a female character swimming, a nod to modern appetites—or, more precisely, the modern erotic aesthetic—also found in Hollywood adaptations of Western classics. The various modern Japanese versions of *Genji* also share something with these popular responses to the tale, since the translator or graphic novelist usually foregrounds that aspect of the text that he or she considers most relevant to the target audience, whatever the "torment" to Murasaki herself.[22] Here, too, however, the most compelling analyses occur in actual fiction. *The Shining Genji Weekly (Shūkan Hikaru Genji,* 1998*),*[23] a spoof of Japanese women's magazines, is a case in point. Unlike other popular studies of *Genji,* this collection of "interviews" with *Genji* characters and character-based personality tests for the reader sold out several times in Tokyo bookstores the week it came out. Part of the appeal, presumably, is the *Weekly*'s creative explanation of readers' favorite parts of the tale, a skillful blend of exegesis and entertainment. Indeed, according to the clerks I questioned, the buyers were as likely to be high school or college students seeking study aids for *Genji* as average community members (typically retirees and housewives) looking for a diversion. The same syncretic spirit suffuses "Tales of *Genji*" (1991),[24] a playful summary of English scholarship on *Genji* written in the style of Boccaccio's *Decameron.* In short, like other great writers, Murasaki Shikibu has inspired many readers to turn author themselves, both to relive her story and to better explain it. In the process, these writers create commentaries that reach beyond specialists to embrace casual but keenly interested readers, the kind for whom Murasaki wrote in the first place.

Genji *and "Late" Heian*

As noted, Murasaki's prompts in "The Perfumed Prince" and elsewhere have encouraged many readers to reflect on *Genji,* including the medieval poets whose formal commentaries became the basis of modern academic work on the tale, both in their specific explanations of confusing details and their generally philological approach to the text. Intriguingly, some of these men—including Teika—also wrote tales, suggesting that even they found the commentary format too restrictive to exhaust their responses to court fiction. While concrete evidence for the attribution is rare, scholars generally agree that Teika composed *The Tale of the Matsura Prince* or *The Tale of the Matsura Palace* (*Matsura no miya monogatari,* ca. 1190), a text that draws on several earlier tales, including *Genji, Hamamatsu,* and *Sagoromo.* Set in the late seventh century and taking place almost entirely in China, *Matsura* is generally seen as rejecting Heian conventions in favor of illustrating one of Teika's pet poetic concepts: "ethereal beauty" (*yōen*).[25] However, Teika's decision to recycle certain character types and plot patterns while eschewing others clearly constitutes a judgment on earlier fiction. Moreover, given Teika's writings on the technique of "allusive variation" (*honkadori*)—the art of putting lines from old poems to fresh use in new ones—and his father's advice that poets study *Genji*, *Matsura* arguably serves as a model for incorporating fictional materials into one's writing.[26] Here, too, *Genji* is treated differently than the other tales; the allusions to it are less direct than in other cases, although this may have been because Teika considered *Genji* already "overworked."[27] The salient point, however, is that Teika—author of numerous poetic treatises—seems to have found tale fiction a useful vehicle for conveying critical opinions, perhaps about the genre itself.

Whatever Teika's intentions or later influence involving writing about *Genji*, Murasaki's text was certainly explored by an earlier group of tale authors: late Heian women. Thanks in large part to *Genji*'s success, the tale genre enjoyed an explosion in popularity and authorship in the late eleventh and twelfth centuries. Records like *The Untitled Book* and *Collection of Wind-Blown Leaves* (*Fūyō wakashū*, 1271), an anthology of tale poetry, suggest that as many as two hundred new tales appeared after *Genji*, although only ten or so percent remain extant. Moreover, scholars believe that many if not most of these writers were women, making late Heian (sometimes subdivided into a further, "final" stage) the golden age of female-authored court fiction. Nearly all of these texts draw on *Genji*, using everything from actual lines of the tale to plot patterns and, as noted earlier, character types. By the early medieval era, this practice—apparently successful enough to keep winning audiences—was so pronounced that modern scholars now refer to that period as the age of "old-fashioned" or "counterfeit" tales (*giko monogatari*), the valence of the term depending upon the scholar who uses it.

In the case of late Heian, however, three tales—*Sagoromo, Hamamatsu,* and *Nezame*—also won early followings of their own. In his *Tale Poetry Contest in Two Hundred Rounds* (*Monogatari nihyakuban uta awase*, ca. 1206), a paper contest matching *Genji* poems against those from other texts, Teika gives these tales pride of place, citing them more frequently than any other sources. Moreover, he limits the entire first half of the match to *Sagoromo* and *Genji*, earning this part of the text the alternate title of the *Genji-Sagoromo Poetry Contest. Wind-Blown Leaves* reprises the pattern, again including more poems from these tales than any other post-*Genji* pieces. Individual tributes, discussed more specifically in the following chapters and ranging from picture scrolls to modern novels, are equally impressive. Shunzei's Daughter summarizes the response best in her *Untitled Book.* After the characters have discussed the tales' individual merits, one woman remarks: "I have seen so many things come out recently that improve upon the style and structure of the old tales, but still nothing compares to *Nezame, Sagoromo,* and *Hamamatsu.*"[28] In short, early medieval readers considered these three tales the best of the best. They were so well-liked, in fact, that although *Hamamatsu* and *Nezame* lost large chunks of their narratives early in their histories—itself a sign of heavy handling, and so, popularity—they continued to be read. *Sagoromo,* meanwhile, inspired dozens of variants, tributes that not even the tale's early commentators (apparently more tolerant than Teika) attempted to put in their place.

This reputation for excellence, or at least special interest, clearly stems from a variety of sources. As the wide range of individual tributes suggests, each of these tales exercises distinctive charms, including unusual plots. *Sagoromo,* which punctuates its "Kaoru-type" hero's love affairs with supernatural apparitions, often reads like a fairy tale; in one passage a heroine leaps into the sea only to be saved at the last minute by her long-lost, one-eyed brother, in some versions by miraculously landing in his tiny boat. *Hamamatsu* sends its own Kaoru-type hero to China, sidelined in Heian life and fiction for a century, to discover that his father has been reincarnated there as that country's Third Prince. Once there, he begins a secret romance with the Prince's mother, later reborn to her own half-sister back in Japan. *Nezame,* finally, pits its female hero against her lover's breathtakingly wicked mother-in-law. To escape her tormentor, the protagonist eventually resorts to faking her own death, resurfacing only to assist her son in his own frustrated love affair. In addition to these plot details, the tales also feature more technical merits: for instance, *Sagoromo*'s celebrated poetry and *Nezame*'s unprecedented illumination of its heroine's thoughts.

Part of the success of these tales also stems, however, from their creative use of *Genji*. As noted above, later fiction borrows heavily from Murasaki's tale. Countless texts, for example, take as their heroes new commoners like Genji or describe searches for substitute-lovers, a key *Genji* topic. *Sagoromo, Hamamatsu,* and *Nezame,* however, also comment on *Genji* in the sense noted earlier: that is, by reinterpreting or otherwise questioning their source. *Sagoromo,* for example, opens with its hero looking out on a pond, wondering if "the Shining Genji had felt like this when he spoke of throwing himself into the blossoms' abyss."[29] While it is unclear whether Sagoromo is referring to Genji as a fictional character or as a historical figure—that is, as someone who lived in the same world that he does—the line clearly demands both knowledge of Murasaki's tale and a willingness to interpret it. One evaluates Sagoromo differently depending on whether he (the reader) believes that the hero understands Genji correctly—or, for that matter, whether the reader is sympathetic to the relevant actions of Genji himself. This invitation to readers to reflect on the story before them is not an innovation. Not only does Murasaki herself, as noted earlier, solicit judgments on her hero. She also—like most Heian writers—does the same with the texts she herself uses to lend her tale depth. This practice, reminiscent of the "allusive variation" technique noted earlier, marks premodern Japanese texts in general, including its accepted masterpieces. Allusion to "old words," as Shunzei and Teika also put it, was a means for the truly gifted writer to display his "new heart."[30]

Unfortunately, modern critics have not usually credited post-*Genji* tales with this impulse, not even texts as formerly esteemed as the three late Heian works in question. Although *Sagoromo, Hamamatsu,* and *Nezame* probably first captured readers' interest with their variations on *Genji,* critics during the Meiji era (1868–1912) who were compiling Japan's first literary histories instead took these debts as signs of imaginative weakness. In the words of one Meiji writer, *Sagoromo* and its fellows were mere "epigones" (*aryū*) of Murasaki's work.[31] As noted earlier, this designation persists even within scholarly circles, the only groups that normally encounter these texts today. When specialists in Tokyo's Tale Research Group (Monogatari Kenkyūkai), for example, decided to create a new annotation of *Hamamatsu* in the 1990s, they announced their meetings in the margins of an insert to the group's monthly newsletter called *Foxes and Badgers' Words at a Glance* (*Korigen shūran*). The reference to foxes and badgers, the notorious tricksters of Japanese folklore, suits the casual news usually contained in the insert, such as music reviews and recent headlines on archaeological digs. In the case of the *Hamamatsu* annotation, however—presumably of serious interest to a tale research group—this location, the playful fonts with which the announcements were written, and their display in the margins humorously signal late Heian's minor status. Bystanders might call the problem simple "belatedness,"[32] the typical struggle of anyone coming after (or working on) a major writer or artist. Some Japanese specialists, however, have a darker name for it: the "*Genji* curse" (*Genji no jubaku*).[33] As this term suggests, the problem for *Sagoromo, Hamamatsu,* and *Nezame* is more than bad manuscripts or unfair comparisons, although these are clearly important. There is also a historiographical problem, implicit in the late Heian rubric itself.

The roots of this second problem lie in the story of yet another heir: Fujiwara Yorimichi (992–1074), son of Michinaga. As noted, Michinaga, also father of Murasaki's employer Empress Shōshi (988–1074), was an extremely successful politician, perhaps the most spectacularly so in Japanese history. Born into an already powerful clan, Michinaga continued the family's ingenious strategy of marrying daughters to emperors and so consolidating power; since children lived with their mothers, even crown princes could be expected to favor their grandfather, essentially yielding control of the court. Michinaga proved to be Japan's most adept practitioner of this "marriage politics" (*sekkan seiji*, literally "regent-chancellor politics"), a fact that he himself recognized. At the apogee of his power, with three daughters bearing the title of empress and a fourth married to a deposed crown prince, the drunken patriarch famously claimed that "this world is my world"[34] and likened himself to the full moon, a conventional symbol of spiritual enlightenment. Not coincidentally, Michinaga and his family were also lavish patrons of the arts, sponsoring everything from Buddhist temples and statuary (offered in exchange for an empress's safe delivery) to elegant concerts and poetry contests—and, of course, *Genji* itself. As a result, his life, like Genji's, has come to symbolize Heian culture at large. Scholars even list Michinaga as one of the models for Genji, a view that Murasaki—who famously complains about the noble in her diary—would probably have detested. Her contemporaries, however, clearly agreed. Describing the noble's death, the narrator of *A Tale of Flowering Fortunes* (*Eiga monogatari*, ca. 1092), a fictionalized biography of Michinaga and his family, remarks, "The entire world went black after Shaka [Sakyamuni, the historical Buddha] entered extinction. Now, with the world's torch extinguished, how many more people wander the long night in darkness?"[35] As with "The Perfumed Prince," the first allusion—a direct reference, this time—is to the death of the Buddha. Michinaga's death, like Genji's before him, is thus made to seem an even grander event, particularly during the long night of the Latter Days. It is hard not to hear, however, the echo from *Genji* itself. Once again, the death of a tale's protagonist plunges the entire world in darkness. According to some scholars, the passage even serves a similar function in *Flowering Fortunes* as the *Genji* passage, marking the end of the main plot: Michinaga's life.[36] Perhaps this should not come as a surprise.

While the authorship of *Flowering Fortunes* is still debated, tradition credits Akazome Emon (fl. 976–1041), one of Murasaki's fellow attendants in the household of the empress and so almost certainly familiar with *Genji* itself.

With Michinaga's death, the world passed to his son Yorimichi. Thanks to his sisters' marriages (arranged by Michinaga), Yorimichi debuted as the best-placed politician in Japanese history, ruling as either regent or chancellor for nearly fifty years. Like his father, Yorimichi also presided over an active cultural scene. The Phoenix Hall of the Byōdō-in—an image of which is still stamped on the back of Japanese 10-yen coins—grew from Yorimichi's luxurious villa on the banks of the Uji River. His three daughters, two of them actually grandchildren born to an adopted princess, sponsored numerous poem contests, the most since the storied reign of Emperor Murakami (r. 946–67), which Murasaki herself takes as one of *Genji*'s mythic backdrops. This hothouse atmosphere produced Japan's only known tale-composition contest (*monogatari awase*), a phenomenon that made the advent of tale criticism still more likely since this contest, like the verse-based events it neatly imitated, contained judgments.[37] But Yorimichi also had a problem, as his multiple adoptions suggest. He could not produce enough daughters to reprise Michinaga's success with marriage politics, a difficulty that grew acute when his sole imperial son-in-law, Emperor Go-Reizei (r. 1045–68), failed to sire a son.

Broader forces also undermined Yorimichi. The aristocracy's clan rivalries, for the most part suppressed in Michinaga's time, had begun to boil over. Powerful families clashed with each other and the newly assertive imperial line over the ownership and taxation of the great private estates in the provinces. Buddhist monks, armed and eager to benefit their temples and monasteries, marched to defend their own lands and to proclaim that the "Latter Days of the Law" had begun in 1052, midway through Yorimichi's tenure as chancellor. These social trends, magnified by natural disasters and, later, open warfare, convinced later historians that, in a sense, what Murasaki's narrator had claimed for Uji was true for court culture at large. As the *Flowering Fortunes* narrator states, the lights had gone out with Michinaga, leaving a "later" and lesser Heian in their wake. In short, late Heian history was an epigone, too. Scholars have branded the last ten chapters of *Flowering Fortunes*, which deal with Yorimichi and his heirs, as "negative and pessimistic" forgeries, perhaps even an outright imitation of the world of Uji.[38] Conversely, Yorimichi is sometimes offered as the model for Genji's own least impressive son, Yūgiri, who takes a backseat even to Niou and Kaoru in the "Perfumed Prince" transition. Whether or not this portrait is accurate is beside the point. Its resonance with the now abandoned view of the Uji chapters highlights another problem: the influence of this view of late Heian history on late Heian fiction.

Overview of the Study

Fortunately for late Heian, history has again begun to shift. In addition to the enthusiastic early reception of the three tales discussed here, there are several heartening critical precedents available. The Uji chapters, as noted, survived similar dismissals in both the medieval and modern eras to become one of the most critically acclaimed parts of *Genji*. The "supplementary" part of *Flowering Fortunes*, meanwhile—that is, the story of Yorimichi and his descendants—could make a similar recovery, since the English translation, while omitting these chapters, observes that they contain "the most extended piece of criticism and interpretation" in the entire tale.[39] This is the same element that rescued Uji, although since the criticism in this case involves the hero of the later chapters—Yorimichi—the analogy is not perfect. Most encouraging of all is the growing, transpacific interest in *Genji*'s reception. Several recent conferences and publications on this and related subjects in the United States alone suggest that late Heian will be in the scholarly spotlight for a while to come, a situation that should inspire a market for studies and translations of late Heian texts.[40] Serendipitously, an earlier vogue in medieval Japanese fiction means that many of the texts illustrating late Heian's own premodern reception are now available in printed annotations, giving experts in later periods a reason to look back. This split focus should help specialists and, eventually, casual readers keep *Genji*'s influence on court fiction in perspective. Finally, a similar revisionist movement in the study of Japanese history now has scholars throughout the world emphasizing the dynamism of late Heian social institutions and politics.[41] Together, these trends, swelled by a more general interest in noncanonical subjects, are lifting the *Genji* curse.

In this study, I hope to contribute to the general reevaluation of late Heian with a reassessment of specific subplots in *Sagoromo, Hamamatsu,* and *Nezame,* subplots that I argue deliberately comment on both *Genji* and the society that produced it. The later tales typically do this by creating simplified versions of a favorite *Genji* motif or storyline, forcing readers to confront Murasaki's less obvious insights about court life and then expanding on the subject. In this sense, the three tales provide fictional commentaries on *Genji* as well as insights into late Heian beliefs and social practices. Since this argument requires that readers have some knowledge of historical context, I begin the study by raising some general issues about the institutional venue of most tale authorship in the Heian period: the "Rear Court" (*kōkyū*) or imperial women's quarters. Chapter 1 describes the complex networks of patronage that sustained Rear Court households and made artistic and political success largely synonymous for male and female residents alike. After this discussion, which draws on research on the Western salon as well as Heian diaries, I examine the household that produced *Sagoromo,* the only one of the three later tales for which we can prove authorship. Since both *Nezame* and *Hamamatsu* are traditionally attributed to a writer from the same era—the reign of Yorimichi's son-in-law Go-Reizei—the discussion is also of more general interest.

In the next three chapters I focus in turn on each of the three late Heian tales mentioned here, analyzing their revisions of *Genji* and the thematic significance of these changes. Chapter 2 explores *Sagoromo*'s most popular subplot, the hero's love affair with the lowborn Asukai. Often cited as further evidence of the tale's imitation of *Genji*, this storyline actually offers a sharp critique of Heian romantic ideals. Here, unlike in Murasaki's text, the relationship is doomed strictly because of the lovers' social gap. Chapter 3 reexamines *Hamamatsu*'s often-derided reincarnation motif. A closer look at hero Chūnagon's relationship with a Chinese woman reveals that each character sees the other as a link to his family; in fact, family interests directly cause the affair, although the lovers themselves do not realize it. This story revisits *Genji*'s famed substitute motif and its inspiration, the Chinese poem "The Song of Unending Sorrow" (Changhenge; in Japanese, Chōgonka; 806) to emphasize the interdependence of individual and household interests in court life. Finally, Chapter 4 discusses *Nezame*'s revision of a key plot convention (*wakei*, that is, a formulaic sequence of events that structures a text) from *Genji*: the "noble in exile" story (*kishū ryūritan*). Murasaki herself plays with the convention, borrowed from *The Tale of the Bamboo Cutter* (*Taketori monogatari*, late ninth century), implying in several subplots that sequences of this kind—which suggest that suffering is both heroic and ultimately rewarded—always go amiss. *Nezame*, still more realistic and perhaps a bit cynical, suggests that life at home and court of itself leads to suffering, regardless of questions of guilt or innocence.

In the postscript, I briefly consider how research on modern fan writing might be useful in rethinking the relationships among Heian texts more generally. The idea comes from my students, who often raise the question after I point out late Heian parallels to *Genji* plots. Although the concept of fan fiction is helpful mainly for its emphasis on the communal ownership of favorite texts, it also implies the potential for fictional criticism of these texts. My conclusions, here and elsewhere, are tentative, since I have in no way exhausted the topic of late Heian's relationship to *Genji*. If this study merely encourages other critics—or casual readers—to pick up *Sagoromo*, *Hamamatsu*, and *Nezame* and start comparing for themselves, then this book will have accomplished exactly what I hoped.

ONE

The Woman's Court: Theory and Practice

Something of her charm for us is doubtless accidental. It lies in the fact that when she speaks of "houses such as you may see anywhere" we at once conjure up something graceful, fantastic, decorated with cranes and chrysanthemums, a thousand miles removed from Surbiton and the Albert Memorial. We give her, and luxuriate in giving her, all those advantages of background and atmosphere which we are forced to do without in England today. But we should wrong her deeply if, thus seduced, we prettified and sentimentalised [her] art. . . .

—Virginia Woolf, "THE TALE OF GENJI"

On the surface, the court fiction of Japan can look very alien to the modern reader. Men effortlessly compose love poems at the glimpse of a woman's sleeve, in the unlikely terms of ducks and dewdrops. Gods descend from the heavens to applaud court concerts, and bodhisattvas suddenly materialize either to ward off demons or to enjoy a particularly fine sutra chant. Occasionally, living souls even quit bodies to mount spirit attacks, usually on romantic rivals. While some of these scenes resonate with medieval European texts, most would startle non-Heian audiences; indeed, even modern Japanese readers marvel at them, as the parodies discussed in the introduction attest.

Beneath these strange trappings, however, we often find familiar themes, such as the pain of loss or frustrated ambition. Murasaki and her peers learned this interest from Japan's early poets. When Ki no Tsurayaki compiled his country's first formal verse anthology, *A Collection of Ancient and Modern Verse* (*Kokin wakashū*, 905), he prefaced it by explaining that "the seeds of Japanese poetry spring from the heart,"[1] equating the genre with self-expression. By focusing on these origins, in other words, the poet's mental state, Heian writers eventually developed the tale genre: first, as accounts of particular compositions, then as inquiries into more general emotional states. The narrative art ultimately proved more translatable; as noted in the introduction, *Genji* is now considered the world's first novel precisely for this attention to the (largely universal) inner life.

I begin with this point about thematic parallels because, as my epigraph warns, Heian's "accidental" charms can also obscure social correlates, correlates that can deepen our literary insights. When Virginia Woolf agreed to review Arthur Waley's early translation of *Genji*—according to *Vogue*'s editor, "the most-talked-of publication of the day"—she could have been forgiven a few illusions about Murasaki's world. The tale's length alone, stretching past a thousand tightly plotted pages in English translation, readily suggests what Woolf termed "advantages in background and atmosphere," perhaps even the "room of one's own" she argued for in her famous lectures on female authorship. Generations of readers have embraced similar fantasies about the writer, if not Heian itself. As noted in the introduction, one fourteenth-century commentator on the tale theorized that Murasaki had begun drafting the tale while on religious retreat near a lake—a tranquil scene quite different from his own, war-torn era. Those admirers who termed her a bodhisattva, meanwhile, implied an even easier composition: divine wit or inspiration, by definition distinct from earthly inconvenience. More broadly, the publishers of Liza Dalby's *The Tale of Murasaki* (2000), a fictionalized biography of the author, describe Heian itself as "an exotic world and time," "the most splendid in Japanese history," in fact, at least according to the dust jacket.

These assertions of difference are certainly understandable. Murasaki's world clearly diverged from interwar England and medieval Japan in many ways, just as it differs from our culture today. Moreover, some of these distinctions were clearly to Murasaki's benefit. Since Heian courtiers (like early modern Western scholars and diplomats) were expected to write in a learned tongue—in this case, classical Chinese—women were essentially ceded use of the native language, which came to be called the "woman's hand" (*onna-de*). In part because of this, as noted in the introduction, women also established an early monopoly on prose, a form better suited to extended reflection than the poetry that men (again, following Chinese models) were expected to write. Given these advantages, and Heian's relative peace, we can hardly fault later readers for envying the *Genji* author; Murasaki and her peers did the same thing when they sent their heroes to the "wild" provinces outside the capital and mythical countries without researching the trip. In most cases, the point of the comparison is the contrast with home—both for fantasy's sake and, more subtly, to proffer social criticism.

Introducing the Rear Court

Woolf herself did not fall for Japan's cranes and chrysanthemums, despite a few unflattering comments at England's expense. Her own ancestors, she observes dryly, were "perpetually fighting, now men, now swine," while Murasaki "danced."[2] Instead, as the excerpt suggests, she cautioned readers against "prettifying" *Genji* by confusing both its foreignness and what she later calls the author's "gifts for invention" with historical snapshots. The British writer might, however, have been amused to learn just how far wrong even her own admiring portrait of Murasaki's world went. To begin with, there was that issue of privacy. Far from enjoying their own rooms to dance in, the vast majority of Heian's (known) women writers lived and worked in a very public institution called the "Rear Court" (also known as the Rear Palace), established as part of the state-funded bureaucracy of the court during the Yamato era (300–710). Some scholars equate the term with an imperial harem, since it literally refers to the consort's pavilions "behind the palace." By Murasaki's time, however, the rubric also encompassed the households of the crown prince, retired emperor, and other imperial family members, including the princesses who served as vestal virgins at the distant Kamo and Ise shrines.

The Rear Court survived the fall of Murasaki's world and the numerous political transitions of the medieval and Edo eras. In fact, the imperial household only completely dismantled the institution in 1952, after Michiko, the first commoner empress, opted not to assign her children the traditional Rear Court wet nurse.[3] Its zenith, however, was unmistakably in the Heian period, both in terms of its numbers and social prominence. Even highly abridged Japanese dictionaries, which gloss the term as any gathering of imperial consorts (including the seraglios of the West), refer readers back to the Heian court, reflecting the imperial family's contemporary importance. Thanks to the large number of women writers working there—most of whom were employed, like Murasaki, as private attendants—we know quite a bit about this epoch in Rear Court history. In fact, in some ways we know more about these women than about the emperors themselves, a situation worth noting given the considerable gender gap in early Japanese history; most official sources, such as courtier diaries and imperial chronicles, describe only formal court events, mostly planned and orchestrated by men. Even genealogies refer to non-imperial women only as the daughters or wives of prominent courtiers, or with sobriquets based on the relative's court rank: the "Kiyo(wara) minor counselor" Sei Shōnagon (ca. 966–after 1017), for example, or the "Fujiwara (in the) Ministry of Ceremonial"—that is, Tō Shikibu, better known as Murasaki Shikibu after her best-loved character.[4] Heian tales and memoirs, however, supplement these cold accounts of court business with portraits of their authors' private lives, what Murasaki wryly calls the "crucial historical details."[5]

Not surprisingly, these texts shed special light on life in the Rear Court. As Sei Shōnagon observes in *The Pillow Book* (*Makura no sōshi,* after 1000), women who remained at home and married—the more common course of action for well-born aristocrats—cannot really understand "the ways of the world" like a woman at court.[6] Shōnagon and others used their memoirs and miscellanies in part to educate such readers as well as entertain them (in Shōnagon's case, with the world's earliest set of top-ten lists, from "hateful things" like clumsy lovers to "delightful things" like cute babies and handsome priests).[7] In fact, so many Heian texts came from these women that critics refer to it as "attendant literature" (*nyōbō bungaku*) written by if not entirely for members of that class.[8] One large topic is the marriage politics discussed in the introduction, which turned consorts into "borrowed wombs" through their fathers' attempts to produce and manipulate a future emperor.[9] As various sources record, however, imperial women were at least as "ferocious" as were the courtiers themselves.[10] Dowager Empress Senshi (962–1001), Fujiwara Michinaga's sister, locked herself in the rooms of her son Emperor Ichijō until he agreed to grant her brother the office of chancellor. A contemporary took time from his court diary to call "Great" Kamo Priestess Senshi (964–1035), so termed for her five-reign tenure in the post, a "subservient old fox" who curried favor with Michinaga and his father despite her supposed isolation from the intrigues at court.[11]

Women writers often did the same thing. Both Murasaki's diary and *The Pillow Book* contain flattering portraits of the authors' patrons, usually read as propaganda pieces intended to upstage rival families; in this case, the rivalry was between the two writers. As noted in the introduction, Michinaga "scouted" Murasaki to help daughter Shōshi compete with Shōnagon's patron Teishi in the first place. The same point can be made for court fiction. *Genji* consort Kokiden, whose desire to promote and protect her son's imperial candidacy prompts her to murderously torment Genji's mother (lest she convince the emperor to favor the hero), all but sends the hero into exile when he sleeps with her sister—the crown prince's favorite. While readers generally see Kokiden as a simple villain, critics take her as further evidence of the Rear Court's corrosive internal competition—although, it must be admitted, this has not helped to improve her reputation.[12] The animated version of the tale, produced in consultation with *Genji* specialists and awarded a prize by Japan's Ministry of Education, depicts her as a kind of ogress, towering menacingly over her cowering son and father and suffering the singular distinction of being the only homely woman in the entire film.

The Rear Court also, however, had subtler influences on its writers. As one Japanese expert puts it, while imperial patronage influenced the arts in many cultures, the Heian "connection is especially deep; on that point, even on a global scale, it must be classed an exception."[13] The observation is in one sense obvious: much of the best premodern Japanese fiction comes from the Heian era, and most of these pieces, in turn, can be linked to the Rear Court. Few other traditions are as heavily dependent on such an institution for their cultural inheritance. The inferences drawn about this relationship, however, are less reliable. Some claims, such as the view that patrons requested the composition of these tales (rather than leaving them to a chance creative impulse), seem obvious. Indeed, we almost have proof of it in the legend, recorded in one of the *Genji* commentaries, that Great Priestess Senshi asked Shōshi to lend her a tale, a request passed along to Murasaki herself. There are also, however, many more romantic notions on this front that court the "advantages" myth noted earlier. One of the most eloquent articulations of it comes from a Western historian of Japan, who claims that in Murasaki's time, "female creativity enjoyed a moment of flowering that may be unparalleled in the history of humankind"—a moment largely synonymous with the Rear Court.[14]

What is less clear, however, is the precise nature of this influence. One longstanding view describes Heian's marriage politics—and the Fujiwara clan's domination of it—as freeing their heirs and competitors alike from worldly concerns, allowing them to develop "purified, increasingly subtle" hearts.[15] A more practical version of this argument emphasizes the economic freedom women writers enjoyed, with Fujiwara prosperity supplementing the relatively generous inheritance laws of the period.[16] In either case, the literary conclusion is the same. These special circumstances helped writers to focus on their craft, producing a "more purely creative literature" expressing their "vibrant feel for beauty" and "introspective melancholy."[17] This sensibility, still evident in much Japanese writing, extended to Heian arts in general, from the intricate color combinations of their lavish kimono to the refined competitions (involving everything from roots and incense to painted shells) timed to religious calendars and the seasons. Such awareness also, however, extends to its literary themes, particularly those linked to "the elegant and elaborate process of courtship."[18] This subject, often viewed as an escape from actual, strategically based alliances, has become the preeminent prism for interpreting Rear Court texts—even in its absence, as the title of one well-known study, *The Splendor of Longing*,[19] illustrates. Dalby's *The Tale of Murasaki* neatly captures this focus for genre and era alike, with a gorgeous artist's rendition of the Heian writer on the cover and a rich purple ribbon, evocative of a leisurely reading experience, stitched into the binding itself.

Revisiting the Salon

The idea of the Rear Court as a preserve of aesthetics is both attractive and, to some extent, accurate; this was undoubtedly a world of both privilege and beauty, as the various competitions and even Shōnagon's lists attest. The anecdotes about the two Senshis discussed earlier, however, suggest a different view of the Heian institution and its writing. As noted, Western scholars offer several translations for the Rear Court, including the women's quarters, imperial harem, and the more literal Rear Palace. There is, however, another word which frequently appears in both Japanese and English discussions of the institution: "salon." This term (used both in Japanese and English) is applied almost exclusively to Heian examples of the institution, and in particular to the great literary circles mentioned earlier, the households of Teishi, Shōshi, and Great Priestess Senshi. (The chief exception to this company involves another Heian woman: Takaiko (842–910), consort to Emperor Uda (r. 887–97) and the sponsor of a group of male poets.) It is not clear where and when the use of the label for the Heian Rear Court originates, although a 1967 Japanese article, "The *Salon* Literature of the Rear Court and Imperial Princesses," omits definition, suggesting a certain level of conventionality to its usage even then.[20] The meaning, however, is clear. In all cases, the label evokes a world of privilege and elegance—and, of course, literary sponsorship.

As it turns out, however, the salon also has a history, one that provides a surprising corrective to the romantic portrait of the Rear Court sketched earlier. Once again, we begin with great ladies and an imperial institution, this time in Enlightenment France. According to Western historians, the word "salon" initially referred to a series of gatherings called *ruelles*, a term which itself denoted the "space between the wall and the side of the bed" where wealthy women received guests.[21] Over time, these visits, which frequently featured leading artists and intellectuals, came to evoke more: skillful conversation, usually enjoyed in opulent apartments and rich dress. The Marquise de Rambouillet (Catherine de Vivonne, wife of Henry IV's Grand Master of the Royal Wardrobe) even built a special domicile, the Hôtel de Rambouillet, in 1617 or 1618 for the express purpose of accommodating her lively circle of acquaintance.[22] In short, the salon strove to present the epitome of elegance—just like the Heian Rear Court.

What is really interesting, however, is the historiography of the French institution. According to one writer, the seventeenth-century salon, its first flowering, was

> like a pause in a party out of the Decameron. Look at its women; they tell the tale: these who are warming their feet by the fire and

their hands on a lapdog; those who are skimming an album of music with flying fingers and listless eyes; these who are playing, indolently, a game of *hombre,* with vagrant smiles; and the young thing turning in her chair to tease the cat with a spool of yarn: is it not an idyll by Watteau, for what were his idylls but the ideal of a French *salon*?—the same peace, the same amenity, the same mannered charm, the same welcoming smile for the moment?

As the salon reached its zenith in the eighteenth century, the writer explains, the scene grew still more lavish.

[H]ere is the caprice of its costumes, here are its women in inviting *négligés,* their white gowns embossed with flowers, their furs, their feathers, their *toques.* Over their books flutters a wit one would vow fled from Boccaccio to alight on the lips of Marivaux. And here and there—where that man is standing, swathed in a mantle, a domino—near a chair, on the muffling Oriental carpet, someone has dropped a velvet gaming purse, or a mask hangs and yawns, the mask of the Regency, black of cheek, white of mouth, Harlequin's mask—the mask of the Ball, the mask of Folly, filched from a night in Venice for a night in old Paris.[23]

This portrait strongly resembles the view of the Rear Court presented earlier, focused as it is on aesthetic codes and what Woolf might have called the "cranes and chrysanthemums" of early modern France. Other historians add a second familiar aspect, the group ethic apparent in the competition between Murasaki's diary and Shōnagon's *The Pillow Book.* Even when on leave from service, salon members wrote their host regularly, creating "a carefully selected and assorted company, its numbers regulated, and so skillfully arranged as to form a homogeneous unity."[24]

The most intriguing parallel, however, is the characterization of the act of writing itself. Surveying the French institution's "marked and happy influence on literature," one of the historians cited above notes:

Not one great writer in the eighteenth century but submitted to the influence of the salon, derived sustenance from it, and composed for it. Montesquieu left his vines to visit Madame de Lambert and Madame de Tencin, Voltaire was a frequenter of the salons and intimate with their most influential leaders, the genius of Rousseau developed under the roof provided by Madame d'Épinay, Buffon's powerful will bent before Madame Necker, and the hitherto untamed Diderot regretted, on her account, the grossness of his writings.[25]

The language here is itself instructive: words and phrases like "submitted," "bent," and "hitherto untamed," while meant to evoke a kind of chivalry, clearly reveal the host's power over her guests. Nonetheless, the writer obviously intends to depict the salon as the sponsor of a rarified ambience, just as in the Heian case. This patronage encouraged its recipients in the pursuit of a familiar theme: "the analysis of the anatomy of that passion of love which will be always, whatever may be said, the material preferred in romantic or poetic fiction."[26] *Genji*, too, contains much about "the passion of love," at least as Heian aristocrats saw it. Some scholars even stress its subtle eroticism, presumably more restrained than the passages the "regretful" Diderot excised from his own work.[27]

As this summary suggests, early portraits of the French salon almost inevitably contain a hint of nostalgia, a tone also familiar in discussions of the Rear Court and, as discussed in the introduction, Murasaki's world more generally. Even chroniclers of more recent incarnations of the salon, such as Dorothy Parker's Algonquin circle, betray this sense, evident in the preface to a recent book.

Forty years have passed since Lady Cunard's death; and I doubt if we shall see her like again. For the salon was the product of a leisured society, and the twentieth century allows us so little leisure that we have begun to forget the art of using it. How agreeably and profitably it was once used, by cultivated people who valued ideas, admired eloquence and delighted in one another's company, is the absorbing topic of the present book.[28]

The sense of loss, patent in both the admiring language and the use of the grammatical past tense ("once used by cultivated people" and so forth), also pervades the anthologized essays, several of which refer to salon sponsors as their artists' "muse." Even the collection's alternate title, *Affairs of the Mind*, conveys this sense of detachment from mundane concerns.[29]

The impulse to "prettify" these texts and their sponsors clearly remains strong, even in distinct areas of study.

There is, however, a second strand in salon scholarship, one of which Woolf might well have approved: that focused on the institution's practical roots and benefits. Again, we return to Enlightenment France. According to one historian,

> Each salon revolved around a woman who for a variety of reasons—poor health, unorthodox political or religious convictions, undistinguished lineage or nonconformist temperament—was unable to figure advantageously at the royal court yet unwilling to forfeit the pleasures and company to be found there, and who created her own private little court instead. The impetus for the foundation of the salons had come from a politically restless class, the aristocracy, faithfully imitated by the bourgeoisie.[30]

In short, the salon grew from political isolation, the same catalyst assigned the Rear Court. Revisionists, however, draw quite different conclusions for the French institution. While status, as the earlier historians put it, may not have "ma[d]e a man welcome unless with it were combined engaging qualities of mind and manner," the resulting mixed milieu was hardly the result of "common intellectual interests."[31] Rather, a patron—even the venerable Madame de Rambouillet, sponsor of the first salon—deliberately chose artists who could "enhance the status of her salon and secure useful protection," whether through "birth or talen[t]."[32] To further her interests, the writer continues, a sponsor might "overloo[k] patent disreputableness," anathema to the idealized salon. Some gatherings, in fact, "engaged, or were suspected of engaging in, subversive activities, and were objects of government surveillance," including, once again, the Hôtel de Rambouillet.[33] In short, the inspirations for the salon were multiple and often entirely unrelated to simple artistic expression.

Not surprisingly, this complex agenda had its effect on salon members. Besides "serving as publicity agents,"

> patronised writers could expect to be tapped for entertainment, erudition and, generally, any commodity for which their patroness felt the need. They had to devise, on order, compositions in prose and

verse on any subject that happened to catch her fancy, regardless of their own natural bent and preferences. It fell to their lot to trace the gallant epistles with which she liked to surprise friends or express gratitude for paeans, gifts and favours received. If she personally was moved to compose, they assisted with the mechanics of literary creation, eliminating errors and polishing style. They racked their brains to invent and arrange diversions for the amusement of her guests, afterwards recording them in literary form for the benefit of absentees or of posterity. They also came in handy to shed lustre, by their learned reputation if not their eccentricities, on her salon.[34]

Writers profited materially from this exchange of "commodities," both in gifts and such occasional posts as the patron's live-in tutor. Moreover, they gained a regular audience for their work, both in the patron and in their fellow affiliates. Inevitably, however, the relationship changed their art. As has been noted of court verse in Tudor and Stuart England, behind their "literary features," sponsored texts betrayed "the personal circumstances of the authors and . . . the social, economic and political milieus they shared with their chosen audiences."[35] In short, they reflected the salon's own shifting identities, springing both from the heart and, as one French patron put it, the "stomach."[36]

Residence and the Rear Court

Certain of these observations about the French salon, such as patronal influence, are immediately applicable to Heian authorship. Indeed, scholars already recognize the influence of the court on many male-authored texts, including Tsurayuki's supposedly heartfelt art of poetry.[37] For example, critics point to political frustration as an impetus for poetic careers that, once started, became springboards for social criticism, much like the modern West's public intellectuals. The same point has also been made for some of Japan's most beloved classical prose: for instance, *An Unsolicited Tale* (*Towazugatari*, better known as *The Confessions of Lady Nijō*; after 1313), the memoir of an attendant from the Kamakura era (1192–1333).[38] These acknowledgments, however, all but fall silent when the subject is Heian fiction, perhaps because of the romantic salon portraits listed earlier. *Genji*, to be sure, inspires such discussions. In addition to the court rivalries discussed earlier, critics discover "subtler critiques of social realities," such as the incentives for self-induced, and even staged, spirit possessions.[39] These insights largely disappear, however, when it comes to other women's fiction, perhaps because they lack Murasaki's skill and, as important, her reputation for genius. Without authorial or obvious literary incentives to study a text, it is easy to call it uninformed or escapist—especially when that is already the consensus on the institution that produced it. As noted in the introduction, the subsequent chapters of this study explore the social criticism hidden in three of Heian's most neglected texts: *Sagoromo*, *Hamamatsu*, and *Nezame*.

The salon comparison also, however, offers deeper insights into Heian texts, beginning with the identity of the writer. Salon writers and artists, as the previous portraits suggest, were usually male professionals, sought out by their patrons (normally women) for their creative talents—despite the mundane uses to which those talents were put. While some writers were financially insolvent, they thus theoretically possessed an independent profession, allowing the more successful of them the regular luxury of private lodgings, as well as, to a certain extent, a choice of company. They often "circulate[d] widely among the different *ruelles*,"[40] presumably experiencing (along with the instability) a range of patronal and collegial influences. The Heian attendant (also translated as "lady-in-waiting" or "court lady") led a considerably different life. Gender alone imposed certain restrictions; wellborn ladies, as Murasaki admits in her diary, were not supposed to venture far from the confines of home and family. One of her chief complaints about court service is the fact that so many men and women can see her face. Moreover, the attendant was a long-term Rear Court resident, typically serving a single patron for months and years at a time. A wet nurse might take up residence with her patron while the latter was still an infant.[41] For a woman marrying into the imperial house, such long-term attendants provided the core of a new Rear Court staff, helping to ease her transition to life at the palace. For a princess, they served as shepherds along a privileged capital orbit and, when necessary, as companions on shrine appointments.[42] In short, attendants enjoyed very little of the French writer's mobility. Should a woman dislike her patron or fellow staff, she had little choice but to adapt, marry, or return home, as Sei Shōnagon's lapses from service in times of political pressure suggest.[43]

Most importantly, however, Heian attendants were not professional writers; indeed, as noted earlier, many of them did not write at all, beyond the requisite occasional poetry. Great Priestess Senshi did, it is true, appoint a "head of tales" and "head of poetry" to her retinue, attendants in charge of producing writing in each genre and organizing contests. Even those women we know as authors, however, spent much of their time performing basic duties like fetching washing water, sewing, and serving meals. In the case of service to an empress, attendants would also participate in formal processions at court.[44] They also served as their patron's hospitality staff, greeting, guiding, and entertaining the stream of courtiers who passed through her rooms after court business was finished. According to one specialist, such work was the attendant's primary responsibility, making her "essentially a hostess," one of the symbols of modern Japanese business entertainment.[45] Hostesses, however, only serve drinks—at least, at reputable establishments. Attendants could be expected to go further, once again in the patron's service. As one historian tactfully puts it:

> Ultimately, the attendant's role was to help her imperial mistress to receive the master's company and bear him a prince, to ensure that she be attractive to the Emperor, and to create a pleasant environment for his visits. In order for the Emperor to find the salon attractive, it must also appeal to other members of the nobility. Beginning with routine interactions with the nobles whom the master sent as his envoys, it was useful, no matter what the circumstance, for the salon to be pleasant always and for every nobleman who stopped by. The attendant worked completely in the service of this effort.[46]

The critic later makes this point more explicit, in an article bluntly labeled "sex."[47] Even here the point is obvious. Attendants had to entertain guests at all costs—in ways that most French writers, even those who occasionally slept with their patrons, could not have imagined.[48] The obvious example is the attendant's role in political intrigue, similar to that discussed for the salon. Experts believe that Sei Shōnagon's relationship with Fujiwara Tadanobu (967–1035), which she claims got her in trouble with her patron in *The Pillow Book*—Tadanobu sympathized with a rival family—may actually have masked exchanges of information between the two factions. One scholar even alludes to "attendant networks" in the Rear Court and the "spy-battles" they conducted for political advantage.[49] Even the attendant's writing, however, had sexual resonance. Michinaga hired Murasaki to "make Empress Shōshi [his daughter] as appealing as possible to the young Emperor Ichijō,"[50] in part by surrounding her with entertaining books. It is not difficult to imagine that *Genji* and other court writing functioned as textual aphrodisiacs, the bodhisattva myth of their composition notwithstanding. Even the beginning of Shōnagon's *The Pillow Book*, a catalogue of memorable moments and seasons, has a carnal backdrop. Critics often argue that this section is guide to proper courtship etiquette, and that one should, in effect, read such statements as "In springtime, the dawn [is most moving]" through a libidinous lens. The textual seduction worked, at least for Murasaki. As noted in the introduction, in addition to fathering several children with Shōshi—including the desired crown prince—Ichijō explicitly praised Murasaki's tale as comparable to Chinese histories, partially explaining his sudden enthusiasm for her mistress.

These extracurricular duties no doubt weighed heavily on the attendant, making her dependent upon and responsible for the good graces of not only her own patron, but those of that woman's benefactor and his envoys as well. The Rear Court also, however, offered rewards the salon writer might recognize—and in some cases, envy. Like the French writer, these women were employees of their patrons, not guests—although they were also sometimes relatives, such as the proverbial poor cousin. This meant that they were used accordingly, as in the story of Senshi's request for new reading material and the duties discussed above. It also meant, however, that they themselves came in search of material benefits. Attendants typically came from middle- or lower-level aristocratic households, families equipped to educate their daughters but unable to finance or otherwise procure politically useful marriages (for lower-level families, birth was the limiting factor). The most famous of such women, like Murasaki Shikibu, were the daughters of provincial governors, courtiers lacking the influence—but not the ambition—for a post in the capital. A clever attendant could become quite prominent within her patron's circle, as the favors recorded in Shōnagon and Murasaki's diaries attest.

Moreover, the woman's family also benefited. A wet nurse earned the most spectacular rewards, due to the intimacy and typical longevity of her relationship. Not only would her husband or father likely receive a favorable post, often a lucrative governorship (some provinces offered better tributes than others, supplementing the governor's court salary), but her own child—also recently born, of course—might become the companion of her charge, in the best scenario, a future emperor. The bond, at least for same-sex children, usually developed into a lifelong patronal relationship that might extend into subsequent generations. Small wonder, then, that so many parents tried to get their daughters the position. Murasaki herself did so for her daughter, winning her the position of Head of the Palace Attendants' Office. Eventually, the girl became an imperial wet nurse. Even ordinary attendants found themselves in a position to benefit themselves and their families through their service. These women, as discussed earlier, spent much of their time entertaining the various courtiers who visited their patron's rooms. Such conversations may not have translated into social mobility for the attendant herself, but in the Heian court's nepotistic bureaucracy, better connections meant better appointments, particularly during the era of Fujiwara dominance. A well-regarded attendant might on the basis of that reputation pave the way for a sister or daughter's service.

Finally, the Rear Court offered attendants artistic benefits, at least to women who played it smart. Women like the Sarashina diarist, who longed in the provinces for the books of the capital, found their hopes exceeded in the well-stocked storehouse of the successful salon. Writers, for all of their additional duties, were also fortunate. As Murasaki suggests in her diary, in the case of instant successes like *Genji*, the writer might also receive the still finer copying materials and collective labor that in their manuscript culture meant the equivalent of publication. They also found an instant group of critics and potential editors. The ubiquitous literary competitions, by definition, entailed judgments, encouraging writers to critique their own work and that of others. Some women, moreover, like Ise (877–940?), filled the "prestigious position" of competition scribe, although the role of official judge was usually reserved for emperors and the courtier elite.[51] The "reading aloud" theory of tale reception, meanwhile, implies what we might call an instant "focus group" for textual revisions. *The Untitled Book*, discussed in the introduction, suggests as much with its fictional depiction of such conversation. In short, Rear Court writers could achieve a measure of fame for themselves and their families, both through these activities and the anthologization of their poetry. (Court prose was not normally collected, at least judging from extant texts.) The final point was particularly important to women from poetic lineages, who arranged for family members to join the competitions and cultivate their own reputations—and fortunes. Madame Rambouillet herself could not have offered a more attractive post.

The Rear Court: A Case Study

Before discussing the effect of this complex working environment on Rear Court writing, I would like to offer a more detailed portrait, centered on the sponsors of *The Tale of Sagoromo*.[52] Unlike *Hamamatsu* and *Nezame*, the other late Heian tales treated in this study, we know the identity of both the author and her patron; we even retain a host of their artistic collaborations, preserved in the records of period poetry contests. Moreover, we command a wealth of details about these women's male relatives, the secondary sponsors so crucial to the assembly and financing of Rear Court households. *Sagoromo* thus presents an unusual opportunity to consider the actual workings of the institution, by connecting these ample particulars to the general trends just discussed. Furthermore, it sheds lights on a historical point crucial to this study: the vivacity of the late Heian Rear Court in general, often overshadowed by the grand households of Shōshi and Teishi, discussed earlier. As the following pages show, late Heian patronage was if anything more complicated than that in Murasaki's time, providing yet another incentive to re-read the era's texts.

Sagoromo's Scribe

As noted in the introduction to this study, for centuries critics believed that *Sagoromo* was written by Murasaki Shikibu's daughter, encouraging the view of the tale as a mere copy of Murasaki's work. As one reference puts it, early readers somehow felt it appropriate that "the author of 'the [so-called] Second Genji' should be the daughter of the author of the first."[53] A series of modern discoveries, however, ended this tradition. Fujioka Sakutarō, the Meiji scholar and literary critic, unearthed an earlier attribution in Fujiwara Teika's *Treatise on Obscure Ideas* (*Hekianshō*, 1226), one of several works by the poet to mention *Sagoromo*: "Senji of the Sixth Street Kamo Priestess's household," a late eleventh-century attendant. Scholars have since confirmed Teika's theory several times over, with such varied evidence as the entertaining *Poetry Contest between Household Articles* (*Chōdo uta awase*, ca. 1214), itself only extant in a sixteenth-century copy. The new ascription again assigns *Sagoromo* a kind of intellectual history, this time more favorable. Senji (1020 or 1022–92) has roughly 40 extant poems to her credit, as well as a positive review for the missing *The*

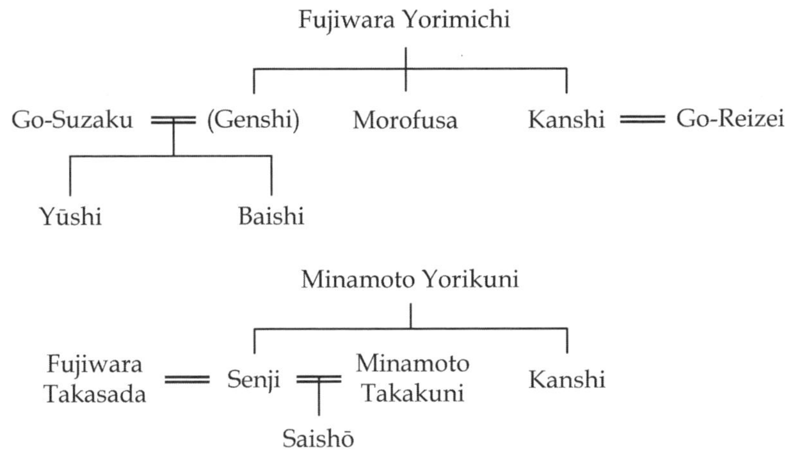

Fig. 1 Simplified genealogy for Senji and her patrons
═ marital or romantic relationship | parent-child relationship ( ) foster relationship

Provisional Counselor Who Dallied in Jewel-Weed (*Tamamo ni asobu gondainagon*, 1055) in *The Untitled Book*. Shunzei's Daughter writes admiringly that, "while there's nothing particularly moving or impressive about the tale, the way it begins with 'although parents scold children for playing' is wonderful. It really makes you want to read more."[54] Modern critics, meanwhile, speak approvingly of Senji's growth as an author, "maturing" in her art from a dependably good competition poet (all but two of her verses come from such gatherings) to the occasional brilliance of *Sagoromo*'s prose.[55] In fact, many readers—including some Edo poets—consider the writer Murasaki's superior in the first art.

The ascription also, however, evokes another image: a patron. As noted above, the *Sagoromo* author's sobriquet is actually "Senji of the Sixth Street Kamo Priestess's household." As I will discuss below, the priestess's household depended on a particularly complex set of patronal relationships, making Senji's position still more complicated than the preceding characterization of the Rear Court suggests and presumably exerting an even greater influence on her writing. Even without these particulars, however, the name implies a special relationship between her texts and her employment. Most of the names given to attendants, as noted earlier, refer to male relatives and their court posts, even in the case of a celebrated writer like Murasaki Shikibu. "Senji," however, is an actual female title, and a high-profile one at that. While the specific duties of the post remain murky, historians describe it as one of the Rear Court's exclusive "three-attendant offices," one for which only attendants from the three highest grades could qualify.[56] Perhaps for this reason, the title often designated imperial wet nurses, one the most elite positions open to attendants.

The etymology of the term is still more suggestive. "Senji" originally referred to an informal court decree, one usually initiated by the Emperor himself. (Most formal decrees, by contrast, originated with his advisory council.) According to some scholars, an attendant could obtain the title merely by delivering the decree, presumably to one of the emperor's relatives or consorts.[57] The august association probably explains the title's prestige, but it also suggests the *Sagoromo* author's role as a writer, authorized by her patron, of "informal" prose fiction. Moreover, it implies her role as a messenger, if again informal, for other interests. Even Senji's noncompetition verse is preserved under this title. For all of these reasons, one could translate her office, and thus her sobriquet, as "scribe," suggesting something of the conflation of the person and message discussed below.

The Princess and Her Attendants

The "priestess" referenced by Senji's title is Princess Baishi (1039–96, Kamo Priestess 1046–58), the fourth daughter of Emperor Go-Suzaku (r. 1036–45) and his second with wife Genshi (1016–39). The link might seem to isolate Senji from the intrigues normally associated with the Rear Court, since, for all of Great Priestess Senshi's "wily" activities (presumably confined to prayers for Michinaga), princesses were supposed to stand clear of court politics. There was little incentive for a regent to marry his grandson to a princess, thus handing the children and political control to her parents. As a result, these alliances were discouraged or actively blocked in Senji's time, although they regained popularity at the end of the Heian period, when strong emperors adopted Fujiwara strategies for themselves. Baishi, at least, never married. Instead, while serving as shrine priestess (which required at least nominal virginity), she devoted herself to one of the most artistically active Rear Courts of the Heian period. Baishi sponsored an unrivaled total of twenty-five known poetry competitions, beginning when she was only ten and extending for nearly three decades until 1078. Nor is volume the only measure of the household's poetic activity. Scholars frequently praise these contests' innovative topics and diction, suggesting the seriousness with which Baishi and her attendants took their poetry—and self-promotion. Senji, as noted earlier, composed all but two of her known verses for these events and sent at least two of them to an impressed competition guest.[58]

The princess took an equally striking interest in prose. In 1055, while serving at Kamo, she sponsored the only known court competition for authoring tale fiction, *The Tale Contest at the Household of the Sixth Street Kamo Shrine Priestess Princess Baishi* (*Rokujō saiin Baishi naishinnō no ie no monogatari awase*), usually abbreviated to *The Sixth Street Kamo Shrine Priestess's Tale Contest* (*Rokujō saiin monogatari awase*). Participants created eighteen new tales for the event, including Senji's *Provisional Counselor.* Unfortunately, only one, *The Provisional Middle Counselor Who Failed to Cross Meeting Slope* (*Ausaka koenu gonchūnagon*), remains extant.[59] Even this limited evidence, however, suggests enormous contributions to court fiction, as well as a reminder of the Rear Court's communal nature. All of the tales clearly responded to an external directive, probably a common theme.[60] For some critics, the contest thus suggests a transformation in the genre from private entertainment to the subject of semi-public debate.[61] In fact, Senji may even have crafted her own entry's elaborate prologue (evocative of *Sagoromo*) to impress the judges, who only had time to hear part of each text.[62] In short, the tale competition, like its verse counterparts, gave Baishi's attendants a forum in which to make and prove their personal reputations, even if the greater glory redounded to the princess herself. Senji, and undoubtedly some or all of her colleagues, took advantage of it.

The Regent

As these events suggest, Baishi's household was an unusually vibrant Rear Court, despite her predecessors' brighter reputations. According to *Flowering Fortunes*, the fictionalized biography of Michinaga and his family discussed in the introduction, not only did the princess herself have a precocious talent for poetry. In the "After the Smoke" (Keburi no ato) chapter, the narrator observes that "her attendants also chose poetic topics and organized competitions, passing morning and night to their hearts' content in this fashion."[63] Indeed, including but certainly not limited to Senji, attendants organized and perhaps initiated these events, particularly during Baishi's childhood. As in the more famous households, this activity reflected more than simple love of the arts, the comments from *Flowering Fortunes* notwithstanding. These events were probably partially meant to cheer Baishi, whom several contemporary accounts describe as an invalid of tenuous sanity.[64] Whatever the princess's mental state, she was undeniably in ill health—a condition normally counterfeited by young women bored with the Kamo appointment—when she retired from her duties in 1058.[65]

Less altruistic motivations, however, also influenced the household's patronage of the arts. As argued earlier, such a prolific Rear Court required the support of the princess's entire family, including its men. Baishi's most prominent male sponsor was Fujiwara Yorimichi (992–1074), Michinaga's son and the era's leading politician. Yorimichi's support for the princess, a non-Fujiwara, reflected the convergence of both political need and generosity. His first wife, the imperial-born Takahime (995–1087), produced no children, a disaster for both her husband and his father Michinaga, who hoped to further cement the clan's domination at court. To Michinaga's frustration, Yorimichi initially refrained from taking a second wife like most aristocrats, in part because of threats from the ghost of Takahime's father.[66] Instead, he adopted Genshi, Takahime's niece, and sent her to serve Emperor Go-Suzaku. *Flowering Fortunes* attributes the decision not only to Yorimichi's fondness for both Genshi and her father, but also to other considerations. Like Takahime, Genshi was a Genji, a former imperial family member forced to become a commoner through Fujiwara manipulation of the succession. More concretely, she was the daughter of deposed prince Atsuyasu (999–1018), Teishi's son, making her the great-granddaughter of Fujiwara Michitaka (953–95), Michinaga's brother and longtime rival. Taking in the girl thus filled several political needs, in addition to expressing Yorimichi's affections (or, in this era of spirit possessions, perhaps easing a guilty conscience). Not only did the courtier gain an essential daughter; he also co-opted a competing lineage, one of the oldest tricks in the book of marriage politics.

The strategy failed; Genshi died bearing Baishi, the second of two politically useless princesses. As the half-siblings of the next two emperors, neither girl could become a consort, adoptive Fujiwara or not. Fortunately, Yorimichi had finally bent to Michinaga's will, married again, and sired his own daughter: future empress Kanshi (1035–1127), who would eventually sponsor her own active Rear Court. He also, however, adopted Baishi and her sister Yūshi, a move that contemporaries like Fujiwara Sukefusa (1007–57) credited to the courtier's affection for their mother. Taking in these "keepsakes," Sukefusa wrote in his diary, was a natural decision for the grieving regent.[67] Once again, however, the decision served several interests. By adopting Genshi's daughters, Yorimichi gained another opportunity to exhibit and extend his own social prominence. During his almost fifty years as either regent or chancellor (1017–67), Yorimichi lent his support (and sometimes, as in poetry contests, his verse) to the households of all three of his daughters, adoptive and otherwise. The support for natural daughter Kanshi, like foster-child Genshi, reflected Fujiwara power politics as usual. By gilding her household, he hoped to encourage imperial visits and the birth of an heir.

Yorimichi's care of the princesses, however, also had a more subtle purpose: the promotion of his cultural authority. The regent supposedly named both Baishi and her sister for classical Chinese references imploring divine assistance for the birth of a prince.[68] The girls ultimately disappointed these expectations: Yūshi "produced" only Baishi, and Baishi effectively killed their mother Genshi in childbirth. Their poetry contests, however, in some sense substituted for the lost prince. Yorimichi boasted an impressive artistic resume even without his daughters: fourteen anthologized poems, a compendium called *The Treasury of Poetry Contests* (*Ruijū uta awase*, spanning roughly the years 1045–68) and at least two personally sponsored events, the second contemporary with those of Baishi herself. It was his influence on the Rear Court, however, that truly captures the imagination. Under Yorimichi's aegis, his three daughters and their attendants (particularly Baishi's group) led a poetic revival unseen since the celebrated reign of Emperor Murakami (r. 946–67), one of the models of the golden age backdrop for *Genji* itself. Nor were these Rear Courts simply prolific. The three "sisters" opened their competitions to the others' households, a practice unheard of in Michinaga's age. Only eight of the entries in Baishi's famed tale-fiction contest came from her own entourage. Moreover, according to the anthology *Later Collection of Poetic Gleanings* (*Goshūi wakashū*, 1086), Yorimichi himself took a personal interest in the guest list, stopping the event midway through so that one of Yūshi's attendants could submit a late entry. In short, Baishi's Rear Court, like Shōshi's before her, was not solely her own. It formed an important part of the "Yorimichi-esque sphere" or "Yorimichi-centered literary world" that buttressed the courtier's political inheritance.[69]

Scholars sometimes point to this unusual cooperation within the late Heian Rear Court at large as evidence of Yorimichi and his daughters' warm affections, a further expression of the tenderness that produced Genshi's adoption. As a partial explanation, this is probably true; one finds little of the personal criticism directed at Michinaga in accounts of his son. Here again, however, there was a practical incentive to be nice, this time for the lower ranks. The male contingent of Baishi's

Poetry Contest between Men and Attendants (*Baishi naishinnō no ie no otoko nyōbō uta awase*), for example, were aware that Yorimichi was their host's ultimate patron: every courtier from the Empress's head-of-household on down had attended the girl's staffing ceremonial when she was an infant.[70] Cooperating with the princess and her guests meant a new chance to impress him and thus win potential personal profit, particularly since he also sponsored the era's other two major Rear Courts. A good performance at one contest might lead to an invitation to another, or even a new post. In short, Yorimichi's expanded Rear Court, while serving his own interests, also enabled a far greater range of second-tier ambitions than the zero-sum campaign to produce and serve a single crown prince. Another aspect of the "Yorimichi-esque" Rear Court was, ironically, the increased politicization of artistic production—particularly when Kanshi, like her dead foster-sister, failed to produce a prince.

The Former Prince

Baishi's household found a second powerful sponsor in Minamoto Morofusa (1008–77), Yorimichi's foster-son. The courtier, Takahime's younger brother, joined the regent's household in infancy with his sister's marriage, despite rumors that his own mother was actually a low-ranking servant. Yorimichi formally adopted him during or just before his coming-of-age ceremony in 1020. Scholars disagree as to the nature of the adoption. Some claim that Yorimichi first made Morofusa his heir but displaced him when a natural son was born. To atone for the slight, the regent reportedly farmed out several subsequent male children to the families of retainers.[71] Others deny that Morofusa was ever in a position to succeed Yorimichi.[72] The delicacy of Morofusa's position, however, is beyond doubt. In addition to the rumors about his parentage, the boy probably faced some hostility as an extralineal foster-child, since the upper nobility generally recruited sons from within the same clan.

Morofusa was not, however, without his defenses. As his surname suggests, the boy was a new commoner, with all of the charisma of his imperial father; in fact, until his coming-of-age ceremony, the boy technically remained a prince. Moreover, Morofusa enjoyed a distinguished pedigree even for one of his birth. He was the grandson of Emperor Murakami, the figure under whom the courtly arts had flourished. Morofusa's father Prince Tomohira (964–1009), meanwhile, commanded his own reputation as a poet in both Chinese and Japanese. Morofusa inherited his line's intellectual affinities. He composed several prefaces and ten imperially anthologized poems, and also sponsored five known poetry competitions. Moreover, he promoted many promising lower-ranking poets, including such celebrated figures as Nōin (988–1058?), including them in his personal contests and even making his home their preferred gathering place. Finally, the former prince became a prominent authority on court custom and precedent, compiling treatises on the subject to which even the regent's family deferred.[73]

In addition to his artistic talents, Morofusa also displayed Murakami's celebrated instinct for power. Through his patronage of the arts, he could challenge the Fujiwara's marriage politics, even as he participated in them as an adopted family member. Moreover, he parlayed both his blood and artistic ties into his own politically useful marriage. In an effort to elevate his own lineage, Michinaga had chosen Genji brides for both himself and for Yorimichi.[74] In 1024 he took Morofusa as a son-in-law, despite an earlier, Yorimichi-brokered arrangement with the current Minister of the Right. By acceding to Michinaga's wishes, Morofusa earned an instant promotion—and also undercut Yorimichi.[75] Despite some initial resistance by the bride's brothers and an interim drought in promotions, the former prince eventually became Minister of the Right himself. His two sons later concurrently served as Ministers of the Right and Left. These efforts made Morofusa's the official Murakami Genji line, one noted for its politically ambitious character.

What Yorimichi thought about Morofusa's ambitions is hard to tell. In 1040, however, he handed his foster-son an additional tool by placing him in charge of the infant princess's household.[76] While Baishi remained close to the regent throughout her life and probably continued to live with him until her Kamo appointment, Morofusa became her immediate sponsor. Most scholars agree that he personally encouraged if not financed the princess's artistic productions: coeval criticism of both men's extravagance notwithstanding, neither Yūshi's five known events nor Empress Kanshi's three could match Baishi's activity.[77] Moreover, like Yorimichi, Morofusa took a hands-on role in the household's activities. The unusual poetic topics mentioned earlier echo Morofusa's own idiosyncratic tastes, and he allegedly organized one contest just to cheer her up.[78] Indeed, he may have inspired her interest in poetry in the first place.[79] Morofusa even gave her household its Sixth Street sobriquet. The former prince and his family were also known as the Sixth Street Genji for their estates in that part of the city, and whether by association or actual residence (a fire in 1068 may have driven Baishi to his home) the name also passed to the princess. Moreover, Morofusa also indirectly preserved Baishi's reputation: works from the princess's events were included in two anthologies compiled by one of his descendants.[80]

The reasons for Morofusa's support of Baishi, like Yorimichi's, were clearly complex. Morofusa probably identified with the princess, given their similar birth and adoptive parentage. His support for so high-profile a Rear Court, however, clearly also redounded to his cultural credit. Baishi's events reached and involved a much greater audience than his own patronage and antiquarian efforts. The former prince may even have launched his sons' "elite course" by including them as children in Sixth Street competitions.[81] This patronage, however much in the shadow of the regent, allowed Morofusa and his family to continue to promote their line's independent identity as literati and cultural stewards, further promoting the former prince's ambitions. The descendant who preserved the princess's contest records, while claiming a number of other events for Morofusa, did much the same thing: he increased his own line's prestige by association.[82] In short, Morofusa mimicked Yorimichi's doubling of aesthetic and political interest in sponsoring Baishi's household. He may even have been more successful at it.

Senji's Family

If Baishi's Rear Court enabled Yorimichi and Morofusa to promote their already healthy reputations and cultural authority, it offered a virtual lifeline for their social inferiors. During the late Heian period, the lesser nobility suffered increasingly straitened circumstances, as the growth of tax-free estates in the provinces stole the revenue supposed to finance, among other things, courtier appointments. The elite families who controlled these posts (and owned most of the estates) shifted the brunt of the shortfall to these middle- and lower-rank aristocrats. The elite even levied extra taxes to pay for things normally covered in the official budget.[83] For families with eligible daughters, court service was one of a shrinking number of paths to advancement.

Senji's family history illustrates this point. Like most attendants, Senji came from the middle ranks of the aristocracy. Her father, Minamoto Yorikuni (?–1058), was an "exemplary" provincial governor, with more than eight separate appointments to his credit.[84] Nonetheless, Yorikuni managed to spend most of his time in the capital, thanks in large part to his father's own ambitions for the family. Senji's paternal grandfather was a grandson of Emperor Seiwa (r. 858–76) and thus one of the prominent Seiwa Genji from whose ranks so many medieval leaders, including the Tokugawa shoguns, would later claim descent. He bequeathed to his sons their own sobriquet, the Settsu Genji (from the provinces that made his fortune); moreover, he passed along his determination for social advancement, symbolized by his gift of a house's worth of furnishings to employer Michinaga in 1018. The noble even took Michinaga's half-brother Michitsuna, whose mother wrote *The Kagerō Diary* (*Kagerō nikki*, after 974), as a son-in-law, effectively making the courtier his dependent.[85] Thanks in part to these efforts, Yorikuni himself received several key appointments in regency households, including those of now Dowager Empress

Shōshi and her son Atsunari, the future emperor Go-Ichijō (r. 1016–36). He also expanded on his father's success, parlaying these initial appointments into still higher offices with the regent's family and then procuring jobs for at least three of his sons there, one with Morofusa.[86]

While his father had earned his credentials—or the money to buy them—primarily in the provinces, Yorikuni appears to have recognized early the political uses of poetic knowledge. In addition to his administrative and security work for the regent's family (including the capture of a renegade priest near Shōshi's apartments), Yorikuni held the post of Scholar of Letters (*monjōshō*), a politically insignificant position that nonetheless lent him a profitable reputation for learning. One modern source describes the courtier as having a "particularly strong air of the literary aristocrat."[87] To judge from his relatives' accomplishments, the governor probably shared a genuine aptitude for verse: one of his brothers and a son were included in the so-called Six Waka Poets of the day, all sponsored by Morofusa. Another son, meanwhile, cosponsored his own poetry contest. Yorikuni and his sons regarded these events, at least in part, as opportunities to expand their bureaucratic careers now that provincial wealth had dried up.[88] In this sense, Yorikuni strongly resembled Baishi's sponsors. While Yorikuni's son Yoritsuna (?–1097), who married into the regent's house, is commonly credited with establishing the line's "aristocratic ambitions," it was Yorikuni, who, like his father and Morofusa, used his position to give the boy and his brothers their elite start.[89]

Yorikuni took a special interest in Baishi's household, which offered the chance to cultivate further patronage from two powerful sources. When Yorimichi adopted the girl, he seized the opportunity and placed one of his daughters in her service, even managing to make her the infant's wet nurse. This nurse's rise to the higher office of Senji, however, required a second sponsor. In between the appointments, the attendant and her family had acquired a third connection to the regent: a second husband, Minamoto Takakuni (1004–77). The nurse's first husband, Fujiwara Takasada (dates unknown), had been exiled for murder, a stigma that would have required remarriage in any case. Takakuni fit the bill perfectly. To begin with, he could claim descent from his own famous emperor, the powerful Daigo (r. 897–930), whose golden age was said to be the model for the world of Genji himself. Takakuni was also something of an artist. In addition to his five extant poems, all anthologized, he compiled an abridged sutra collection and was traditionally credited as the compiler of *Tales of Times Now Past* (*Konjaku monogatari*), perhaps in an earlier version called *Tales of the Uji Major Counselor* (*Uji dainagon monogatari*). While scholars now reject the ascription, it nonetheless records Takakuni's reputation as a writer and anthologist.

Poetry and perhaps prose, however, were not Takakuni's only strong suit. His family was also close to Yorimichi; one brother had even been the regent's foster-child for a time.[90] When that brother entered the priesthood, Takakuni became Yorimichi's closest retainer, managing Kanshi's household for decades. He eventually retired near the regent in Uji, giving his tale collection its title. While Takakuni already had a powerful "main wife" (*kita no kata*), he made an attractive match for Yorikuni and his daughter, especially in light of her first husband's fate. Yorimichi may even have arranged the marriage on Yorikuni's behalf.[91] Of course Senji herself, as wet nurse to Baishi, arguably possessed additional claims on the regent's goodwill—and perhaps even the opportunity to meet Takakuni and encourage his affections herself.

Whoever arranged it, the new marriage bore fruit in the form of social connections. By 1046 (four years after Takasada's exile), Takakuni's influence had won Senji her promotion, awarded concurrently with the princess's own appointment as Kamo Priestess. That Takakuni, not her father, engineered the advancement seems clear when one considers the fates of Senji's sisters. The only other of the nine girls to leave an independent record, as a participant in one of employer Kanshi's poetry competitions, did so with the sobriquet of her father's latest provincial post, Mino. With only her father's support, Mino (1041?–1129) proved unable to earn a titled post, despite bearing two sons to a future regent. Takakuni's influence on Senji's behalf is the most plausible explanation for her distinct fate, even given her own artistic prowess. The real beneficiaries of the promotion, however, were Senji's siblings. When Baishi's entourage set out for the Kamo Shrine in 1046, the attendant's older brother Yorisuke (?–1066) came with them as the assistant head of household, an appointment directly attributed to his sister's influence.[92] Five years later, Yorisuke and brother Yoritsuna also participated in one of Baishi's poetry contests. (Some scholars cautiously credit the younger Yoritsuna's role in this and later events to his siblings' combined influence.[93]) Nor does the family's influence end there: other brothers appeared in Morofusa and Yorimichi's contests, as well as some sponsored by Baishi's sisters. In fact, the Settsu Genji were so active in court literary pursuits that they are now considered "a large force behind the poetry contest revival" at large.[94]

The rewards for Senji's husband Takakuni were less spectacular, probably because he already enjoyed greater benefits from his own relationship with the regent than those accessible through an attendant. His standing with Yorimichi clearly did not suffer, however, from having a wife in Baishi's service, particularly one who contributed so heavily to the princess's (and so the regent's) reputation in the arts. Moreover, Senji bore Takakuni his own daughter, Saishō (dates unknown), whom he later placed as wet nurse to another shrine priestess.[95] Through this child, Senji's support of both Takakuni and her family extended into the next generation. When Saishō's mistress later sponsored her own poetry contest, for example, Senji's brother Yoritsuna participated, no doubt thanks to his niece's efforts.

The End of Sixth Street

When Baishi retired as Kamo Priestess in 1058, her Rear Court fell silent for over six years. Even when the contests resumed, they never regained their old regularity, no doubt because of her sponsors' deaths. Yorimichi, who had been officially retired from politics for almost a decade, passed away in 1074; Morofusa followed three years later. Baishi herself lingered nearly another twenty years, probably still in the care of Morofusa's family and perhaps after acting on the Buddhist impulse which influenced her final events. Her last recorded poetry contest, notable for its spiritual flavor, took place in 1078. As argued earlier, however, any individual member of a Rear Court was less important than the confluence of interests the entire group represented. Baishi's particular date of death is in that sense irrelevant. The network of patronage that truly constituted Baishi's Rear Court had dissolved much earlier.

The men and women who made up this particular Rear Court exemplify the complex interests outlined in the first half of this chapter. Yorimichi, Baishi's foster-father but also the regent, may have adopted the princess out of affection for her dead mother, but he acted in his own interests as well, relying upon her gatherings to an unprecedented extent to display and consolidate his cultural and political authority. Morofusa, his foster-son and Baishi's official guardian, added to these motives another purpose: the recuperation of his own lineage, both as an intellectual and (imperial) patron. Even Senji's husband and family used the princess and her gatherings to promote their careers, if only by rubbing elbows with the powerful at poetry contests. Within this setting, Baishi and her attendants also exercised a kind of authority, capitalizing on their male sponsors' ambitions both to finance their activities and, in the case of the lower-ranked women, to obtain their privileged positions in the first place. Moreover, as Senji's case plainly illustrates, these attendants actively promoted their family interests. In short, the competitions supposedly intended to entertain the princess served a range of men and women from across the (aristocratic) social spectrum. In a different and perhaps more suggestive sense than those quarters focused on imperial childbirth, Baishi's Rear Court highlights the growing fusion of the political and the aesthetic in late Heian Japan. In Baishi's rooms, even more than the world that produced *Genji*, fiction and poetry served as keys to court appointments, appointments that in turn brought further opportunities for "artistic" success.

Poetry, Fiction, and the Rear Court

I hope that the previous pages convey at least some of what we miss when we "prettify" Heian history. The same households that allowed attendants to cultivate their authorial talents also enabled, and in some cases forced, them to satisfy a range of political ambitions. Families of all levels mined relationships and texts alike for political benefits. They did the same with writers' reputations, which, in addition to aesthetic glory, brought the prospects of further opportunities for material advancement. This tendency was especially marked, however, at the social margins, among aristocrats unable "to figure advantageously"—like the members of the Hôtel de Rambouillet discussed earlier—at court. Here a final comparison with the French case is fruitful. Earlier I quoted the view that the middle class imitated the aristocracy in founding salons, hoping to advance their "restless" ambitions. The same thing, clearly, is true of Heian, particularly in the concluding decades of the period. As provincial posts grew scarce, middle-level aristocrats schemed as relentlessly as the Fujiwara elite to stock the Rear Court with their daughters: not in the proud positions of consort or empress, but in the more accessible ranks of such women's attendants. This competition was particularly intense for positions within artistically active households, given the networking opportunities afforded by poetry contests and similar events. Would-be attendants and their families would have found these Rear Courts irresistible, making the pressure to keep and profit from such posts intense.

It is hard to believe that these concerns simply disappeared when attendants paused to write, read, or narrate their texts. As Woolf recognized, personal concerns inevitably influence our readings, whether of Murasaki's world or of history in general. The same is clearly true for authors, as the following chapters argue at length. The patronage networks discussed above, however, suggest several general conclusions for Rear Court texts, particularly tale fiction. In addition to the shadows of official marriage politics noted earlier in *Genji* characters like Kokiden, for example, we can now recognize lower-rank intrigues. Genji's servant Koremitsu, for example, who sticks with his master even during the latter's exile, seems at least as pragmatic as loyal; as one critic points out, as Genji's "breast brother" he has been raised to rely on the relationship.[96] These calculations ultimately prove correct, when Koremitsu manages to marry one of his daughters to Genji's son as a secondary wife and so secures both her future and that of his grandchildren.

There are, however, subtler lessons to be gleaned from Rear Court history. The forces that compelled attendants to write about their environment—from patronal requests to authorial ambitions and perhaps a psychological desire for mental detachment—also influenced the ways in which they wrote about court life. One predictable effect is a striking cynicism about courtship and marriage, already evident in private (that is, non-attendant-authored) texts. Michitsuna's mother, for example, mentioned earlier, writes in her *Kagerō Diary* that she will offer a corrective to all of the romances she grew up with, based on her personal experience of elite courtship. With their constant participation in the competitive Rear Court, attendants were naturally still more critical, as the generally grim endings of court fiction indicate.

The *Kagerō* diarist's failure to recognize the clouds in the romances she criticized suggests the Rear Court's second major influence on its writers: subtlety, based as much on self-interest as the "purified" aesthetic discussed earlier. As noted, unlike the relatively mobile members of the French salon, Rear Court attendants generally relied on a single patron or family of patrons, often for their entire professional lives. By so doing, they hoped to spread their good fortune to their children and even grandchildren, to say nothing of anxious parents, brothers, and sisters. Fear of reprisals, particularly given the substantial expense families might incur to get them these positions, almost inevitably forced court writers to tread lightly in their criticisms. An attendant, as even Sei Shōnagon admits, was believed to sacrifice her modesty in court service, and once a patron's support faded, she lost the compensatory benefit to her family. In short, along with their authorial ambitions, Senji and her counterparts had a finely tuned sense of audience. Writers who wished to make unpopular points were careful to camouflage or otherwise moderate them. Murasaki Shikibu, who wrote *Genji* itself as a kind of aphrodisiac, mastered this balance, crafting a tale that readers can enjoy either as social criticism or an unusually skillful romance. While her heirs were less successful at this fusion, striking modern critics as either escapist or derivative of *Genji* or both, this does not mean they did not attempt it. When we keep the back side of court service—and "private" courtships—in mind, we stand a better chance of seeing these efforts.

TWO

The Tale of Sagoromo *and Midranks Romance*

Those born into the ranks of the elite are so well taken care of that a lot about them is hidden, which naturally makes them seem superior to everyone else. In the middle ranks, though, you start to get a sense of different personalities, and that gives you some choices. When it comes to the lower levels, well, there's not much worth talking about.

—Murasaki Shikibu, *The Tale of Genji*

The class criticism found in late Heian tales can shock modern readers, particularly those used to the playful approach used by Murasaki. Midranks romance—my term for the love affairs between courtiers like *Genji*'s Tō no Chūjō, quoted above, and the "middle ranks" (*naka no shina*) daughters of their social subordinates—is a staple of most Heian fiction, court-based and otherwise. *The Tale of Ochikubo* (*Ochikubo monogatari*, tenth century), for example, recounts how its middle ranks heroine, forced to work as her stepmother's maid, wins the heart of a nobleman and so regains and even surpasses her social place. *The Tale of Utsuho* (*Utsuho monogatari*, also tenth century), while generally interested in elite courtship, includes a similar rescue. With *Genji*, as usual, things become more complex. In contrast to these earlier usages, Murasaki begins by re-characterizing midranks romance as male fantasy. In the "rainy night's discussion on ranks" (*amayo no shina sadame*) quoted above, Tō no Chūjō notes that men profit most from these affairs, temporarily escaping both the monotony of formal marriages—typically depicted as loveless political alliances—and their behavioral restrictions. As he has learned from experience, midranks women stay "touching[ly]" silent through neglect or betrayal, even in cases where the man himself admits cause for complaint.[1] Murasaki rejects even this more plausible fantasy. Most of *Genji*'s midranks relationships end badly for both partners. In the worst cases, the woman succumbs to the toxic effects of the envy of others or their own isolation (Kiritsubo, Yūgao, Murasaki, and Ukifune), while their lovers (notably Genji and Kaoru) risk emotional collapse. In the best, as with Utsusemi and Suetsumuhana, the relationship fades into benign indifference, with the hero financially supporting his old lover but reserving his romantic attentions for newer candidates.

If Murasaki is openly skeptical about midranks romance, however, her reasons for being so remain opaque. Tō no Chūjō's rainy night remarks clearly suggest a social criticism: courtiers, however heedlessly, exploit their standing, treating these women in ways that highborn brides will not permit. The few happy midranks stories in *Genji* highlight this point, since by episode's end any class-crossing passions have been exorcised and the social order firmly restored. But Murasaki also offers a wealth of additional reasons for these failures. Some of the stories, as just noted, indict jealousy; others seem to implicate male rivalry or even, in the case of Ukifune, misplaced guilt. The reader is free to choose from several explanations for each tragedy or, conversely, to dissolve all of these affairs in the tale's broader pool of failed relationships. As a result, the troubling social dynamic evoked by the "midranks" label shrinks into shadow, only one in a seemingly endless list of reasons why romance goes wrong.

While contemporary readers may celebrate this complexity as a sign of Murasaki's realism, not everyone in her premodern audience was equally pleased. Even writers otherwise influenced by *Genji* reverted to midranks fantasies, as with the lost *Tale of Sumiyoshi*'s (*Sumiyoshi monogatari*) medieval revision and any number of coeval short stories. This is true even for authors who, like Murasaki, questioned the convention's happy ending. In *Nezame,* for instance, the evil mother-in-law mentioned in the introduction to this study torments the heroine in large part because she considers Nezame insufficiently deferential to the woman's own daughter, a princess. It is *The Tale of Sagoromo,* however, that presents the most thorough rebuttal of the midranks romance. Senji devotes most of *Sagoromo*'s first book (unlike *Genji,* the story is not subdivided into chapters) to her hero's own affair with midranks heroine Asukai. Like Murasaki, Senji emphasizes the encounter's tragic potential: Asukai eventually disappears from the tale, an apparent suicide. Unlike Murasaki, however, the later writer provides us with a single, unmistakable explanation for the tragedy. In *Sagoromo,* unlike *Genji,* there is one overwhelming reason for the failure of the romance: the lovers' social gap and the obstinacy of the "young nobles" (*waka kindachi* and *hoso kindachi*) who refuse to pay it heed. To make sure that the reader appreciates the contrast, Senji deliberately plays on some of the most celebrated midranks stories from *Genji*—ironically precipitating the dismissals discussed in the introduction.

The Tale of Sagoromo: *A Brief History*

As noted in the introduction, *Sagoromo* is not a readily accessible text. While the original prose is no more complex than Murasaki's, a modern Japanese translation has appeared only recently, and versions in other languages remain incomplete or nonexistent. Ironically, this neglect may be due to the tale's earlier success. Unlike most Heian tales, *Sagoromo* boasts a wealth of surviving manuscripts, well over a hundred by recent counts. As with medieval judgments ranking the tale "second only to *Genji*" and its poetry "outstanding,"[2] these numerous copies suggest *Sagoromo*'s warm reception, but they also present scholars with a challenge. Manuscripts often diverge at key points in the narrative, making it difficult to speak definitively about *Sagoromo*'s plot, much less subtler points of characterization, theme, and tone. Equally troubling, from a modern standpoint, is the tale's heavy debt to *Genji*. Plot structures, character types, and actual passages are lifted directly from Murasaki's text, a Heian commonplace that has nonetheless tarred *Sagoromo* as a footnote to *Genji*. The text's current position as a minor classic—frequently listed but rarely read—reflects both problems.

Happily, neither *Sagoromo*'s variants nor its alleged imitative character seem to have troubled medieval audiences, who continued to rework it in stories and commentaries well into the Edo period. Intriguingly, these readers took particular pleasure in the Asukai subplot. Like many court tales, *Sagoromo* is nominally focused on an elite relationship, the hero's unrequited love for his foster-sister Princess Genji. Sagoromo pines for this character throughout the twelve-year span of the narrative, worrying first that she will marry the Crown Prince and then, when she suddenly becomes Kamo Priestess, that he will lose her forever to the gods. Despite her constant rebuffs, Sagoromo continues to be obsessed with the princess, even after he discovers a virtual look-alike and, upon his stunning elevation to emperor, makes that woman his empress. This element of the narrative, lightly plotted and late in the tale, is a fairly insipid variation on Genji's love for Fujitsubo, complete with quasi-incestuous and subversive overtones but lacking the encounter that gives them force. It may also, ironically, allude to the obsession of readers with *Genji* itself. Either way, readers unsurprisingly devoted most of their attention to Sagoromo's romance with Asukai, the orphaned daughter of a noble who has fallen on hard times and the hero's first real conquest of the book. Shunzei's Daughter saves most of her praise for *Sagoromo* for this subplot, marveling that Asukai "could have so captivated such a man"—an apparent reference to their social distance—and wishing that the heroine "could have lived just a little longer and seen the depth of his affections."[3] The only female character from *Sagoromo* that *The Untitled Book* gives more attention is the Second Princess (*Onna Ni no Miya*), whose decision to become a nun better suits its religious subtext. Muromachi writers, who fashioned an entire cycle of "Sagoromo stories" (Sagoromo no sōshi, literally "books about Sagoromo") from the episode, echoed this enthusiasm, raising Asukai from the grave for a joyful lovers' reunion and ultimately revealing all parties involved as manifestations of popular deities.[4] Even *Sagoromo*'s variants confirm the subplot's special reputation. Not only do the earliest manuscripts suggest that Senji herself got carried away with Asukai, undercutting her opening focus on Princess Genji; many of the most divergent passages in later texts come from this story line, attesting to the ongoing fascination with it among subsequent readers.[5] One dimension of this divergence concerns Asukai's nurse, who figures in some versions as the villain of the story. The nurse also serves another narrative purpose, however: she is the center of Senji's midranks critique. If Tō no Chūjō and his remarks represent the elite male perspective on such relationships, the nurse and her doubles speak for the midranks themselves, regardless of gender, and with considerably more authority than anyone present that rainy night.

Asukai's Nurse and the Question of Class

Before discussing Asukai's nurse more specifically, it will be helpful to make a quick review of the subplot and its relationship to the midranks ideal. The beginning of the affair is structurally conventional if a bit livelier than usual. Late one night, as Sagoromo and his men return home from the palace, they meet and nearly collide with a speeding ox-cart. A priest, it turns out, has kidnapped one of his temple's pretty pilgrims, and he is rushing to find a place where he can get her alone. Sagoromo gallantly chases the man off and escorts her home, but by the time they get there he is himself infatuated, in typical midranks fashion. Soon he is making nightly visits to "Asukai," the woman's apologetic term for her shabby residence, in quiet defiance of the marriage offers that await

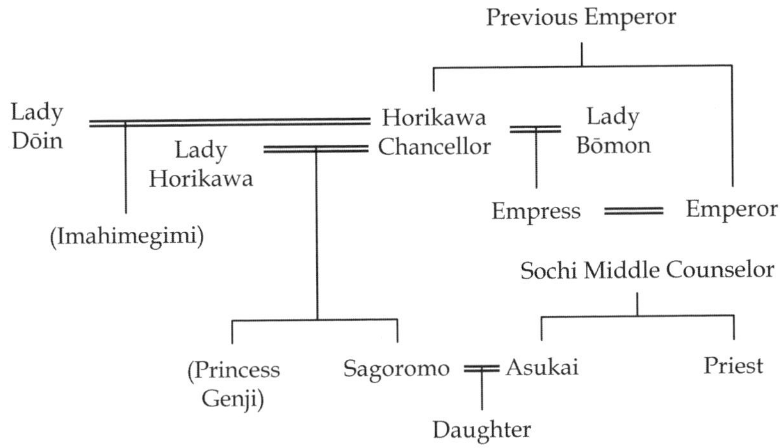

Fig. 2 Simplified genealogy for *The Tale of Sagoromo*
═ marital or romantic relationship | parent-child relationship ( ) foster relationship

him back at court.[6] Asukai, too, is smitten, again in keeping with the convention. She even comes from an appropriately collapsed lineage. Although we learn little about the heroine's parents, the narrator does reveal that Asukai's father was the Sochi Middle Counselor (*Sochi no chūnagon*), that is, the middle counselor in the Sochi's employ. Sochi was the name awarded to the prince put in charge of Dazaifu, the imperial compound in Tsukushi (modern Kyūshū) associated with exiles like Sugawara Michizane (845–903). While the Sochi and his retinue did not usually go to Dazaifu, it seems clear that Asukai's father served an unfortunate patron. The association neatly explains Asukai's midranks status and, perhaps, her wit and beauty, conventionally associated with women of good birth.

Here, however, the midranks story takes an unpredictable twist. While Asukai quickly falls for her rescuer, her nurse, an aging widow, is less impressed. Despite his passion, Sagoromo will not identify himself to Asukai and put the affair on a more stable footing for fear of offending Princess Genji. The pragmatic nurse soon loses her patience. "These young nobles," she grumbles to the heroine, "will abandon a girl if her parents can't provide for them" (100). Since she is Asukai's sole support, and not an effective "provider," she decides preemptively to sabotage the relationship. First she tries "accidentally" (and repeatedly) barring the gate, but Sagoromo's persistence—and Asukai's pregnancy—soon move her to more drastic action. After wearily advising the lovesick heroine to tell Sagoromo about her condition and see if this sways him, the nurse turns to her own male acquaintances. She reluctantly contacts the priest, a former benefactor; when he fails to reply, she turns to an amorous general, who offers to marry the nurse and move them all to the provinces. The nurse, who sees no other choice, curtly informs Asukai of her decision. The heroine may stay if she wishes, but the rest of the household will shortly be leaving the capital.

As Asukai agonizes over what to do, the subplot reaches its shocking climax. One of the heroine's earlier suitors, Michinari, informs the nurse that he is also moving to the provinces; his father has just taken a post in Dazaifu, and he anticipates a related appointment. (For midranks men, apparently, the city of exiles was a desirable posting.) Arguing that it "will be to [her] advantage" to help him, he presses the nurse to let him take Asukai as his wife (93). Impressed by his prospects, the nurse immediately agrees. She abandons her general and tricks Asukai onto Michinari's boat, "beaming with satisfaction" at the wedding gifts that await them (103). Asukai, understandably, is less pleased, particularly when Michinari inadvertently (and completely innocently) reveals that her mysterious lover is his patron, Sagoromo, the toast of the court. Rather than betray the hero, she leaps overboard, briefly wondering before her death what will happen to her nurse once she is gone. Although Sagoromo later finds both Asukai's child and her diary, and ultimately offers a memorial service for her, in most versions of the tale we never see her alive again, nor do we learn what happens to the nurse.[7]

Medieval readers and modern critics alike, despite their general enthusiasm for the subplot, have had a difficult time with the nurse. The problem seems to stem from her contradictory behavior, at least in the early manuscripts summarized here. On the one hand, the nurse is clearly the episode's antagonist. Contrary to generic convention, which makes nurses the helpmates of court romance, this woman harasses the lovers, ultimately sending Asukai to her death.[8] The protagonists, generally the reader's surrogates in the story, react with horror to this betrayal. Asukai, fending off Michinari, "despairs that she had ever thought of her [nurse] as a parent"; Sagoromo, arriving to Asukai's empty house, assumes with dismay that the "the nurse must have done something" and berates himself for his lack of foresight (107–8, 109).

On the other hand, the nurse clearly also has her virtues. Unlike stock villains such as the stepmother in *Ochikubo*, who plots to have the heroine raped, or *Genji*'s Kokiden, who lobbies for the hero's exile, the nurse believes herself to be acting in the heroine's best interests. She raises Asukai after the girl's parents die, exhausting her own resources and apparently, judging from Asukai's later sense of betrayal, treating her quite affectionately.[9] Moreover, when the nurse does decide to separate the lovers—something she attempts only when it becomes clear that the mysterious noble will not make the affair public—she takes pains to justify herself. "I can't do much more for you, as a woman, on my own," she argues, trying to convince Asukai to quit the affair and go into court service (73). Later, she returns to this point, insisting that "even a thousand parents and wet nurses are worthless for a woman. We can only help until you get a husband" (90). It is difficult to imagine Ochikubo's stepmother or Kokiden stopping to explain herself to her victim, and the contrast again makes the nurse look good. Nor is the nurse's final deception of Asukai totally without redeeming features. Although she has a few early twinges of conscience—"It really is too bad," she worries while packing, "to hand Asukai over to a stranger and send her so far away"—Michinari's lavish shipboard reception seems to justify the nurse's decision (101). Certainly her fellow travelers, Asukai's new attendants, think so. "I hear that everyone wants him for a son-in-law," one gushes, admiring Michinari. "She is so lucky!" marvel others, looking at Asukai. "Why is she being so difficult?" (104–5) Small wonder, then, if Asukai spares a thought for the nurse before she jumps. Both in terms of her past and in comparison to her fictional colleagues, Asukai's wet nurse comes across as a relatively sympathetic figure.

In short, Asukai's nurse appears in the earliest versions of *Sagoromo* as a complex character, one of the rounder figures in a generally flat roster. Rather than considering the significance of this portrait, however, later readers attempted to rewrite Asukai's nurse to match their simpler expectations. A few of *Sagoromo*'s early variants attempt to soften the character, adding an account of her remorse after the heroine jumps ship.[10] A far more popular choice, however, was to make the nurse a more conventional villain. Many copies of *Sagoromo*'s first book—the heart of the Asukai story—omit sympathetic passages about the nurse, such as her tears for the heroine or Asukai's own parting thoughts for her, while others feature expanded descriptions of Asukai's suffering.[11] Both changes transform the nurse into a more wicked character, an assessment that Satomura Jōha (1524?–1602), the noted linked-verse master, apparently shared. In his commentary *Sagoromo's Sash Strings* (*Sagoromo no shitahimo*, 1591), Jōha accuses the nurse of colluding with the priest in Asukai's initial abduction, despite textual evidence of her shock at the incident.[12] Even some modern critics adopt this position, linking her to the wicked stepmothers of *Ochikubo* and *Genji* despite the differences noted earlier.[13] The "bullied stepchild story" (*mamako ijimetan*, sometimes abbreviated to *mamakotan*) is another common plot convention. One also posits a failed love affair with the priest, making the nurse's alleged cruelty to Asukai a matter not only of malice but sexual jealousy.[14] As suggested earlier, these decisions have interpretive implications for the subplot as a whole. To varying degrees, they recast the Asukai affair as a kind of fairy tale, pitting the heroine against a malicious or spiteful guardian.[15]

Other readers, meanwhile, perhaps disconcerted by the nurse's inconsistency, choose to ignore the character altogether. Shunzei's Daughter, for example, omits the nurse from her lengthy discussion of the subplot, despite specific references to the roles of both the priest and Michinari in the heroine's suffering.[16] The "Sagoromo stories," divergent in other parts of the story, go even further. After briefly describing Michinari's first contact with the nurse, they have Asukai's (now living) parents arrange the shipboard deception, apparently reintroducing them into the story expressly for this purpose.[17] Here, too, literary history has repeated itself in more recent interpretations. One view, while granting that the nurse may have betrayed Asukai, downplays her behavior as a kind of financial panic.[18] Another shifts the discussion from simple villainy, framing it instead as bad judgment; had the nurse known Sagoromo's identity, the argument goes, she would never have acted as she did.[19] Instead, these critics group the nurse with *Sagoromo*'s nurses in general, a group of more or less innocuous "stagehands" who advance the narrative and connect its subplots.[20]

Enter the Middle Ranks

Despite these ambivalent views of the nurse, when we reconsider the episode in terms of its midranks contours, we make an interesting discovery. Senji repeatedly juxtaposes the nurse with two other (lower) middle ranks figures: Michinari, Asukai's southbound suitor, and the "mother-substitute," a character from a related subplot. These characters, who, like the nurse, are given extensive opportunities to speak, invariably echo or favorably counterpoint the nurse's judgments. Their observations and actions make the nurse seem more sympathetic, and suggest Senji's commitment to the complexities of the original character. In effect the juxtaposition also confirms the nurse's—and author's—rejection of midranks romance itself.

Michinari

Michinari, Asukai's suitor, is a fairly traditional literary double; despite the difference in gender, he is clearly associated with the nurse through their negotiations for Asukai, and this association confirms key points in the nurse's character. It is important to notice then, before dismissing the nurse, just how sympathetic a figure Michinari is. To begin with the obvious, he is described as strikingly good-looking, literary shorthand for virtue in most Heian texts. Michinari is so "refined and handsome" that people "even prefer him to some members of the upper nobility" (92). Asukai and Sagoromo separately echo this assessment. Even while spurning Michinari's advances, the heroine reflects that "people would probably call him attractive" (103). Years later, when Michinari returns to the capital to receive his promotion, Sagoromo makes the same observation. "His downcast appearance," the hero notes, listening to his former retainer discuss his wife's suicide, "was really much more attractive than the young nobles one saw around court" (178). Sagoromo understandably becomes rather less fond of Michinari when he realizes that the wife in question was actually his lost lover, Asukai, but his favorable account of the man's looks remains nonetheless.

Trivial though they may seem, these descriptions of Michinari tend to improve our opinion of the nurse. For one thing, they flatter her judgment. Although the nurse is described by Sagoromo as "old, ugly, and unimaginably coarse"—traits that would typically be associated with a villain—she knows a good-looking man when she sees one (69). Moreover, many more "refined" (i.e., attractive and virtuous) people agree with her, including both the heroes and, according to the shipboard attendants quoted earlier, some equally elite courtiers looking for son-in-laws. Earlier, the nurse reacts with horror when she hears that Asukai has been kidnapped by the priest, physically caricatured by the narrator as a "bald head" or "bad haircut" in stole-flapping flight (65, 70). The nurse's decision to wait for someone like Michinari, despite the household's worsening financial straits, speaks to her discernment, however little Asukai may like the results. To the extent that looks reflect ethical worth, Michinari's attractiveness lends the nurse a kind of moral credibility.

Michinari's physical depiction prompts us to reconsider the nurse's portrait—and, more significantly, the perspective that informs it. As just noted, we get several confirmations of Michinari's good looks, from a variety of people of different backgrounds. The nurse's physical appearance, however, is known to us only from Sagoromo's observation when he escorts Asukai back to her house, and the nurse peeks into the carriage with a blinding torch. Given Sagoromo's desire to remain anonymous, it is hardly surprising that he views the pushy bystander negatively. Indeed, when she draws closer, the hero actually pushes Asukai (his new lover!) from the carriage, just to make the nurse leave. As his fascinated view of the "hot-looking, cramped-looking gate" and "desolate-looking" mosquito fires betrays, Sagoromo sees the whole episode as a kind of social safari, with the squalor of the place forming a crucial part of its appeal (69). If the hero sees the nurse as "unimaginably coarse," then—particularly after so brief and confused a meeting—it is arguably because his imagination demands it. Considering that the nurse does, after all, receive a second marriage offer and once served in a wealthy household, we may wish to give her person the benefit of the doubt. Indeed, even critics arguing for the nurse's affair with the priest suggest that she is probably younger than Sagoromo thinks.[21]

Michinari's prospects, as tantalizing as his physical presence, also do the nurse credit. As he boasts to Asukai, Michinari works for Sagoromo, one of the capital's most distinguished courtiers, suggesting that he is probably fairly distinguished himself; Heian aristocrats, at least in fiction, tend to assemble equally worthy attendants. Moreover, as the narrator points out, Michinari is a child of Sagoromo's wet nurse, and the most impressive of them at that. As Michinari tells Asukai, this relationship and the patronage it implies make him an excellent catch.

> You may say that your lover is better than I am, but that's nothing to be proud of; it's just plain foolish. Do you really want to spend your days as the mistress of some minor captain or the other, wearing your heart out worrying about what people think? I may be low-ranked, but you should keep in mind that I will be absolutely de-

voted to you. These young nobles are nothing but trouble; they never settle down. As long as my master is around, though, even a nobody like me will come out ahead of men like that. If I put my mind to it, I could become a minor captain or an assistant captain in the middle palace guards, too. Just wait and see. Next year, when I return to the capital, I'll become a fifth-rank chamberlain, with court privileges and everything, and then we'll see how your lover compares. People like him are going to come begging to work for me. It's your decision. . . . I may not be a young noble, but people don't think I'm so bad." (103–4)

Michinari's speech, self-serving though it is, is also accurate. As noted earlier, his father has just received a provincial appointment, probably on the strength of those same connections; that is why the nurse finally accepts his suit. Moreover, when Michinari returns to the capital, the occasion for his sad conversation with Sagoromo, he comes to accept a new post himself. Although Michinari's words also resonate ironically—one cannot imagine Sagoromo asking his retainer for work—the emphasis on class, particularly on the uselessness of "young nobles," also encourages a kinder view of the nurse. Asukai is poor; Michinari's patronage makes him rich. To a nurse responsible for her charge's physical as well as emotional needs, the choice between him and an irresponsible "young noble"—a term familiar from her own complaints—is obvious.

Michinari's views on romance, and his contrast on this front with the hero, provide a final sympathetic perspective on the nurse. As noted earlier, some critics attempt to defend the nurse by blaming bad judgment, rather than malice, for her behavior. Michinari's own thoughts on the affair, alongside his attractive physical and social profile, argue for an even more positive interpretation. As he reveals in the speech just quoted, Michinari does not take midranks romances seriously either; in his words, such clandestine relationships are "nothing but trouble" and simply cause the woman involved to "wear her heart out with worrying." He makes the same point while unwittingly describing Asukai to Sagoromo. "She was pregnant, in her seventh month or so, by some minor captain or the other, but I thought that rather than leaving her to the affections of that young noble, it would be better if I married her myself" (179). Like the nurse, Michinari recognizes that midranks fantasies can never result in real marriages; in fact, he is even more pessimistic than she is, since he thinks that even a child will not make a noble take Asukai seriously.

By contrast, Michinari offers both Asukai and her child his formal support. As he tells the nurse during their first discussion, "It would be a shame to leave her as the secret mistress of one of those young nobles. Just wait and see what I'll do for her" (93). Michinari's gifts of trinkets and attendants bear him out, as does his attentiveness to Asukai's physical condition; it is difficult to imagine a noble hero, conventionally ignorant of such things, estimating the length of his lover's pregnancy or personally attending her aboard his ship.[22] Once again, Michinari's words reveal more than self-interest. These repeated, credible offers of a more stable relationship echo the nurse's own criticisms of midranks affairs, forcing us to reconsider her viewpoint.[23]

In the speeches just quoted, of course, Michinari also presents an unconscious criticism of the hero, something that he would presumably never do if he knew the truth. Lest we miss the point, in introducing Michinari, the narrator explicitly invites us to compare the two men.

> In his heart, Michinari suffered from no unrequited longings in particular; in fact, he was quite a playboy, and he thought only of finding a truly exceptional beauty to be his wife. Because of this, he refused to go anywhere near the various households that wanted him as a son-in-law, instead devoting himself entirely to doing what his master did. He never missed a chance to join Sagoromo on his midnight rambles, and during his own trips home he was always poking into corners himself. (92)

Like Sagoromo, Michinari was once a playboy of the kind immortalized in *Tales of Ise* (*Ise monogatari*, tenth century) and the midranks romance's typical hero. Like Sagoromo, who rejects the daughter of the reigning emperor rather than risk his hopes for Princess Genji, Michinari once shunned marriage for private dalliances. Unlike Sagoromo, however, Michinari takes Asukai seriously, and this response directly reflects the men's social gap. As a lower-ranking courtier, Michinari is free to choose Asukai as a wife, even as he thrills to her romantic appeal. Sagoromo, by contrast, cannot possibly marry Asukai; as noted earlier, this mismatch between desire and social reality is the fictional prerequisite for their romance. Given Asukai's social distance, the only option Sagoromo has is to place her in his family's service as an attendant, something that Asukai herself unwittingly rejects when the nurse suggests it. Not that Asukai's thoughts on the subject matter. Sagoromo abandons the idea even before broaching it to her, convinced that Princess Genji will slight him if she finds out. As the nurse and Michinari both realize, however, the real obstacle is Asukai's social class. In acting on this knowledge and ending the relationship, the nurse may be cruel, but she is also, as Senji implies through the sympathetic Michinari, a fountain of midranks common sense.

The Mother-substitute

If Michinari serves as a double for Asukai's wet nurse, allowing us to appreciate her good judgment, the character also has a darker angel: the "mother-substitute" (*hahashiro*) caring for Asukai's cousin, Ima Himegimi (Imahime). Senji does not directly link the two characters; the substitute appears in Asukai's story only briefly, and then after Asukai and the nurse have vanished. Like Michinari, however, the substitute shares the nurse's midranks background, accented this time by the women's common profession and their charges' own family tie. The mother-substitute thus emerges as a counterpoint to the nurse, both in terms of her social views and her professional competence. Both comparisons highlight the nurse's good judgment, once again complicating our view of the midranks subplot.

Like Asukai, the mother-substitute and her charge enter *Sagoromo* almost as a digression. During a description of Princess Genji, the narrator casually mentions that Lady Dōin, one of Sagoromo's father's wives, wishes to adopt a child.

Sagoromo's mother, guardian to Princess Genji, and Lady Bōmon, mother of the current empress, enjoy public acclaim for their beautiful, successful daughters, and Dōin is jealous.[24] "If only there were someone appropriate," she spends her days brooding. "I would take her in and raise her myself" (37). Dōin is partially hoping to regain her husband's affections with the adoption, a stratagem also memorably employed by the Kagerō diarist.[25] Dōin's desire to pit someone against her rivals' children, however, clearly also parodies Heian marriage politics. Even Dōin's language betrays this agenda, as she literally says, "I would take her in and . . . *stand her up*" (*tateru*, emphasis added), a phrase normally used for the elevation of an empress or crown prince. From its inception, then, the subplot foregrounds the class concerns so pivotal to the Asukai episode.

Here the substitute enters the story. In a scene strategically placed just after Sagoromo's meeting with Asukai, Dōin, having heard that a late attendant's daughter may be her husband's, impetuously brings the girl home. Dōin quickly showers the girl with rooms and ornaments, and since the girl has also lost her nurse, provides a "mother-substitute." Imahime or "the new lady," as the rumormongers enviously call her, is poised to conquer the court, making her story seem the perfect antithesis to Asukai's. Before long, however, disaster strikes, and here the parallels with the earlier subplot turn to the nurse's favor. Imahime's new caretaker manifests almost no aptitude for her role, and her failures repeatedly foreground the nurse's unnarrated success in the same.

The substitute's first failing is her snobbery. According to the narrator, "although she had some elite connections, the substitute had always bemoaned her own insignificant status" (82). The woman's newfound prominence in Dōin's household intoxicates her. Despite her inferior background, the substitute is soon walking around with "a smug, self-satisfied expression, pretending to know everything and acting as if she has first-hand knowledge of things she has never even seen." She displays the same intemperance in her decorating, "collecting things together in a shocking manner and doing everything with seemingly no sense of restraint." Even Dōin, too intent on her own ambitions to pay much attention to Imahime, senses that the substitute "is not settling in properly." The contrast with Asukai's nurse is striking. Like the substitute, the nurse has a taste for sermonizing, as her frequent lectures to Asukai attest. The scene on Michinari's boat, meanwhile, suggests her comparable delight in trinkets. The two women's attitudes regarding this matter, however, are entirely different. When the nurse lectures Asukai or praises Michinari's gifts, she does so at least in part to help the heroine to what she considers the right decision. Moreover, even Sagoromo, so critical of the nurse herself, mentions no lapses in the household furnishings, despite the nurse's meager resources. The mother-substitute's quirks, by contrast, are both painfully obvious and self-serving. As Senji stresses, the substitute, like Dōin, is a social climber, and one who commits the considerable sin of not knowing her place—something that we suddenly realize we cannot say about the nurse.

If the substitute, like Michinari, confirms the nurse's good judgment, she also illuminates her professional competence. Imahime, the narrator notes dryly, is "overly informal and immature" for her twenty years, a serious liability for a potential consort (82). One of the substitute's most pressing responsibilities is to correct or at least camouflage this flaw; that, as Genji and his friends famously complain in the rainy night's conversation, is part of a guardian's job.[26] Instead, the substitute exposes Imahime to potentially ruinous court gossip by putting her flaws on display. Among other things, the substitute hires the wrong kind of attendants to run the heroine's household. Armed with Dōin's resources, she could presumably hire the cream of the attendant class. Instead, she calls her old friends into service—women who likely are as unsavory as she is—and "lies to her heart's content" to get some gullible younger ones (83).[27] Even Imahime, despite all of her flaws, recoils from the "worthless" group that results. Sagoromo, stopping by her rooms unannounced, echoes the assessment.

> The standing curtains were all scattered about, and a large number of attendants spilled out in front of them. Very inappropriate, he observed, watching them intently. He had heard that Dōin's sister the consort was sending over quite a few of her women; could this really be them? He stepped closer, intrigued, since he had never seen Imahime's household, and some of her attendants saw him and panicked. How bizarre! They were bringing out screens from the back with a crash and trying to set them up, yanking hurriedly on the tangled strings—there must have been twenty women at work, rushing about and making a racket. The noise of the screens, along with the rustle of their robes and trousers, was almost deafening. (84–85)

Although the ease with which Sagoromo peers into the room in itself condemns Imahime's new entourage—in *Genji*, for example, it takes a typhoon to throw the heroine Murasaki's women off their guard—the view betrays a far more serious lack of wit and composure. Like the mother-substitute, these new attendants are obviously *not* from the consort's household. Sagoromo's attempts to engage them in conversation only make things worse. Arguing noisily over which one of them should provide the expected poem, the women literally bolt from the room, tearing hems and toppling screens in the process. Sagoromo, who had earlier only with difficulty controlled his laughter, now feels as if "he could die laughing" (87). The attendants' clumsiness also has a somber side, as a second lapse demonstrates. Not long after the women have regained their composure, a gust of wind blows through the curtains and knocks over a screen, again exposing the household to view. Rather than straightening things up, the women only cry out and "tumble to the ground, their Chinese robes thrown over their heads" (88). They also thoughtlessly expose Imahime herself, a serious breach of etiquette. Sagoromo, shocked, actually makes eye contact with the girl, who, to make things worse, is standing, a particularly inappropriate pose. Kashiwagi, who betrays Genji with the Third Princess, initiates the affair because he is so inflamed by the sight of her doing the same thing—a lapse the text also blames on careless attendants. These mistakes clearly fall on the head of the mother-substitute, as does the shamelessly audible commentary Sagoromo hears through the women's screens. The comparison again flatters Asukai's wet nurse. Asukai may not have many attendants, but Sagoromo certainly never sees them behave like this. We likewise never hear of anyone catching a glimpse of Asukai in the nurse's presence; both the priest and Michinari apparently spot the heroine during retreats, and Sagoromo meets her in the extraordinary scene at the intersection. The contrast with Imahime's household helps us to appreciate this discretion.

The substitute's few attempts to educate Imahime are similarly revealing. The Heian elite expected its women to be adept with poetry; it allowed men to imagine their beauty, otherwise ideally screened from view, and gave women a rare acceptable means of complaint. The Kagerō diarist, for example, manages to have her husband read and respond to a long poem on her concerns, although he usually leaves when she raises them in conversation. But when the nurse takes advantage of Sagoromo's presence to coach Imahime in the art, she once again invites his censure. Noticing that the younger attendants have yet to answer Sagoromo's conventional complaint that they are ignoring him (a claim that, given their very noticeable reaction to his presence, is itself highly ironic), the substitute swoops into action.

"Don't you know that the elite can get a reputation from the people who work for them?" she hissed at them, wearing her usual smug expression. "At this rate, you youngsters might as well not be working here at all." Still glaring, she sidled over near to where Sagoromo was seated on the other side of the curtain. "What an unexpected honor! Did you perhaps make a mistake?

> What brings you here, crossing Yoshino River?
> Sibling Mountain may sound reliable,
> but the name is all that drifts this way." (87)

The poem, a rebuttal of Sagoromo's complaint, is fairly conventional, but the substitute's "breakneck," "hoarse," and inappropriately "youthful" delivery shames the entire household. As Sagoromo reflects afterwards, Imahime "may not have very good manners, but at least she's better than those attendants" (88). The substitute's music lessons, another educational responsibility, fall still farther from the mark. Even after the earlier visit, Sagoromo had taken a sympathetic view of the heroine, intrigued as he is by her undeniable beauty. But when, several years later, Dōin requests that he give Imahime a music lesson, he makes an unpleasant discovery. Not only do the attendants remain unchecked, stampeding before him "like so many wild horses," poor Imahime herself has regressed. As the substitute herself smugly announces, Imahime's technique has developed into something "not just anyone can appreciate. It's in a class of its own" (233, 235).

While the woman is describing Imahime's music, the speech, like some of Michinari's comments, redounds ironically. Under the substitute's active if unwitting tutelage, the heroine has gone as wild as the attendants themselves. Her performance, shrewdly left to our imagination, is apparently appalling and subsumes a host of additional flaws. As the narrator explains, the substitute had "called in some strange person as a *biwa* (lute) teacher, and so the girl, terrified, played exactly as he said" (237–38). Sagoromo can only conclude that his sister "is not at all what I thought" (235–36). Here, again, the contrast with Asukai's wet nurse is striking. While we never see her in the classroom, she obviously develops Asukai's talents to the utmost; they are as much a part of the midranks fantasy as the heroine's beauty. Once again, we are compelled to admit the nurse's virtues and to reconsider her other actions in the process.

The substitute's final favorable contrast with the nurse involves Imahime's odd fate. Not surprisingly, Dōin's new daughter does not end up going to court. After that singular concert, Sagoromo resolves to do everything he can to prevent her from doing so, worrying that "it will be scandalous, a complete disaster" for the entire family (236). In the event, he never has to lift a finger. Not long before Imahime is to go to the palace, Dōin's older brother, a ranking noble, sneaks into the girl's quarters and sleeps with her.[28] The seduction itself does not necessarily ruin her chances at court; as Dōin later observes, "At times like this, you quietly escort the man out," a strategy used successfully by Oborozukiyo and her women until her father finds Genji in her bed (252). Unfortunately, the mother-substitute's typically unmeasured response rules this option out. "Hey," she yells out, noticing movement from the heroine's corner of the room that night. "There seems to be a man in here! Everyone, get candles and come over here, quick! Some thieving rascal has snuck in!" (251) Before long the entire household is staring at the embarrassed couple. Nor does the substitute stop there. As the narrator relates,

> She came over to where the girl was lying down and, dragging her from bed, began to scold her. "So you're just going to throw away the good fortune that our lady threw all of her riches into gaining for you—and as fast as she could, too! You take up with some provincial governor just because you can't wait a few days! Even really low-born girls with lots of needs to consider worry about their reputations and make up their minds as children not to get involved with some man who just takes after them like that. I don't care where you go, just get out of here quick. Don't you have any sense of shame?!" The sight of her scraping her nails together in fury was so terrifying that Imahime threw her hair over her face and wept. (252–53)

By trumpeting the presence of the man to the entire household—she even emphasizes it, calling him, literally, a "provincial governor *man*"—and, moreover, mistakenly demoting him to an inferior rank, the substitute does more than just frighten Imahime. She sabotages her protégé's chances at court, since the emperor can hardly ignore the resulting gossip.[29] Despite an unusual happy ending (after a misguided tonsure, Imahime marries her seducer, who is actually quite devoted to her), the episode again confirms the worth of Asukai's nurse, recalled here by the substitute's nosy waving of her torch. As noted earlier, the nurse manages to protect Asukai until the priest's shocking kidnapping, and even once Sagoromo begins visiting she tries to keep him away, locking him out until his men threaten to call in the Heian police.[30] Given the nurse's much thinner staffing and resources, this is no small feat, and the substitute's ineptitude helps us to appreciate it. Finally, the substitute's comments highlight the nurse's wisdom in choosing Michinari. No matter what her tormentor says, Imahime obviously does not choose the seduction any more than—at the ripe age of 20—she rushes into an early marriage. The nurse, however, does both on Asukai's behalf. In contrast to her cousin, Asukai does have "a lot of needs," and Michinari, unlike Sagoromo, clearly promises to fill them. If the nurse's decision to act on this knowledge makes her the episode's antagonist, it nonetheless reflects favorably on her professional commitment. Her distance from the mother-substitute—a stock malefactor—makes this point unmistakable.

The Asukai Subplot and The Tale of Genji

Before concluding this look at Senji's critique of midranks romance, and the nurse's special role within it, let us consider the subplot from one final perspective: its *Genji* templates. As noted earlier, Murasaki also reflects on the midranks convention in her tale; almost every significant romance plot in *Genji*, aside from the hero's affairs with Fujitsubo and the Third Princess, invokes this storyline at some level. Senji, like many of Murasaki's successors, draws heavily from two of these stories in constructing her own midranks episode: Genji's affair with Yūgao and his heirs Kaoru and Niou's love triangle with Ukifune. (There is a third substantial parallel between Imahime and Tō no Chūjō's awkward daughter Ōmi no Kimi, better known as the Ōmi Lady, which I will not discuss here.)[31] The debt is so striking, and so often remarked upon, as to make discussion of it tedious. Senji also, however, deliberately rewrites certain portions of these episodes, underscoring her innovation on the midranks theme.[32] Even a brief review of their effect on the nurse's character confirms what the figures of Michinari and the mother-substitute already make clear. Senji, even more than Murasaki, wants the reader to recognize the essentially exploitative nature of the midranks relationship.[33]

Senji's innovations on the Yūgao episode, one of *Genji*'s "rainy night" stories, rely on several important parallels. Tō no Chūjō's introduction to the heroine reveals most of these almost immediately.

"I'll tell you a fool's tale," said Tō no Chūjō. "I had just started seeing someone very secretly, not the kind of affair you expect to last, but as I got to know her, I started to care for her, until even when I hadn't visited for a while, I still kept thinking about her. As time went by, it became clear that she relied on me, but although by then even I realized there must be times when she resented my behavior, she acted as if nothing was wrong, even when I hadn't come by in a long time. She treated me as if, instead of being a long-lost visitor, I had been with her morning and night, and I found this so touching that I ended up telling her she could always rely on me. Her parents were gone, so things were hard for her, and the occasional glimpses I had of this feeling for me were very appealing."[34]

Tō no Chūjō notices two key traits in Yūgao, traits that directly color the portrait of Asukai. First, Yūgao is, in social terms, utterly insignificant. Tō no Chūjō refers to his story as a "fool's tale" (*shiremono no monogatari*), and while he may be referring to himself (scholars differ on this point), its applicability to the heroine is obvious. In an aristocrat's view, only a fool would devote himself to a poor orphan, whatever her attractions; Tō no Chūjō admits as much. As noted earlier, however, this poverty is an integral part of the midranks heroine's charm. Tō no Chūjō later speaks nostalgically of Yūgao's shabby lodgings, and her sobriquet, an allusion to the "evening faces" flowers blooming on her fence, evokes both them and her more general fragility. Asukai shares this trait, right down to her humble sobriquet.

Second, and equally important, Yūgao is completely devoted to her lover, despite his dismissive treatment. By acting as if he "ha[s] been with her morning and night," rather than visiting sporadically, she acquiesces to the young noble's midranks fantasy, effectively agreeing not to complicate it with her own practical or emotional concerns. Tō no Chūjō finds this response, which he takes as a sign of her trust, "very appealing." Genji, who later becomes involved with Yugao and is again mesmerized by her shabby surroundings, also notes how much easier she is to be with than more demanding lovers.[35] Here, too, the influence on Asukai is obvious. Like her model, the *Sagoromo* heroine remains silent about her troubles, although she at least thinks about them, rationalizing that her inferior status on some level justifies the hero's treatment of her.[36] She cannot even bring herself to tell Sagoromo of her pregnancy, despite the fact that the nurse briefly drops her resistance to the affair and urges an appeal for help.

Unlike these heroines, however, the antagonists in both stories reject this supposedly romantic behavior—and it is here, against another seeming parallel, that Senji's innovation stands out. In Yūgao's case, the antagonists are her sexual rivals. As Tō no Chūjō relates, when his main wife—tellingly described as "the place [he] humbly visit[s]"—learns of the affair, she frightens Yūgao off with some "cruel, heartless" notes.[37] When Genji takes up with Yūgao, years later, he invites a more dramatic version of the same thing. Rokujō—his lover and the widow of a crown prince—mounts an involuntary but fatal spirit attack on the heroine, disgusted that Genji would neglect her for "someone with nothing to distinguish her."[38] As these remarks suggest, Tō no Chūjō's wife and Rokujō react as much to the slight to their status as to the sexual betrayal. Crucially, however, the men interpret the episodes romantically. Tō no Chūjō, remembering how visits to Yūgao were "like something out of an old tale," imagines her burdened with regret for leaving him.[39] Genji, who glimpses the spirit generally identified as Rokujō at Yūgao's pillow, comes to a similar conclusion. Briefly reflecting that "this is exactly the kind of thing one finds in old tales,"[40] he later blames the whole thing on female jealousy: "It must have happened because something that haunted the ruined place saw me and was attracted to me."[41] In a way, Genji and Tō no Chūjō are correct. Tō no Chūjō's wife and Rokujō are jealous. Yet their jealousy reflects not just wounded affection but the value ascribed hierarchy and status. Aristocrats are supposed to command more respect than do women like Yūgao. By striking out at her, Tō no Chūjō's wife and Rokujō act at least in part to restore the social order that midranks romance rejects.

Asukai's nurse, arguably, does the same thing—and here Senji's deliberate evocation of the *Genji* story bears fruit. Critics typically judge the nurse by her peers in *Genji* (that is, Yūgao's attendants), a comparison that tends to put the nurse in a negative light. Unlike Yūgao's attendants, who have Genji's carriage followed, Asukai's nurse does not make any obvious efforts to discover Sagoromo's identity; unlike Ukon, Yūgao's nurse who eventually makes the heroine's daughter's fortune, she never does anything for Asukai's child. Critics have thus written her off as malicious or lazy or, at best, dully realistic.[42] When we compare the nurse to Tō no Chūjō's wife and Rokujō, however, we gain a new appreciation for her perceptiveness. Like Yūgao's romantic rivals, the nurse acts as she does in part because she cannot accept the hero's midranks fantasy. Like them, in a sense, she also works to restore the social hierarchy, this time by giving the heroine to a man that can formally accept her. Structurally this decision makes her a villain, since it forces her to resist the hero and a widely held romantic ideal. Her action, like that of the Yūgao villains, is not without its darker side; when the nurse strikes her bargain with Michinari, she is clearly also defending her own interests. By making her a nurse, however, rather than Asukai's romantic rival, Senji forces us to discount jealousy as a motive for her actions. Unlike the *Genji* antagonists, she does not attack the heroine, either literally or by letter; in fact, she finds her a husband. Once again, we have to admit a more favorable profile, no matter what we think of the decision or its tragic results.

By removing jealousy as a potential explanation for the nurse's action, in short, Senji narrows our focus to the practical costs of midranks romance. It is worth noting that the nurse's late husband was not simply any middle-ranks bureaucrat, but the head of an office concerned with taxes and other fiscal affairs.[43] Some critics use this in support of their negative views of the nurse, claiming that this relatively privileged position would have given her a dangerous taste for luxury.[44] Senji's internal advocates for the character, however (i.e., Michinari and the substitute), suggest a quite different perspective. With these subtle but significant changes, Senji uses the Yūgao intertext to reinforce her pragmatic criticism of the midranks convention: if, as Arthur Waley famously concluded from *Genji*, "hate kills," then fantasy can, too—whether midranks heroines like Asukai admit it or not.

Senji uses her other key intertext, *Genji*'s Ukifune story, to make an abbreviated but similar point. Here, too, the writer first prepares us to appreciate her variation with a series of structural parallels. Ukifune, the unrecognized daughter of a prince, famously tries to drown herself rather than choose between the nobles (Kaoru and Niou) who relentlessly pursue her. When she survives the suicide attempt, thanks in part to the efforts of some traveling priests, she retreats to a mountain hideaway and takes the tonsure. This story, another failed midranks romance, clearly inspires Senji, although some of the parallels (the heroine's tonsure and seclusion) unfold only in the Asukai plot's epilogue. Senji even includes a nod to Ukifune's mother, who, like the nurse, shows a taste for both baubles and social commentary, at least until she herself is swept off her feet by her daughter's suitors.[45]

Senji does not, however, borrow the Ukifune intertext's key motif: the rivalry between the suitors. As noted in the introduction, Niou and Kaoru compete over everything in their lives, right down to the fragrances that give them their names.[46] This competition may lead the reader to conclude (as have many critics) that the men's interest in Ukifune has more to do with their rivalry than romance. One popular view argues that Kaoru and Niou really desire each other, at least metaphorically, with Ukifune merely providing an excuse for their closer connection.[47] Senji, however, pointedly omits any such backdrop. Not only do Sagoromo and Michinari not consciously compete for Asukai, but Sagoromo does not even know that he has a rival until after Asukai's death. All the reader gets are Michinari's unwitting observations about nobles in general, completely divorced from any sense of personal animus or jealousy. Nor does Asukai herself encourage any rivalry, since she—unlike Ukifune—has no difficulty choosing between her would-be lovers. These revisions, like the new status gap between the suitors themselves, force the reader to confront the only other explanation Senji offers for the tragedy: the lovers' own social distance.

These changes once again spotlight the nurse. Whereas Asukai may have no problem choosing between suitors, the nurse finds it a more difficult decision; it is because she vacillates for so long in this regard that the affair has time to develop in the first place. Sagoromo, however, never enters into these calculations. As noted earlier, once the nurse realizes that the hero will never put the affair on a formal footing, she turns to other men, men who can offer her and Asukai material support: the priest, the Michinoku general, and, once he seems poised for promotion, Michinari. Romantic appeal, either to Asukai or herself, is beside the point; we never get a physical description of the general, and the attributes of the priest, as already mentioned, are laughable. Practical considerations also figure in the *Genji* episode. Ukifune wavers between her suitors in part because she realizes that, although she prefers Niou, Kaoru is the more reliable of the two, a perception that the text clearly supports. Ukifune's attendants take part in the contest, one advocating for Kaoru, the other aiding and abetting Niou, although mostly for emotional reasons. Ukifune's mother, on the other hand, tells the girl's nurse that while the heroine probably deserves better, "the only man you can really trust is the single-minded sort"—that is, a man with only one lover, like her own midranks husband.[48] Ultimately, however, the women in the *Genji* episode either duck the choice (Ukifune) or succumb to the impractical option, Niou. By contrast, Asukai's nurse speaks in and acts on purely practical terms. The nurse prefers Michinari expressly because he, unlike some "young noble," will make Asukai his wife. As before, this change has thematic implications. *Genji*'s concluding chapters, including the Ukifune story, have been called a "denial of romance," since the heroines there generally choose literal or metaphorical deaths over their lovers.[49] As noted earlier, Murasaki offers various explanations for this denial, diluting her social criticisms for the sake of a more complex portrait of human life. Senji makes a different choice. Without jealous rivals and the heroine's inner conflict to distract us, the nurse's judgments assume a larger weight. In *Sagoromo,* unlike *Genji,* the writer explicitly endorses the nurse's view of the world, whatever the literary cost.

The Rear Court and the Nurse

Later readers did not accept Asukai's wet nurse, despite all of Senji's internal and intertextual support for the character. Medieval and modern audiences alike (the latter mainly scholars) have chosen almost without exception to overlook the nurse or to elide her complexities, as if in punishment for her fictional sins. As I have argued above, these approaches entirely mistake the character's purpose and her author's thematic aims. The nurse is admittedly the antagonist of the Asukai subplot, at odds with its hero and ultimately responsible for its heroine's death. Considered in context, however, the character assumes a far more favorable aspect. The nurse literally embodies Senji's critique of the midranks fantasy, a view already visible in *Genji* but made much more explicit in *Sagoromo* by the author's narrower and more sustained social focus.

The failure of so many of Senji's readers to recognize this point suggests more than a simple series of misunderstandings. It points to profound changes in *Sagoromo*'s audience, specifically to its increasing distance from the Rear Court. Many of the inferences Baishi's own group would have drawn from the tale have no effect on the theme, functioning instead as inside jokes. Senji's original readers, for example, obviously identified Sagoromo's foster-sister Princess Genji with Baishi. The fictional heroine, like Baishi, serves as Kamo Priestess, and the descriptions of Princess Genji's procession to her post directly reflect Baishi's own trip.[50] Moreover, Princess Genji never marries, again like the real princess. Sagoromo, two generations removed from the imperial family—his father was born a prince but stripped of his rank—presents a fictionalized version of Baishi's guardian Morofusa. The hero's final ascension to the throne, engineered by the goddess Amaterasu herself (the mythical ancestress of the imperial family), probably nods to the former prince's own fantasies on this point. (Whether Morofusa cherished an unrequited passion for Baishi, making the parallel complete, is sheer speculation.) Later readers did not need to recognize these historical models to appreciate the story—although such knowledge does add a certain tabloid interest.

Imahime's story relies more heavily on familiarity with the Rear Court environment. As noted earlier, Lady Dōin adopts the girl not only to get the attention of her husband—the current chancellor—but to compete with her fellow wives, Lady Horikawa and Lady Bōmon. This situation itself evokes court rivalries, especially since Dōin attempts to give Imahime to the emperor, a conspicuous reprise of Fujiwara marriage politics. The Horikawa Chancellor's own family, the backdrop to this story, deepens the parallel. The narrator introduces Dōin as one of Horikawa's "three main wives," an extremely unusual situation in Heian life and fiction (32); normally, aristocrats only had one, treating the other women as mistresses. Moreover, we learn that all three women live in the same compound, a situation that recalls not only Genji's Rokujō estate, discussed in my introduction, but the imperial palace. As many scholars have noted, the Horikawa Chancellor thus appears as a kind of secular emperor, surrounded by his consorts. Indeed, Horikawa's rule of his estate is even starker than Genji's, since unlike Murasaki, who describes the Rokujō residents by the seasons in which their gardens bloom (e.g., the Lady of Spring, the Lady of Autumn), Senji refers to these women by their street address. Lady Horikawa, who shares Horikawa's own building, is thus the undeniable favorite, making Dōin's jealousy more understandable—and desperate.[51] Without understanding this backdrop, one misses much of the episode's social satire.

Asukai's wet nurse differs from all of these characters, since she speaks for a less obvious stratum of the Rear Court. Senji was herself a nurse, as well as (by definition) a bona fide member of the aristocracy's middle ranks. Moreover, she includes a number of nurses in her story, causing one critic to label

Sagoromo a "nurse's tale," in contrast to the attendant-based *Genji*.[52] It is thus tempting to identify Senji with all of these characters solely on the basis of profession. However, Senji clearly invites us to sympathize with only one of these women: Asukai's nurse. No one would accuse Senji of treating Baishi like the nurse did Asukai, even for the princess's own good. The patronage stakes were too high for attendants in elite households, and in any case Baishi (at least until her sponsors' deaths) never wanted for money. Senji and her colleagues, however, undoubtedly identified with the pragmatism of Asukai's nurse, and probably her social views as well. Rear Court attendants, writers or not, made similar calculations every day, both in their professional lives and, as we have seen, their marriages. Heian social structures required as much. Without recognizing the pressures placed on attendants, nurses or not, we risk misreading *Sagoromo*—and its thoughtful response to *Genji*.

THREE
Family Substitutes in The Tale of Hamamatsu

Chigirishi o	Our vows,
kokoro hitotsu ni	sworn with all my heart,
wasurenedo	I will not forget.
ikaga wa su beki	But how can I honor them now,
shizu no odamaki	without control of life's slim thread?

—*The Tale of the Hamamatsu Middle Counselor*

Whereas Senji criticizes the ideals of midranks romance, emphasizing their cost to the lower-born lover, the author of *The Tale of the Hamamatsu Middle Counselor* (*Hamamatsu chūnagon monogatari*, ca. 1050) targets the Heian family and household networks discussed in Chapter 1, particularly the instrumental use of children. *Hamamatsu* begins, like *Sagoromo*, by revisiting *Genji*: this time, its theme of romantic obsession. Murasaki borrows Tang poet Bai Juyi's (772–846) "Song of Unending Sorrow" to frame this part of her tale. The "Song" describes how Emperor Xuanzong (685–762) neglected his rule for the company of consort Yang Guifei (J. Yōkihi), swearing that the two of them would be as "two birds with the wings of one, two branches of one tree" for all time to come.[1] When rebels sensed weakness and attacked, an angry military made Xuanzong put Yang to death. The "Song" takes its title, however, from subsequent events. Once his army repels the attackers, Xuanzong sends a wizard to bring Yang back from the dead, hoping to renew the affair. The effort fails, leaving Xuanzong to grieve "on and on forever," presumably even in the afterlife.[2]

Murasaki echoes this lesson throughout *Genji*, most pointedly in the opening story of the hero's birth. According to the narrator, Genji's imperial father favors the hero's mother Kiritsubo so heavily that "the example of Yang Guifei [is] bound to come up,"causing considerable consternation at the court.[3] Eventually, the hostility of her rivals drives Kiritsubo back to her mother's home, where she dies of nervous exhaustion. The references to Yang, one of Heian Japan's favorite heroines, serve several functions in *Genji*. First, they lend Kiritsubo's story "the grandeur of classical archetype," elevating the consort's less impressive (and hastily sketched) romance.[4] Moreover, by underwriting the story of Kiritsubo, the "Song" underwrites the entire tale's association of love and death.[5] Even here, Murasaki makes changes, blaming Kiritsubo's death on women rather than a loyal army. In a sense, one may consider the tale Murasaki's "answer" to the Tang poet, shifting the focus from epic tragedies to the daily cruelties of the Rear Court.

The *Genji* author also uses the "Song," however, to introduce a new point: the effects of unresolved passions on later relationships. According to Bai Juyi, while Yang cannot return to Xuanzong from the afterlife, she does send him half of a box and a hairpin he gave her, pledging them as tokens of her lasting affection. Structurally, the ruined trinkets underscore the lovers' failed promises. Yang actually repeats Xuanzong's oath about shared wings and branches when she breaks the gifts. Murasaki darkens even this ironic ending. While Genji's father initially mourns Kiritsubo, re-reading the "Song" for comfort, he eventually finds a replacement: the princess Fujitsubo, whose striking resemblance to the consort allows him to pretend that she is Kiritsubo. Actually, Fujitsubo improves on her predecessor, since Kiritsubo's tormentors are cowed by the princess's rank. Nonetheless, Fujitsubo ultimately proves as poor a substitute as Yang's hairpin and box. In an unnarrated scene (one of the so-called riddles of the tale), she betrays her husband with Genji and conceives a son, the future Emperor Reizei.

Novelist Tanizaki Jun'ichirō implies in his story "The Floating Bridge of Dreams" (Yume no ukihashi, 1959), titled for the final chapter of *Genji*, that the Kiritsubo Emperor intends for this to happen. In the story, the protagonist's father ignores a budding sexual relationship between his son and second wife, allowing (and perhaps requiring) her to nurse him much later than normal children. (The boy still occasionally plays with her breasts as a college student.) On his deathbed, the father even tells the protagonist to "give [the stepmother] all his love" and "tak[e] [his, i.e., the father's] place with her" after he dies.[6] Murasaki focuses her own narrative upon the effect of the stepmother's rejection. After Fujitsubo gives birth, she refuses to see Genji, spurring him to seek out his own "substitutes" (*katashiro*), also known as "keepsakes" (*katami*). These surrogates, too, fail; one even betrays Genji, just as Fujitsubo betrays his father. In short, for Murasaki the true endless sorrow is not loss per se but our inability to accept it, and the havoc this wreaks on our later relationships. To sharpen her point, the writer includes a missed chance for happiness in each story line. After forcing Fujitsubo to allow the young Genji into her rooms, counter to Heian etiquette, the Kiritsubo Emperor bans personal visits at the boy's coming-of-age ceremony. Had he done this earlier, he might have prevented Genji's infatuation in the first place. Genji's later decision to forbid all contact between his love Murasaki (Fujitsubo's niece) and his own son Yūgiri shows that the hero, at least, recognizes this.

Genji's portraits of obsession heavily influenced later tale fiction. The hero of *Sagoromo*, for example, wastes his life pining for Princess Genji, crippling his relationships with other women (including Asukai) and souring his miraculous installation as emperor at the tale's end. The heroine of *Nezame at Night*, meanwhile, spends years brooding over a chance encounter with her brother-in-law, ignoring the happiest formal marriage in Heian fiction. Nezame's husband, a kindly aging regent, continues to cherish the heroine although he knows she is unfaithful to him; he even adopts Nezame's son by her lover. *The Tale of the Changelings* (*Torikaebaya monogatari,* twelfth century), the story of two siblings with crossed gender identities, also preserves the pattern. At the end of the tale, the heroine reverts to wistful thoughts of her childhood as a boy, undermining her conventional triumph as empress.

No text examines Murasaki's theme as closely or creatively, however, as *Hamamatsu,* the story of a courtier's search for his father's reincarnation in China—and the romance he finds once he gets there. Once the eponymous Chūnagon meets his unforgettable woman, the Heyang (Hoyang) Consort (Kōyōken no kisaki), he spends the rest of the story chasing substitutes for her, across huge spans of time and distance. At the end of the tale, we see him awaiting the Consort's rebirth in the womb of her sister back in Japan. *Hamamatsu* thus enshrines an even more epic obsession than that found in *Genji,* as even my epigraph, from Chūnagon's brief affair with a midranks woman, suggests. The poem alludes to an episode from *Tales of Ise,* in which the hero wishes in vain that he could "spin time's thread back to the past" and resume an old relationship.[7] *Hamamatsu,* however—informed by Murasaki's bleak view of attachment—is still more pessimistic. Here it is the woman who, in response to Chūnagon's overtures, refers back to the past. Since the readers knows that this character has never been in control of either her life or the relationship, the verse thus resonates ironically. There is nothing she can do to change either present or past—and Chūnagon knows it.

The Tale of Hamamatsu: *A Brief History*

As noted in the introduction, we still do not know who wrote *Hamamatsu.* The traditional attribution to the Sarashina diarist (b. 1008), if true, would link *Hamamatsu* and *Sagoromo,* since the diarist briefly worked for Baishi's sister Yūshi at the famously close Go-Reizei court. This would in turn suggest that Yorimichi actively supported fictional reworkings of *Genji,* his father's great trophy—at least, if one accepts my readings of the two texts. *Hamamatsu*'s manuscript trouble, unfortunately, is more firmly established. The tale is currently missing at least one book, the crucial introduction; all forty extant copies share the gap. As in the case of *Sagoromo,* these textual problems probably reflect the tale's early popularity, since the first book was the most commonly circulated part of a text, and thus the most easily lost.

Unlike *Sagoromo,* or, as we will see, *Nezame, Hamamatsu* did not inspire any medieval revisions that we might use to guide our own approach to the tale. The chief extant tributes are a poetry collection written by the mother of a priest studying in China (*Jōjin ajari no haha no shū,* ca. 1070), inspired by Chūnagon's own visit to the continent, and an anonymous genealogy of the characters from the Edo period. Fictional family trees remain a favorite homework assignment in the Japanese classroom, since they encourage students to pay more attention to these relationships, often important to tale plots. Otherwise, these two texts only foreground *Hamamatsu*'s obvious points: Chūnagon's travels to China (the first adventure set outside of Japan since *The Tale of Utsuho*) and the tale's two reincarnations, which make the genealogy unusually complicated. Shunzei's Daughter is also unhelpful, exclaiming in *The Untitled Book* that "*everything* about *Hamamatsu,* beginning with its language and structure, is ingenious. If I were going to write a tale, I would make it just like this."[8] Even *Hamamatsu*'s title, usually a good indication of what readers liked about a story, fails us, since it emphasizes an event related in the missing book: Chūnagon's affair with his stepsister Taishō no Kimi. The title refers to a poem in which Chūnagon describes her as the "beach pine" that "pines for" him after he leaves home, drawing on a pun similar to that found in English. The alternate title, *Hamamatsu at Mitsu* (*Mitsu no Hamamatsu*), does the same thing while adding an additional pun on the phrase "I saw" and the place Chūnagon sails from. In full, it reads *The Beach-Pine I Saw (Which Pines for Me) at Mitsu.*[9]

Taishō no Kimi remains important in the extant text, which opens as the hero arrives in China. Chūnagon longs for her throughout his three-year sojourn on the continent, and when he returns home, he insists on visiting her despite her new life as a nun. Nonetheless, despite her general enthusiasm for *Hamamatsu*, Shunzei's Daughter spends little time on Taishō no Kimi, praising even minor heroines as much or more than her.[10] Modern tributes, and the more plentiful academic reviews, are equally contradictory. At the end of *Spring Snow* (*Haru no yuki*, 1968), novelist Mishima Yukio credits the "tale of dreams and rebirth" for inspiring his final tetralogy *The Sea of Fertility* (*Hōjō no umi*, 1968–71).[11] Mishima uses the dream and reincarnation motifs, which bracket *Hamamatsu*'s existing narrative, to explore the effects of time on both friendship and passion. Most critics, however, mock the series as derivative fantasy—a charge also leveled at *Hamamatsu* itself.

Mishima does contribute one thing to our understanding of *Hamamatsu*, whatever we think of *The Sea of Fertility*. Like the authors who rewrote Asukai's wet nurse, he highlights an aspect of *Hamamatsu* central to its reworking of *Genji*: the tale's supposedly fantastic elements. For all of its supernatural ambience, *Hamamatsu*'s main plot draws heavily on *Genji*. As noted in the introduction, this is another reason some critics call the tale decadent. The most obvious debt is to the obsession theme discussed earlier, specifically to Genji's pursuit of Fujitsubo. At the end of the tale, as noted, Chūnagon is literally awaiting the Consort's rebirth as her own niece, a satirical twist on Genji's own affair with heroine Murasaki. It is worth noting how this story line inverts the *Genji* plot. As one critic points out, thanks to the magic of reincarnation, Chūnagon can actually resume his relationship with the Consort rather than replace it, in the process restoring the original meaning of the "Song of Unending Sorrow."[12] (The critic takes Xuanzong's vow to be two wings of one bird and so forth as a literal wish for shared rebirth.) In this sense, *Hamamatsu* returns our focus to the suffering endured after losing a lover, if only while waiting for a reunion, rather than the impossibility of finding a substitute.[13]

Hamamatsu also, however, redirects the *Genji* story, emphasizing the familial obsessions noted earlier. Here a brief return to my epigraph for this chapter is useful. Daini's daughter, the verse's author, first meets Chūnagon when he visits her father in Dazaifu, the famous exile site discussed with respect to *Sagoromo*. (Daini is the name of the second-in-command there, although the nominal leader usually stayed at court. In *Sagoromo*, it is the position that Michinari's father takes.) Daini sends the girl to Chūnagon disguised as a masseuse, hoping to spark an affair between the young people and so gain the hero's patronage, a less lofty version of elite marriage politics. When Chūnagon refuses to be seduced, Daini's wife convinces her husband to marry the girl to a lower-ranking man: Chūnagon's uncle, a union sparking the daughter's regret.

The episode clearly echoes *Sagoromo*'s criticisms of the mid-ranks romance, including the stories of Yūgao and Ukifune. After renewing the affair, for example, Chūnagon reflects that, "Instead of someone completely out of reach, who can only bring sorrow, I should have fallen for a girl of muddled rank, someone who would be sweet and yielding like this."[14] As the annotator points out, Chūnagon is here thinking of his painful affair with the Consort. The phrase translated as "muddled rank" (*kakimaze no hodo*), meanwhile, is a clear synonym for *Genji*'s "middle ranks" (*naka no shina*), discussed in Chapter 2. In short, Chūnagon—like Tō no Chūjō in the rainy night's conversation—is longing for the ease and informality of a mid-ranks relationship. Once Chūnagon tires of Daini's daughter, meanwhile, he admits that her mother was right. "Marrying my uncle really is an extraordinary piece of luck for her. No matter how much I care, I could never make such a fuss over her. Even if I were truly devoted to her, the best I could do would be to hide her in some dreary mountain village for the occasional visit. I'm sure she would be miserable."[15] The girl's poem, written before their reunion, underscores this point. Despite the sense of helplessness expressed in her verse, Daini's daughter does find a way to "control life's thread" and arrange a second meeting with Chūnagon, effectively returning them to the past. At this point, predictably, the hero reverts to his old indifference. The scene revisits a point central to *Hamamatsu*'s main plot. As discussed in Chapter 2, Heian fiction typically depicts relationships between social equals as loveless unions, the fruit of the aristocracy's marriage politics. As a result, the romantic ideal becomes the unequal, impractical relationship between a courtier and a woman of lower or otherwise problematic status. (Genji's affair with Fujitsubo, an imperial consort, exemplifies the alternative group.) Both categories of relationship are tragic, as Genji's marriage to Aoi and Sagoromo's affair with Asukai in their different ways illustrate.

Murasaki gives Kiritsubo both problems. Genji's father, as noted, loves her more than he should for her status, a romantic detail. As Kiritsubo's mother points out, however, it was her husband's "last request" to send the heroine to court and fulfill his political ambitions that exposed Kiritsubo to this fate in the first place.[16] In short, paternal obsessions play as large a role in Kiritsubo's life as romantic ones. The same is true for Genji and any number of other characters, including, notably, Genji's own final substitute for Fujitsubo, her other niece the Third Princess. As noted in the previous chapter, the Third Princess slips into an infamous affair with Kashiwagi (Tō no Chūjō's son) after her attendants carelessly allow the courtier to see her. The relationship eventually produces Kaoru, driving the princess to become a nun. As Fujitsubo's niece, the Third Princess clearly continues the motif of romantic obsession discussed earlier. It is Genji's disappointment that the heroine looks and acts nothing like Fujitsubo that causes him to neglect her, allowing Kashiwagi to realize his hopes. But the princess's father, Retired Emperor Suzaku, is also responsible for the disaster, since he arranges the marriage to Genji in the first place. Suzaku later admits as much, blaming himself for "entrusting her to Genji with such limitless confidence."[17] As with her midranks romances, however, Murasaki supplements this explanation with additional reasons, such as Kashiwagi's own desire "to surpass everyone in every way"[18] and the machinations of an evil spirit, possibly that of the dead Rokujō.[19]

Hamamatsu gestures toward this complication in the Daini subplot. During the brief affair with Chūnagon, Daini's daughter conceives a child, threatening to expose the lovers and ruin her marriage; in Heian fiction, children born of adultery, like Genji's son Reizei, usually inconveniently resemble their natural fathers. Since Daini's daughter does not serve as a substitute for anyone, however (other than in a brief comparison to a woman Chūnagon knew platonically in China), the writer does not further develop the parallel. Instead, as noted above, the episode emphasizes Daini's own responsibility for this chain of events. It was Daini who introduced Chūnagon to the heroine in the first place. Had he not done so, Chūnagon would never have thought to visit her later. In short, the ultimate cause of the affair is not desire but paternal misjudgment. The same is true for Daini's daughter; had Daini never exposed his daughter to Chūnagon, inspiring a kind of crush on him, she might have tried to fight him off. The brief comparison to a Chinese woman, Wu Jun (Wu Chün; J. *Go no Kimi*), underscores this point, since the latter character falls in love with the hero after a single glimpse of him, forcing her father to invite him to the house.[20] The story of Daini's daughter, minor though it is, taps both stories, neatly introducing the theme of the main plot: the extent to which family and household ambitions dictate even "private" relationships at the Heian court. *Hamamatsu*'s contribution, like *Sagoromo*'s, is thus to simplify *Genji* by focusing our attention on a single source for the problem—using the allegedly fantastic elements just discussed.

Prelude to a Substitute: Chūnagon, Taishō no Kimi, and the Third Prince

As noted, *Hamamatsu* currently begins with Chūnagon's arrival in China, en route to his reunion with the Third Prince. Like the opening reference to the hero's "deep filial piety"—literally the first words of the extant text—this setting reflects

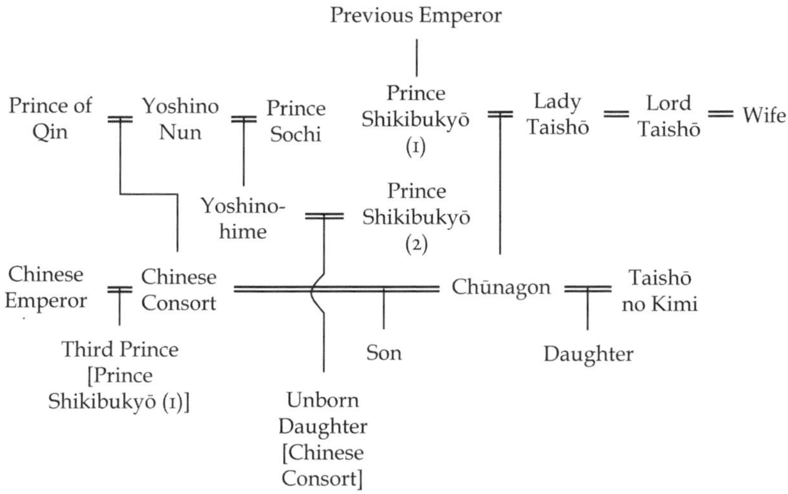

Fig. 3 Simplified genealogy for *The Tale of Hamamatsu*
═ marital or romantic relationship | parent-child relationship [ ] reincarnation

a shift from Heian courtship tales to a nascent medieval interest in the family.[21] Sagoromo's fixation on what his parents would think of his passion for Princess Genji fits the pattern, as do *Nezame*'s idealized portraits of the heroine's father and her much older husband. In *Hamamatsu*, however, these details serve an additional function. Like Fujitsubo, *Genji*'s "original substitute,"[22] the Prince introduces the importance of family history in the tale's later romantic relationships, illustrating structurally as well as figuratively that, in this tale, father always comes first. In this sense, as with Fujitsubo, "it would not be hyperbolic to suggest that [the Prince] embodies the principle dynamic forces of the work."[23]

The initial point to consider about Chūnagon's meeting with the Prince is his complex motive for seeking it. Chūnagon first learns of his father's reincarnation in the tale's missing introduction, either in a dream or through reports from traveling monks; the extant text notes only that Chūnagon somehow heard of the event (165; Rohlich, 65). Traveling to China was difficult in the Heian era, both because of unrest on the continent and the dangers of the sea voyage itself. The trip had not been officially attempted since Sugawara Michizane's failed embassy in 895, well over a century before *Hamamatsu* was written. Even in Michizane's time, moreover, these trips were rare; over half a century had passed since the last successful mission, and some scholars speculate that no one, including Michizane, intended for this one to happen either.[24] Chūnagon's decision to make the trip, particularly on such slight evidence, suggests extraordinary affection for his father. The narrator encourages this view, speculating in the opening line that the hero's devotion causes the winds to blow "in the direction they wished" and speed the trip (153; Rohlich, 55). Later in the tale, Chūnagon himself remembers his shock at his father's death, recalling that he was "too upset to think straight" (337; Rohlich, 177). In short, *Hamamatsu* suggests that the main reason Chūnagon goes to China is his unusually strong desire to see his father.

There are also, however, a number of less admirable reasons for the trip. After Chūnagon's return from China, stepfather Lord Taishō recalls that the hero "had never liked [him], since the boy considered the marriage inappropriate" (305; Rohlich, 158). Lord Taishō also remarks that Chūnagon would hardly even look at him, even though they naturally met during the older man's visits to the residence (305–6; Rohlich, 158). The hero's mother, for her part, remembers feeling "mortified" by Chūnagon's response to the marriage (306; Rohlich, 159). The narrator offers no explanation for the hero's initial dislike for Lord Taishō, although the framework suggests the "bullied stepchild" convention discussed in Chapter 2. Such stories were apparently so common in Heian fiction that Genji makes heroine Murasaki ban them from her foster-daughter's nursery, worried that they will frighten the child and ruin her relationship with her new mother. Chūnagon probably also suffers from a more personal animus, misplaced grief for his father. It is not hard to imagine that the hero thinks of Lord Taishō as an interloper and makes the trip to find his idolized father in order to escape.

In addition to his dislike for Lord Taishō, however, Chūnagon clearly has another reason to go to China: the affair with stepsister Taishō no Kimi. As noted earlier, Chūnagon becomes involved with Taishō no Kimi sometime during the first book, and when he sets sail, she is already carrying his child. Lord Taishō, however, had "dreamed of raising her to the highest rank since she was an infant" (241; Rohlich, 118). That is, Lord Taishō hoped to marry his daughter to an emperor. In fact, when Chūnagon seduces Taishō no Kimi, she is already betrothed to the future crown prince. Chūnagon's affair with his stepsister and her subsequent decision to take the tonsure ruin Lord Taishō's ambitions, likely causing considerable bitterness. The narrator evokes *Genji*'s "Suma" chapter when Chūnagon arrives on the continent, evoking Genji's own escape from Kokiden's wrath after the hero's affair with Oborozukiyo.[25] Chūnagon's affair with Taishō no Kimi also borrows Genji's mixed motives. On the one hand, Chūnagon truly loves his stepsister, if not in a fraternal way. He had hoped, once he returned from China, to "make her his closest confidante, with or without her father's permission" (226; Rohlich, 107). Moreover, as noted earlier, when Chūnagon does get home he insists on face-to-face visits with the girl, behavior that is both mutually frustrating and highly inappropriate now that she is a nun. However, in the tradition of tale heroes in general, Chūnagon also seduces Taishō no Kimi as part of a formulaic rivalry with the future crown prince. The men's later competition for Yoshino Himegimi (Yoshinohime), and the prince's envy at Chūnagon's tales of his continental adventures betray as much. Chūnagon may even become involved with his stepsister in part to spite Lord Taishō, judging from his frequent references to his sense of guilt toward both parties (e.g., 233; Rohlich, 112).

This backdrop, probably related in greater detail in *Hamamatsu*'s missing first book, connects Chūnagon's affair with Taishō no Kimi and his subsequent trip to China to a host of practical interests, establishing the general complexity of the characters' relationships. Once Chūnagon arrives in China, however, the writer narrows her focus to family influences. Here she reworks a famous *Genji* subplot: the story of heroine Murasaki. After several days as the Chinese Emperor's guest, during which Chūnagon demonstrates his talents (and the general superiority of Japanese culture, according to the narrator), the hero receives an invitation to visit the Prince. Scholars argue that the missing book built to this meeting, probably by focusing on the difficulty of Chūnagon's voyage.[26] Even in the extant text, however, the meeting in Heyang (a suburb of the Chinese capital Luoyang) stands out. As the narrator puts it:

> The site was spectacular, with the hue of the water, layout of the rocks, approach to the garden and even the branches of the trees all more captivating than those of the other estates. Servants brought Chūnagon to the Prince. He was seven or eight years old, and very winning in his formal hairstyle and robes. Although it was not the face he knew, Chūnagon instantly sensed their connection and felt the tears welling up. The Prince, too, was visibly moved, and while offering only casual greetings, he managed to convey both his memories of the past and his deep emotion at this reunion in a silently scribbled verse. Chūnagon, while careful not to betray the truth, could not refrain from weeping. (156; Rohlich, 57)

The passage, only the first part of the reunion scene, is interesting for several reasons. To begin with, the depiction of reincarnation sharply contrasts with that found in contemporary Buddhist fiction. Collections like *A Record of Marvelous Happenings in Japan* (*Nihon ryōiki*, ninth century), *Miraculous Tales of the Lotus Sutra* (*Hokke genki*, ca. 1040), and *Tales of Times Now Past* (once attributed, as noted in the first chapter, to Senji's husband Takakuni) typically equate rebirth with sin, particularly the sin of attachment. According to Buddhism, attachment is the source of all suffering, since it tempts people to forget the inevitably transitory nature of life and material wealth. This attachment, in turn, leads to various crimes as well as the simpler "lapse" of grief. The authors of these tales, probably priests, use reincarnation as a device to warn people of this chain of events.[27] *Times Now Past* (XIV: 3), for example, relates the famous Dōjōji story, in which a girl lusts so strongly for a traveling priest that both are eventually transformed into snakes. Characters who gain positive reincarnations, meanwhile, usually do so thanks to the merits of a sutra or bodhisattva, achieving appropriately spiritual ends. *Miraculous Tales* (III: 94), for instance, describes a snake reborn as a man after hearing a priest recite the first six chapters of the *Lotus Sutra*. More commonly, such characters are reborn into a Buddhist paradise.[28]

Hamamatsu, too, links rebirth to attachment; indeed, the writer probably borrows the idea of reincarnation across countries from Buddhist stories describing priests reborn in this manner in order to spread the faith.[29] In *Hamamatsu*, however, these reincarnations are strictly secular in nature. After meeting Chūnagon the Third Prince admits to his mother that, "since he had only had one child" in his previous life, attachment to the hero kept him from rebirth in even the lowest level of the Pure Land (*Jōdo*), a Buddhist paradise (165; Rohlich, 65). The Consort says the same thing near the end of the tale, when she appears in Chūnagon's dream to foretell her own rebirth. Despite their spiritual cost, these rebirths also have benefits. The Prince takes great pleasure in his reunion with Chūnagon; indeed, he spends so much time in Heyang with his guest that the Emperor grows lonely and summons him back to the palace. (In an interesting reversal, the Prince here thinks of Chūnagon as a substitute parent, since the Consort soon leaves Heyang in accordance with dream warnings.) Furthermore, as the description of his estate makes clear, the Prince enjoys numerous creature comforts, quite unlike most punitive rebirths. In fact, Chūnagon's father has arguably improved his status. In Japan, he was merely Prince Shikibukyō (Shikibukyō no miya), head of the Ministry of Ceremonial, but now he is the favorite son of a Chinese emperor and thus heir to a vastly greater empire. As if to reinforce this point, at the end of the tale, the Chinese Emperor names him crown prince. One critic, noting that another Prince Shikibukyō in *Hamamatsu* ultimately becomes Japan's crown prince, asserts that this would have happened anyway; the rebirth of the hero's father is merely a deferred version of the natural conclusion.[30] Even so, the rebirth is a positive one, reinstating what was lost. Religiously speaking, then, rebirth in *Hamamatsu* is something of an advantage, allowing the "victim" to revisit secular goals or relationships. This alone makes the passage worth reading, not least for the lighter portrait it paints of audiences during the Latter Days of the Law. *Hamamatsu*'s author, and perhaps some of its readers, were not too concerned about it.

More interesting—and thematically significant—is the use the *Hamamatsu* passage makes of *Genji*. In *Genji*, as noted, surrogate relationships always fail, even when the surrogate seems to be a perfect copy of her predecessor. Chūnagon, however, literally resumes his relationship with his father. In this excerpt, the Third Prince "convey[s] both his memories of the past and his deep emotion at their reunion." The narrator later repeats the point, remarking that the Prince retains the same "heart of old" and an "unchanging" concern for the hero (168; Rohlich, 68). Even the Prince echoes this detail, explaining to his mother that he seeks out Chūnagon's company because he himself still "thinks of Chūnagon with the same heart of old" (165–66; Rohlich, 65). As noted earlier, this pattern inverts Murasaki's own use of the substitute motif; in *Genji*, the substitute normally bears no inner connection to the person she replaces. *Hamamatsu*'s real inversion, however, is how the search for the substitute ends. Instead of aggravating Chūnagon's longing for his father, as the earlier critic predicts, the meeting with the Third Prince completely satisfies it: the boy's company not only "consoles" Chūnagon; it "makes him feel happy and secure" (156–57; Rohlich, 57),[31] reinstating the (idealized) father-son relationship. Thereafter, references to Chūnagon's grief for his father all but disappear from the narrative, even after the hero leaves the Prince and returns to Japan. The contrast with Genji's own endless search for Fujitsubo or, for that matter, with Yang's useless hairpin, is perfect.

This does not mean that the transition from the old relationship to the new one is seamless. As the excerpt notes, the Third Prince does not look like his predecessor, a point that the author stresses. Just after this passage, the narrator observes that "the Prince had changed his appearance" upon his rebirth (156; Rohlich, 57). Describing another meeting between the characters, the narrator again states that Chūnagon's father "looks completely different" in his new body (168; Rohlich, 68). Even the Prince alludes to this contrast, worrying that Chūnagon is neglecting "the parent who has not changed her appearance"—that is, the hero's mother—on his account (194; Rohlich, 86). The narrative is a little muddy here. When the Prince confesses his relationship with the hero to the Consort, he begins by reporting the general amazement at how much Chūnagon looks like him, implying some kind of family resemblance and thus a physical connection to his former self (165; Rohlich, 65).[32] The Consort echoes this point in her reply, although both comments may simply refer to the men's shared good looks (166; Rohlich, 66).[33] The subplot thus affirms Murasaki's critique of obsession: since the only way to truly replace someone would seem to be to find his reincarnation—something normally impossible—one should not even try less obvious substitutes. Moreover, even reincarnation has its problems. As noted earlier, the tale closes with Chūnagon awaiting the Consort's rebirth to her sister, naturally as an infant. It will be years before he can continue the love affair, assuming that he does not die first.[34]

The more important *Genji* allusion, of course, is to the story of young Murasaki, noted earlier. As close readers may notice, Chūnagon's reunion with the Prince strongly resembles Genji's meeting with the heroine, narrated in the tale's "Young Murasaki" (Wakamurasaki) chapter. In this episode, Genji, suffering from a mysterious ailment known as "child's sickness" (*warawa yami*), goes to the northern foothills of the capital to seek the help of a famous healer. During a break in treatment, Genji notices a "charming house" amid the "artfully planted trees" below the healer's cave.[35] Spotting several attractive attendants there, Genji sneaks down for a closer view and spies a young girl "of about ten," standing with "her hair fanned out over her shoulders" and "rubbing her tears away until her face flushe[s] red."[36] Despite the girl's childish dress and behavior, Genji quickly realizes that "she looks very like the person who has caused him so much pain":[37] Fujitsubo, for whom he continues to yearn and who, he soon learns, is the girl's aunt. There are several subtle but fascinating parallels between this episode and the *Hamamatsu* scene. Both Genji and Chūnagon find themselves in charming isolated settings, different from and aesthetically preferable to the imperial capital. Heyang, like Kitayama, even has a legendary recluse, albeit one known for his poetic rather than healing gifts.[38] Both men discover children who strongly evoke lost loved ones, children carefully distinguished by their clothing, hairstyles, and even a shared blush from everyone around them. Indeed, Murasaki is actually Fujitsubo's niece and the most famous of *Genji*'s surrogate "links" (*yukari*), characters with a blood tie to their precursor.[39] As the actual reincarnation of Chūnagon's father, the Prince represents the culmination of this pattern, just as he typifies the trend, which peaks in *Genji*'s Uji chapters, of blood substitutes declining in physical resemblance to their predecessors. After lover Ōigimi's death, for example, Kaoru suddenly thinks that the heroine's sister Naka no Kimi resembles her, even though during an earlier night with the younger woman, he had only noticed difference.[40]

What binds the *Genji* and *Hamamatsu* scenes in thematic terms, however, is their heroes' shared emotional state. As noted, Genji suffers from "child's sickness," a condition the narrator links to recurrent fevers and general malaise. Modern critics tentatively identify the complaint with malaria, but as they also suggest, the disease's name itself implies a spiritual ailment. Genji's illness stems from his guilt-ridden relationship with stepmother Fujitsubo, as well as an obsessive tendency inherited from his father; when Genji learns how much the princess resembles Kiritsubo, he, like his father, "can't help wanting to visit her constantly and strike up a more intimate acquaintance."[41] Genji may even inherit his father's disappointment at the demotion to commoner status, a problem the Kiritsubo Emperor remedies (consciously, Tanizaki would say) with his new favorite, Reizei. There is thus no way that the hermit's prayers for physical health can cure the hero, any more than the priests who treated him after Yūgao's death, the immediate catalyst of this trip. Genji's decision to adopt the young

Murasaki after his treatment is supposedly finished, so that "she can serve as a constant consolation in the place of *that* person," in short, Fujitsubo, proves the point.[42] While the *Hamamatsu* author does not assign Chūnagon a medical condition, he clearly suffers from a similar spiritual burden, characterized by his inability to accept his new father and the unfavorable order this man, who has promised his stepsister to a prince, represents. By alluding to "Young Murasaki," the *Hamamatsu* writer hints that Chūnagon's reunion with the Prince is an attempt to exorcise this problem. More darkly, she implies that this, or another family problem, will continue to plague him throughout the book.[43]

Here a final point from *Genji* seems useful. At the beginning of "Bamboo River" (Takekawa), one of the contested parts of the tale, the narrator declares that what follows "will not resemble the lavender links" from earlier chapters.[44] That is, the story will be unlike that of heroine Murasaki, named for a plant that produced lavender dye, and Fujitsubo, whose sobriquet comes from her similar-hued wisteria at her palace residence. The line alerts us to a change in cast: the focal character of this episode will be Yūgao's daughter Tamakazura, largely absent since her sudden marriage a dozen chapters earlier. It also, however, underscores a deeper continuity. While "Bamboo River" interrupts the sequence of Fujitsubo substitutes, it does relate several similar stories, including the marriage of the now retired Emperor Reizei to one of Tamakazura's daughters. Reizei, who had hoped for a relationship with Tamakazura years earlier, accepts the daughter in her stead, reprising the old pattern.[45] Genji's support for Tamakazura, meanwhile, depends in part on his earlier love for Yūgao. In short, the narrator's claim in "Bamboo River" is ironic; Tamakazura's story strongly resembles that of the heroine Murasaki, right down to her adoption by Genji. By inviting us to compare the two characters, "Bamboo River" reminds us that in *Genji*, love always involves family, at least for the hero and (as becomes clear later in the tale) his heirs Niou and Kaoru. While the *Hamamatsu* writer does not directly allude to the chapter, she makes the same point through her general allusion to Murasaki—preparing the way for *Hamamatsu*'s heroine, the Consort.

The Mother of All Substitutes: Chūnagon and the Chinese Consort

As already noted, Chūnagon's romance with the Consort generally follows *Genji*'s substitute pattern. After "losing" the heroine (he briefly makes love to her in the provinces, directed by another dream vision), Chūnagon pursues several women who look like her, first in China and then in Japan. Moreover, he essentially adopts the Japanese substitute, Yoshinohime, promising to care for her after her mother's death. There is a parodic edge to the hunt's conclusion. As noted earlier, by the time Yoshinohime's unborn child comes of age, the hero will be old, rendering any sexual bond grotesque. (Of course, by the logic of reincarnation, the Consort is already Chūnagon's grandmother, making even their "original" love theoretically distasteful.)[46] The message here seems simple: erotic obsessions can be disastrous. *Hamamatsu*'s extended portrait of Chūnagon's relationship with the Consort, however, reveals that pragmatic concerns are the writer's real target.

As with Chūnagon's trip to China, the writer begins by depicting the complicated roots of the love affair. During a visit to Heyang, the hero hears music in the garden and stumbles into a scene straight out of "the Chinese paintings the masters once made": a gorgeous pavilion, flanked by a waterfall and chrysanthemums and filled with beautiful women (159; Rohlich, 60). Most intriguing of all is the mysterious musician herself, the Consort:

> She looked to be about twenty, with a beautiful profile: neither lean nor plump, and with strong features. Chūnagon compared her skin to the celebrated crystal jade and decided that she far outshone it; indeed, she seemed to radiate charm until even her eyebrows appeared to be the most elegant he had seen and her lips seemed stained scarlet. She was flawless, brightening everything around her, as she gazed out on the garden with her beautifully upswept hair and strummed her zither. Chūnagon was stunned to find such

a scene in China. Reflecting on his own long-standing preference for the free, flowing hairstyle favored in Japan, he found that this more elaborate, pinned coiffure, perhaps because of its wearer, had its own appeal. (159; Rohlich, 60–61)[47]

In some ways, this is a typical "fence peeping" (*kaimami*) scene, a stock element in Heian fiction. After accidentally seeing the heroine, Chūnagon is mesmerized by her beauty. Just after this passage he reflects, this time referring to both the Consort and her women, that "this must be what the heavenly maidens from the past looked like" (160; Rohlich, 61). The line evokes a series of unearthly women, from *The Bamboo Cutter*'s Kaguya Himegimi (Kaguyahime) to the dancers who appeared before the future Emperor Temmu in the mountains of Yoshino to endorse his claim to imperial succession.[48] This second reference seems especially strong, given Yoshino's broader associations with imperial power and the fact that Chūnagon later finds the Consort's Japanese half-sister there.[49] More immediately, Chūnagon feels the conventional draw of the Consort's status. When he learns that the Consort must live away from the capital to appease her enemies at court, he competitively concludes that the Chinese Emperor "lacks the strength of character" to defend her (187; Rohlich, 81). This follows on the heels of the equally insulting speculation that the Emperor "may have devoted himself too much to pleasurable pursuits and so compromised his judgment" (187; Rohlich, 81). The writer underscores the point when Chūnagon returns to Japan. After reporting on his travels in China to the Japanese emperor, the hero wanders to the empress's quarters and thinks to himself,

Omoi dani	Is it possible
yoramashi mono ka	that even my burning thoughts
murasaki no	would reach out to you
kumo no kakaranu	were you not one who is tied
narai nariseba	to the clouds of lavender?

(251; Rohlich, 124)

This poem, which unfortunately has a number of grammatical problems that make interpretation difficult, nonetheless highlights two things about Chūnagon's interest in the Consort. First, it reiterates the formulaic nature of her appeal as an imperial intimate. "Lavender clouds" are poetically associated with the rank of empress, who dwells "above the clouds" in the palace. In one sense, then, the hero is asking himself if he would be attracted to the Japanese woman were she not of that rank, a point that applies equally well to the Consort. Unfortunately, Chūnagon's idiosyncratic grammar can also imply the opposite meaning: that he would be longing for the empress if she did not have that title. The annotator, who uneasily endorses this reading, therefore suggests that the pair were involved before the woman ascended to that rank.[50] If this is the case, of course, then Chūnagon's feelings for the Consort also become suspect, since along with his seduction of Taishō no Kimi it establishes an earlier pattern of pursuing women intended for the court. This pattern also resurfaces in *Hamamatsu*'s fourth and fifth books, where Chūnagon competes with a prince for the Consort's half-sister. In short, either way, the poem reminds us of the Consort's formulaic significance, a far cry from Chūnagon's own conscious descriptions of incomparability. Moreover, by comparing the empress to "lavender" clouds, the hero also invokes the color of romantic affinity and reminds the reader of something discussed below: the Consort's again formulaic role as an object of obsession.

The Consort's own reaction to Chūnagon, dispensed with in a couple of lines, is also conventional. On the "night of the chrysanthemums" (*kiku no yūbe*), as the narrator refers to it, the Consort weeps upon hearing him perform on the Japanese zither (*koto*). "How talented he is at everything! I hate to think of how sad I'll be when he returns home and I can no longer see him" (161; Rohlich, 61). At his farewell banquet, staring at this man who "truly seems to radiate light," she thinks the same thing (197; Rohlich, 89). Both episodes emphasize Chūnagon's own stock allure as a man of unusual talents and Genji-like radiance, a claim that the narrator has already introduced.[51]

As we continue reading *Hamamatsu*, however, we discover a less conventional side to the budding romance. After Chūnagon's initial shock at his glimpse of the Consort, he presents her with a chrysanthemum, declaring,

Furusato o	What makes me forget
kouru kokoro mo	all the yearnings of my heart
wasururu wa	calling me back home
kono hana mitsuru	is none other than this night
yūbe narikeri	and the sight of this fair flower.

(160; Rohlich, 61)

The verse, which strikingly dismisses Chūnagon's earlier joy at the reunion with his father, again has several meanings. First, and obviously, it describes Chūnagon's general delight at the beauty of the scene, which he had earlier compared to a masterful painting. It also recapitulates the Consort's formulaic allure, since the chrysanthemum, while generally associated with China in the Heian imagination, was more particularly considered an imperial flower. Deeper forces, however, are also at work here. As Chūnagon recites his poem, the ladies open their fans and quietly listen, "no different than the people of his own land," and then respond with a Japanese verse of their own (160; Rohlich, 61). It is important to remember here, since the narration is Japanese, that these women are supposed to be from China. That was why, earlier, Chūnagon was so shocked to find them attractive. Critics often point to this scene as evidence of the author's ignorance of China or weak imagination, but it soon becomes clear that these details foreshadow a surprising plot development. The Consort, who—although playing a Chinese zither (*kin*) when the hero first meets her—had earlier wept at Chūnagon's Japanese melodies, is actually half-Japanese. To be precise, she is the child of a Chinese diplomat and the daughter of an exiled Japanese prince. Moreover, she spent her first five years with her mother in Japan. Small surprise, then, that after that night in the garden, she "never leaves Chūnagon's thoughts" (165; Rohlich, 65), even—or especially—when he thinks of home and Taishō no Kimi.

This lineage, repeated twice more in the tale, makes the Consort a "link" for Japan, if not in the conventional sense of the motif. That is why Chūnagon specifically mentions his yearning for "home" (*furusato*) in the poem quoted earlier. While the narrator first speculates that Chūnagon fixates on the Consort "because she cannot help being moved by him" (165; Rohlich, 65)—in effect, invoking the Heian belief that lovers fill our dreams because *they* miss us—she quickly makes this conflation of homesickness and desire explicit. "While Chūnagon never stopped missing his home for a moment," the narrator asserts, "he kept her so much in mind that he naturally felt distracted" (167; Rohlich, 67). The verb rendered here as "distracted" (*magiruru*), furthermore, can also be translated "confused," underscoring the identification of Consort and birthplace in Chūnagon's head. This association signals *Hamamatsu*'s innovation on the substitute pattern familiar from *Genji*. For Chūnagon, the Consort—like Fujitsubo—is both original and substitute at once. This time, however, the substitution is for a place, not a person—a pairing that recalls an earlier usage of the surrogate motif. According to scholars, pre-Heian poets wrote about places like Yoshino, mentioned earlier in this chapter, in part to eulogize patrons associated with them, effectively making those sites "spatial keepsakes."[52] Consciously or not, the *Hamamatsu* writer inverts this connection, making the Consort the keepsake of the land Chūnagon has "lost."

The point, if possible, is still truer for the Consort. Intriguingly, *Hamamatsu*'s expansion of the *Genji* motif begins here with a heavily emphasized comparison between the Consort and Yang Guifei, Murasaki's own emblem of obsession. The narrator begins by drawing our attention to the Consort's "upswept," "pinned" hairstyle, describing the same kind of ornaments that Yang sends Xuanzong from the grave: hairpins (*kanzashi*). The ornaments are themselves suggestive, since Xuanzong clearly found them inadequate replacements for Yang's company. The Consort's problems at court, however, are also likened to those of the earlier heroine, with the hostility of her rivals "inevitably dredging up that example from the past, Yang Guifei" (162; Rohlich, 63). Chūnagon echoes these comparisons. Back in Japan, the hero reports to the court that the Consort "like Yang Guifei and others, enjoys great favor with the Emperor but is hated by his ladies, beginning with the First Consort [*Ichi no Kisaki*]" (310; Rohlich, 161), essentially the empress. The hero then notes, as discussed earlier, that the Consort was forced from the palace as a result, once again like Yang. As he warms to his topic, Chūnagon claims that "even such celebrated women as Yang Guifei and Wang Zhaojun (Chao-chün) may have been noteworthy for their formal perfection, but none of the women I saw who were compared to them could compare to" the Consort and her retinue (312–13; Rohlich, 163). The reference to Wang, a beautiful consort who was unwittingly traded to the Huns by another emperor because she refused to bribe the court painters like the other women, reinforces the sense of the Consort's innocence and bad luck. However, the main purpose of the line is clearly to strengthen the association with Yang herself. Even the Chinese Emperor, who perhaps ought to know enough to learn from the comparison, links Yang with the Consort. Right after the heroine's introduction, the narrator relates that the Emperor "vows continuously to the Consort that 'if they become birds'" they will still remain lovers, a direct reference to Xuanzong's famous oath (164; Rohlich, 64). The Emperor quotes the entire vow during a poetry gathering on Tanabata, the proverbial night for lovers' meetings and the supposed anniversary of Xuanzong's statement (187; Rohlich, 82).[53]

It comes as a bit of a shock, then, when we learn that the Consort is not equally devoted to her husband. In fact, "she does not even consider his endless vows awe-inspiring" or auspicious (*kashikoshi*), a sentiment that may extend to Xuanzong's vow itself (164; Rohlich, 64).[54] In short, the Consort is either unimpressed with the Emperor's vows or, sensitive to Yang's example, afraid of them—perhaps both. Moreover, the Emperor seems to sense and accept this. When the Consort retreats to the mountains to hide her pregnancy—the result of a surprise encounter with the unwitting Chūnagon—the Emperor mistakenly believes that she is planning to take holy orders and offers her father a political prize to stop her. "As long as I am on the throne," the Emperor pleads, "things are beyond my control, and since I can't take holy orders, I have been doing what people want to keep the peace. But in a little while, when I step down and let the Third Prince take the throne, there will be nothing to worry about. Please, just put up with things for a little longer and wait for the reign of the Third Prince" (183–84; Rohlich, 78–79). Later the Emperor makes the same promise to the Consort herself in order to persuade her to perform at Chūnagon's farewell party, this time adding that, if she does what he wants, he will keep his word without regard for the "upheavals" it will bring at court (198; Rohlich, 89). The Consort's response—"Well, in that case, I will do what you ask"—underscores the pair's emotional distance, raising the question of what motivates any of her less-storied, supposedly romantic relationships.

Once again, the Consort's family history provides the answer. Even though the Consort left Japan as a young girl, the narrator observes,

> since she had lived alongside her royal mother, she was more serious than other children and could clearly remember things from that time, including how her mother had hugged her the day they parted. "Since this is the last time we will see each other, you will probably not know when I die. Please think of this as our last goodbye." Those words and the tears that followed them had stayed with the girl long afterwards, and as she grew up she took to staring out across the ridges of the eastern mountains, wondering what had become of her mother and wishing she could join her if only in death. (163–64; Rohlich, 64)

This experience has a lasting effect on the Consort. For one thing, as the narrator pointedly observes, the heroine remembers what it was like to live as the child of an orphaned "royal mother" (*haha miya*), an experience of isolation and perhaps even poverty that explains her unusual maturity as a child. Moreover, the Consort's attachment to her mother swells her distaste for court life, already suggested by her lack of faith and even interest in the Emperor's promises. Despite both his affection and the hostility of her rivals, the Consort "spends her time worrying about her mother's fate and grieving that she cannot hope to meet her again in this life" (164; Rohlich, 64). These thoughts echo Chūnagon's feelings for his father when he sets sail for China. One might even say that the Consort suffers from a version of Chūnagon's "child's sickness," recalling the links between Genji and the heroine Murasaki: like Genji, Murasaki loses her mother at an early age, exposing her to the abuse of a wicked stepmother. (When Genji finds Murasaki in Kitayama, she is living with her grandmother because her father fears bringing her into the house.) Intriguingly, this also puts the Consort, despite her general association with Yang Guifei, in the position of the bereaved Xuanzong, changing the romantic obsession to a filial one.

This psychological burden has an enormous effect on the Consort's attitude toward Chūnagon. As the narrator observes, the Consort "craves any news from Japan, even from the wind" (164–65; Rohlich, 65), and is constantly asking Japanese monks visiting temples in China about her mother. Not surprisingly, then, when she learns that Chūnagon is in China, "she cannot help wanting to speak with him" (165; Rohlich, 65). The Consort's fear of scandal keeps her from arranging such a meeting even though the Third Prince encourages it; presumably the handsome hero poses a greater threat to her reputation than do the monks. However, she takes pains to observe Chūnagon's visits with the Prince, thinking of him as "someone from the place she always thinks about" (167; Rohlich, 66). If Chūnagon initially sees the Consort as a substitute for Japan, in short, she does the same with him. In this case, however, she sees him as a surrogate for a specific person from that place: her mother. Here again, Chūnagon and the Consort reprise Genji and his love, who at least initially see each other as shadows of their parents—hence Murasaki's shock when Genji initiates their sexual relationship.

The pattern of seeing each other as substitutes for places and relatives, rather than lost lovers, continues once Chunagon and the Consort become involved. Months after the encounter in

Heyang, Chūnagon decides to distract himself from his passion by traveling to the provinces, only to once again find himself drawn into a garden by the echo of music (this time a lute or *biwa*). In the moonlight he glimpses a woman and "suddenly thinks of the Heyang Consort that night of the chrysanthemums," although he cannot conceive of finding the Consort so far from her estate (178; Rohlich, 75). Instead, rejoicing that "there *is* someone like her after all," he sneaks into the house and makes love to the stranger in the Consort's place. Chūnagon's luck is not what it seems. The encounter, which he fondly labels his "spring night's dream" (*haru no yo no yume*), essentially reprises the "night of the chrysanthemums," with the hero thinking of Taishō no Kimi and his family in Japan both before and after the meeting. Moreover, here, too, Chūnagon transfers his affections to a new replacement when his mystery woman disappears. After that "spring night's dream," the Consort—who has conceived Chūnagon's child—vanishes from the provincial estate, determined not to let the hero discover the truth. Chūnagon has no choice but to return to Heyang, morose. Here again, the narrator initially depicts the Consort as a link to Japan. Noting Chūnagon's depression, the Third Prince speculates that the hero's "longing for home"—and the difficulties of life among foreigners—"has overwhelmed" the appeal of the exotic (182; Rohlich, 77). Chūnagon's new infatuation, however, also deepens the allure of the Consort. After the "spring night's dream," Chūnagon begins to think that the Consort "looks very much like the woman he saw" earlier and "wishes that he could see her [the Consort]" as a result (184; Rohlich, 79). In short, the Consort becomes a potential substitute for the woman Chūnagon first loved in the Consort's place. This pattern recurs when Chūnagon sees an attendant, again actually the Consort, perform at his farewell party.[55] Watching the woman play her instrument—a Chinese zither, not the lute—Chūnagon is again reminded of "the Consort that night of the chrysanthemums" (199; Rohlich, 90). Since the hero again cannot imagine the Consort in this new setting, however, he concludes that she must be the woman from that "spring night's dream" and pursues her. In a sense, the Consort thus becomes a substitute for a substitute for herself. Once again, Chūnagon's devotion—to any of these women—seems suspect. The same is true of the Consort's feelings for Chūnagon. It is only at the farewell party that she is able to forget the bitterness she feels toward the hero and the "deplorable vows" of that spring night (197; Rohlich, 89). These mixed emotions clearly mimic Fujitsubo's feelings for Genji, but in the context of the passages just discussed, they also remind us of all the competing reasons given for the relationship.

The final point to consider about Chūnagon's romance with the Consort is its supposedly inevitable quality. As noted earlier, when Chūnagon first sees the heroine, he becomes so obsessed, and so homesick, that he visits a temple to pray for another glimpse of her. In response, a priest appears in his dream and recites the following poem:

Ima hito me	Only one more time
yoso ni ya wa min	and at a distance at that
kono yo ni wa	would you meet again?
sasuga ni fukaki	In this world despite the odds
naka no chigiri zo	your vows are fated to be deep.
	(175; Rohlich, 73)[56]

In short, Chūnagon's wish is not nearly ambitious enough; the pair are destined to be lovers and even parents, as a common pun on "this world" (*kono yo*) and "the world of the child" hints. The spring night's meeting occurs shortly after this revelation; after the farewell gathering, when Chūnagon learns the truth about his mystery women, the *Hamamatsu* writer reiterates the point. Reflecting on the oracle, Chūnagon concludes that "what even he had considered a surprisingly bold decision"—that is, the decision to travel to China to find his father—"had actually been the pull of his bond" with the Consort (203; Rohlich, 93). Back in Japan, gazing at the son the Consort sends back with him, he recapitulates the sentiment (334; Rohlich, 175). In short, by the end of the first book Chūnagon rejects all of the personal motives earlier attributed to his trip to China, including his filial duty toward the Third Prince. For Chūnagon, the relationship with the Consort has been all about romance. The Consort, however, ultimately comes to the opposite conclusion. While resolving to send the child back with Chūnagon, lest someone discover the affair, she recalls her own parting from her mother and laments, "My mother must have felt the same way then that I do now. There really is such a thing as karmic retribution" (208; Rohlich, 96). Unlike Chūnagon, the Consort ultimately blames the affair on her relationship with her mother, a point that the narrator later confirms. The Consort's mother, now a nun in the mountains of Yoshino, learns in a dream that the heroine "has such a strong filial spirit" that she has "pledged herself to someone from this world as an expedient means" so that he will take care of the nun herself (283; Rohlich, 144). One does not need to choose between the explanations; the complexity of the relationship is the point. The Consort's story illustrates that Heian romances always serve other people's interests, whether or not the lovers recognize it.

Yoshinohime and the Consort's "Niece"

The priest from the Yoshino Nun's dream offers a third explanation for Chūnagon's relationship with the Consort: the Nun's prayers to find someone for Yoshinohime, a rationale that removes both love and the lovers from the equation entirely (283; Rohlich, 144). This new heroine, whom Chūnagon pursues for the last two books of *Hamamatsu*, presents a final challenge to *Genji*'s portrait of romantic obsession. The later writer crafts Yoshinohime from characters in several relevant *Genji* subplots. I have already noted Yoshinohime's role as a surrogate for her sister, a point the narrator confirms. Once Chūnagon finds the new heroine, he tries to "cool the flames that burn throughout his breast" for the Consort by writing the girl letters, "but since there is no path which can take him to Yoshino, either, this has no effect" (308; Rohlich, 160). This facet of the character clearly draws on *Genji*'s Naka no Kimi and Ukifune, two of the Uji sisters. When Yoshinohime is born, the Nun first considers drowning herself, then desperately instructs her attendants to "cast the child into a deep river" (280; Rohlich, 142), a striking variation on Ukifune's attempted suicide. It is worth noting that even here, the parent is responsible for what in *Genji* is a crazed lover's action. In her calmer moments, the Nun worries that Yoshinohime is "buried deep in the mountains in a hovel that can't even keep the dew out" and thus has no chance of attracting suitable attendants (281–82; Rohlich, 143). Both comments reflect similar descriptions of Ukifune and Naka no Kimi, as well as their sister Ōigimi. (Not surprisingly, most scholars link the Yoshino Nun herself to the Uji heroines' father, the Eighth Prince.) Once the Yoshino Nun dies, Chūnagon becomes Yoshinohime's guardian, just as Genji did with Murasaki; a prophecy warning that the 17-year-old will die "if she becomes pregnant before age 20" even forces Chūnagon to mimic Genji's initially innocent care of his charge (358; Rohlich, 189).[57] Finally, in *Hamamatsu*'s last chapter, Prince Shikibukyō—Chūnagon's old rival for Taishō no Kimi—steals Yoshinohime and makes love to her, reprising Niou's theft of Ukifune from Kaoru. All of these layers make Yoshinohime one of the most effective symbols of the displacement and triangulation of passion in Heian fiction.

The *Hamamatsu* writer does not, however, limit Yoshinohime to merely romantic (or erotic) significance. During the girl's formal introduction to the tale, we learn that even the Nun thinks of Yoshinohime as a substitute for the Consort. Noting that her new daughter "resembles the one whom she [the mother] never forgets," the Nun takes to stroking the child's hair between prayers, and then to seeking her company to lighten her "unrelieved gloom" (281; Rohlich, 143). The detail does more than simply underscore the mother's grief at losing her child. Even watching the 5-year-old Yoshinohime at play, the Nun had thought the girl "looked just like" the Consort when she went to China (280; Rohlich, 142). Now, she also mourns the life the Consort might have brought her. As the priest who serves as her spiritual advisor has already told Chūnagon, the Nun "believes that the fact that she cannot shelter in her daughter's shadow"—that is, enjoy her daughter's patronage—"must be retribution for her actions in a previous life" (268; Rohlich, 135). This belief lends the Nun's "embittered" view of the fate that separates her from her daughter a distinctly worldly cast (269; Rohlich, 136). Her dismay at Yoshinohime's beauty, which "shines brighter each day than the last" (281; Rohlich, 143), suggests that she would have had equally practical hopes for the girl had she been able to give her the right backing. It also lends a darker side to her growing affection for Yoshinohime, particularly in contrast to her initial (at best) disinterest.

Lest we miss this, the *Hamamatsu* writer hints that the Nun feels the same way about Chūnagon, whom the Consort urges her mother to rely on as completely as if "she [the Consort] had even been reborn as him" (270; Rohlich, 136). The Consort makes this request in a letter that Chūnagon reads and then repeatedly thinks about, betraying the importance of the new substitution for all parties concerned.[58] At first, Chūnagon and the Nun view each other as merely emotional substitutes for the Consort, albeit in the non-erotic sense. At their first meeting, the pair immediately see each other as "links and keepsakes of that peerless woman," despite the lack of a blood tie between Chūnagon and the Consort (270–71; Rohlich, 137). The writer restates this claim frequently. Chūnagon, for example, looks at the Nun as "a lingering reminder of the distant Consort" (270; Rohlich, 136), whereas the Nun impatiently awaits his visits because "she thinks of him as a keepsake of her daughter in China" (319; Rohlich, 166).[59] This designation of Chūnagon as a keepsake of the Consort again highlights the text's emphasis on practical (as opposed to romantic) substitutions. When the hero directs officials from his provincial estates to supply the Nun's household, she is happy to accept the material assistance, although she refuses to let him move her to the capital. The narrator later reiterates this point. On her deathbed, the Nun, watching Chūnagon "hover about her like a child, . . . promising to provide for her in this world and the next," thinks, "This is just as it was in that dream. He is the real keepsake of the Consort in China, an expedient means of the Buddha himself" (331; Rohlich, 173). Here the Nun, like the Consort, equates surrogacy with financial support, a view also endorsed by the older woman's religious advisors.

Once we notice the Nun's practical hopes for the Consort, and her reliance on Chūnagon's support in their place, we note a final parallel between the Consort and Yoshinohime. When the Nun first asks Chūnagon to care for her second daughter, sensing that she herself is close to death, she begins by alluding to her family history, which she assumes her confessor has already related to him. The Nun's version of the story is elliptical: since "the person [she] knew as her father did not seem to be likely to prosper in the world" to begin with, his death left her destitute, and she does not want Yoshinohime to suffer the same fate (320; Rohlich, 167). She therefore begs Chūnagon to look in on the girl after her own death. The version of the story that Chūnagon heard from the monk during his first visit to Yoshino, however, is more complex. "There was once someone called the Prince of Kōzuke," the man had begun.

> Although he was more learned than the others at court and very intelligent, he somehow came to be charged with scheming against the realm and was exiled to Tsukushi. Now, he had one, motherless daughter, and since he had nowhere to leave her he was forced, despite his forebodings, to take her with him. When he died there, she clung to a single, hapless wet nurse and, while still in Tsukushi, met the Consort's father, the minister. (266; Rohlich, 134)

The reader already knows this story, since it was first introduced with the Consort herself. The writer even reminds us that we know, since the monk starts his narrative by remarking that Chūnagon "[has] probably already heard about this" somewhere else. All three accounts explain the Consort's mixed parentage. Tsukushi, home to Dazaifu and thus to the exile tradition discussed earlier (Senji's first husband was sent there, after the murder), was also the center of Heian trade with Korea and China. It is natural that the Consort's father, a Chinese envoy, should meet her mother there once the prince died.

The *Hamamatsu* writer is not, however, merely repeating herself. As the monk continues, once the Chinese envoy returned home with the Consort, the girl's mother found herself "secretly and enthusiastically pursued" by Prince Sochi (267; Rohlich, 135), another political exile, since holders of that rank typically governed Dazaifu in absentia when given the choice. The affair results in the birth of Yoshinohime, although her mother takes the tonsure during pregnancy to escape the governor. Both Yoshinohime and the Yoshino Nun, in short, are the children of princes with failed ambitions. Moreover, as the narrator adds when she repeats the lineage a third time in Yoshinohime's own introduction, the Prince of Kōzuke's own mother was "an aging princess for whom things had never gone as she wished at court" (279; Rohlich, 142). This also explains why the Prince himself "had hardly any success" in court circles, making it impossible for him to escape exile to Dazaifu himself. It also, more importantly, defines Yoshinohime as a woman born to a completely frustrated lineage—and a resentful one, as the Nun's confessor points out. It takes little imagination to guess that the man's "crime" (*tsumi*) like Chūnagon's, was to sleep with a (future) empress (279; Rohlich, 142). Chūnagon uses the same word to describe his relationship with Taishō no Kimi (248; Rohlich, 118).[60]

This history of failed ambitions, or at least social disasters, brings us full circle to the Consort. I have already noted that the narrator mentions the Prince of Kōzuke while introducing the heroine; he appears as a "prince who had been exiled to Tsukushi, then died there" leaving his daughter to cling to her equally desperate nurse (161; Rohlich, 62). (This nurse, like Asukai's, presumably takes matters into her own hands and lets the Consort's father in.) There is also a similar story, however, about the Chinese envoy himself. In fact, the narrator begins her introduction of the Consort with this point. "The Consort's roots," she explains, "lay with the last descendant of the Tang Emperor Taizong (T'ai Tsung) [597–649, r. 626–649], a man called the Prince of Qin (Ch'in). Since he was handsome and of exceptional learning, he was sent to Japan as a special envoy to attend to certain matters of concern between the two countries."[61] Annotators do not identify the prince with any historical figure, but he clearly comes from a powerful family; Heian aristocrats looked to the Tang dynasty as the peak of continental culture. For the descendant of such a lineage to be sent to Japan—a mere tributary state, from the Chinese perspective—is a shocking comeuppance, no matter how the narrator tries to sugarcoat it. Once again, the implication is a political failure of some sort. The Consort's father manages to send the heroine to court when she grows up, suggesting that he is not entirely without resources. Moreover, he has the support of the mythical Dragon King, the same figure who helps *Genji*'s Akashi Priest realize his ambitions for his daughter. The Dragon King tells the father in a dream that "because the child is meant to be a consort in China," he will allow them safe passage rather than taking the girl as his usual tribute. Nonetheless, like both her mother and Yoshinohime, the Consort ultimately becomes an orphan, if only in a figurative sense. Once her father sees the hostility of the other consorts and their families, he "grows disillusioned with the world and resigns as minister," retiring to the mountains to live out his days in peace (162; Rohlich, 62–63).

The point matters because, as with Chūnagon's ill will toward Lord Taishō or the Consort's own grief for her mother, this history informs more than the heroine's romantic relationships. It dictates the entire course of the Consort's life. As noted earlier, she cares little for life and still less for the splendor of the palace. Instead, as she admits to the Third Prince, "the real reason [she] serve[s] at court . . . is to lift the appropriate people to exalted ranks" (166; Rohlich, 66). In short, the Consort claims to have chosen to go to court, or at least stayed there, in order to help the people who matter to her, presumably her father and son. Murasaki never makes this claim for Kiritsubo, whose mother famously blames her husband for the girl's fate. Whether or not the Consort really has a choice is beside the point. The passage stands as a final reminder of the pragmatic concerns underlining all of *Hama-*

matsu's allegedly romantic relationships. It is no accident that, in this story of substitutes, the narrator refers to lineage as the Consort's "roots" (*hontai,* literally "true form"). Practical obsessions, not romantic ones, are the tale's true constant.

Daini's Daughter and the Sarashina Diarist

It is tempting here to return to the theory, mentioned at the beginning of this chapter, that the Sarashina diarist wrote *Hamamatsu*. In her memoir, the diarist famously longs for "a man like the tale's Shining Genji to hide [her] away in a mountain village like Ukifune for even an annual visit."[62] One view of this passage holds that the diarist deliberately reinterprets Ukifune's fate (her attempted suicide and later life as a nun feigning amnesia) as a kind of happy ending in order to create a "plausible precedent for her own prospects and destiny."[63] That is, the diarist idealizes and attempts to emulate Ukifune's transformation from a marginal woman to one important to elite men but ultimately sheltered from sexual jealousy. In the critic's phrase, this "rhetoric of exaggeration" about the virtue of abstinence mimics that found in *Hamamatsu*'s Taishō no Kimi subplot, perhaps confirming *Hamamatsu*'s attribution to the diarist. The Sarashina diarist's reference to "someone like" Genji, rather than the hero himself, tends to confirm this argument, since it suggests an interest in substitution—as we have seen, a crucial part of *Hamamatsu*'s response to *Genji*. The allusion to Ukifune also raises the issue of surrogates, particularly given the juxtaposition with Genji. While Murasaki's hero never meets Ukifune, his narrative surrogate Kaoru does, and it is precisely his failure to act as Genji would have and take Ukifune into his home that leaves her vulnerable to Niou, precipitating her suicide. This reading, of course, depends on one's view of Genji. One might also argue that Kaoru treats Ukifune exactly as his "father" would have and so causes disaster. Both interpretations, particularly the latter, evoke *Hamamatsu*'s own theme of family obsession.

Whether or not the Sarashina diarist wrote *Hamamatsu*, one further historical claim seems plausible. *Hamamatsu*'s author clearly gives considerable thought to the notion of substitution, both romantic and familial. While Murasaki inspired this interest with her portraits of obsession, the Rear Court environment discussed in Chapter 1 undoubtedly provided the later writer with more grist for her mill. Attendants, from whose ranks *Hamamatsu*'s author almost certainly came, went to court hoping to further family ambitions as well as personal ones. More precisely, these women were sent to achieve them. Regents and princes, like Yorimichi and Morofusa, adopted and sponsored higher-ranking women and their art to similar ends. In reality, these different goals for the women and their writing—artistic, affective, and instrumental—inevitably blurred. Murasaki, "answering" the "Song of Unending Sorrow," weaves all of these motivations into her narrative, but as we saw with *Sagoromo*, not all Heian readers were content with her complexity. In *Hamamatsu*, the only truly inescapable burden is the presence—and often absence—of parental influence. In this sense, the tale serves as an answer to *Genji* and a critique of late Heian society itself.

FOUR

Nezame at Night *and the Exile Plot*

Ama no hara	The high plain of heaven
kumo no kayoiji	its old pathway paved with clouds
tojitekeri	has forever closed.
tsuki no miyako no	Now not even she who came
hito mo toikozu	from the moon will visit me.

— *Nezame at Night*

Nezame at Night (*Yoru no nezame,* late eleventh century) is in many ways the most difficult of the late Heian tales to discuss. As detailed below, *Nezame* has severe manuscript problems; some scholars estimate that as much as three quarters of the original text has been lost. Although some measure of this missing content can be reconstructed—as with *Hamamatsu*—from descriptions of the tale in other sources, *Nezame*'s "mutilated" state precludes extended analysis.[1] Indeed, unlike *Hamamatsu,* even specialists refrain from referring to book-length divisions in the tale and instead divide it into "parts." The larger, conceptual challenge with *Nezame,* however, is its relative isolation within the tale genre itself. Despite its reputation as part of the derivative late Heian cluster, *Nezame* is not especially indebted to *Genji*—or to other examples of court fiction. To begin with, there is the unusual title. As noted throughout this study, Heian authors usually left their work unnamed as well as unsigned, forcing later copyists to invent labels for easy reference. Most of these ad hoc titles simply identify the text's genre and author or, in the case of fiction, its protagonist: "the diary of Murasaki Shikibu," "the tale of Genji," and so forth. Sometimes several titles coexist, reflecting disagreements on one or more of these fronts. *Tales of Ise,* for instance, also appears as the "poetic collection" and "diary" of its famous hero, Ariwara no Narihira, while *The Tale of Hamamatsu*—more properly called *The Tale of the Hamamatsu* [Beach Pine] *Middle Counselor*—also appears in some records as *Hamamatsu at Mitsu.* As we saw in the last chapter, this second title redirects our attention from hero Chūnagon to his first lover Taishō no Kimi, the metaphorical "beach pine." *Nezame at Night* has two alternate titles, the "old-fashioned" *Nezame at Midnight* (*Yowa no nezame*) and the simple *Nezame.*[2] All three titles, however, make essentially the same point. Instead of linking the text to a particular genre, they foreground an emotional setting: the hours that the protagonist and her lover spend "lying awake" (*nezame*) worrying about their relationship.

This phrase, conventionally used as the heroine's sobriquet, also has a problem. Typically, Heian heroes get their names from an emblematic poem they recite early in the text. Sagoromo, for example, earns his name from a verse complaining about the "narrow robes" (*sagoromo*) he sleeps in, an allusion to his lonely nights without Princess Genji.[3] (In fiction, Heian lovers normally use their robes as bedding, meaning that someone who sleeps alone loses blankets as well as companionship.) The word *nezame,* however, appears dozens of times in *Nezame at Night,* describing both Nezame and her lover, Gonchūnagon. In short, even the heroine's sobriquet alludes to a general setting rather than the pivotal scene typical of the tale genre. Scholars continue to debate the precise significance of the words "night" and "midnight" in the two longer labels. Some people believe that one refers to late nights spent awaiting faithless lovers, while others posit a more general reverie for the past.[4] Either way, the word and thus the title are unconventional, on two levels at least.

Even Nezame is unusual, at least for a tale heroine. Female protagonists as such are not rare in court fiction. *The Tale of Ochikubo* and *The Tale of Sumiyoshi* both feature them as part of the "bullied stepchild story" discussed earlier, perhaps inevitably; well-born women were relatively restricted in their movements, making them more vulnerable to household tyrants. Many critics also consider Ukifune the true hero of *Genji*'s Uji chapters, despite the nominal focus on Niou and Kaoru. In fact, female characters generally outnumber male characters in tale fiction, reflecting the genre's predominantly female audience. It is important, however, to notice how radically Nezame differs from these women in both rank and circumstance. Fictional heroines, unlike heroes, are typically marginal figures, buffeted by social and/or financial uncertainty. As a result, their adventures, like those of Ukifune and *Sagoromo*'s Asukai, frequently involve the vicissitudes of poverty and provincial life. Even elite heroines endure unusual difficulties, such as Rokujō's plunge from imperial consort to commoner's mistress and her related, uncontrollable spirit attacks. The interest in these stories comes, in a sense, from the incongruity of the woman's past and present experience.

Nezame, however, leads a fairly normal life for a well-born aristocrat. In fact, her story is, in most senses, enviable. She spends her entire life at the center of court society, first as the favorite child of a powerful minister and, later, as the wife and widow of a loving retired chancellor. Moreover, for the decades-long duration of the narrative, Nezame barely sets foot outside of her comfortable home in the capital, leaving only occasionally to visit her now retired father at his villa in Hirosawa, a favorite spot for viewing the moon and cherry blossoms. In this sense, Nezame is more like a fictional hero than a heroine, since these men typically begin with an exalted rank: either "middle captain" (*chūjō*), like Genji and Sagoromo; or the even higher post of "middle counselor" (*chūnagon*), which gives both the *Hamamatsu* hero and Nezame's lover their sobriquets. (To avoid confusion, I refer to the latter character as Gonchūnagon or "provisional middle counselor," a post he also holds.) The only scenes that show Nezame in a truly atypical situation, two early visits by a celestial music teacher, occur at the beginning of the text in an undeveloped plot line. This is not to suggest that Nezame does not suffer. The affair with Gonchūnagon—her brother-in-law—is strikingly ill-starred: as the narrator notes at the start of the tale, "of all the relationships I have heard of, none brought more heartache than that of this sleepless pair, despite the depth of their commitment."[5] In addition to fatally alienating her sister, Nezame's relationship with Gonchūnagon leads to a near-rape, arranged by the now-widowed Gonchūnagon's new mother-in-law, the Dowager Empress. Moreover, the heroine must endure the pain of hiding her affair and the resulting children from her father and formal husband, the most sympathetic characters in the text. The latter character, known as the Old Chancellor (*rō kanpaku*), even adopts the lovers' son when he learns the truth, a compassionate gesture that makes the heroine feel worse. The majority of the narrative, however, concerns Nezame's navigation of the more prosaic straits of pregnancy and household management, successes that again frame the heroine as a conventional, if idealized, aristocratic woman. To quote Shunzei's Daughter, this is a "touching and unusual" choice for a tale plot—and hero. Heian writers usually relegate such details to diaries or expository backdrop.[6]

Given this unlikely emphasis, and the confusion it caused later copyists, *Nezame*'s long-standing reputation as one of the best tales after *Genji* comes as something of a surprise. The view dates to at least Shunzei's Daughter, who particularly admires the "uninterrupted" focus on Nezame.[7] Modern critics go still further, calling the heroine "the true heir to Ukifune";[8] some name the writer herself Murasaki's best student, at least in the realm of the interior portrait.[9] In fact, Nezame inspired a series of elite heroines, perhaps because she combines aspects of *Genji*'s principal female characters: Kiritsubo, Fujitsubo, and Murasaki.[10] Novelists' claims for the text are still more extravagant. Despite Nezame's general conformity to Heian gender norms, these readers assert that the tale contains "something dangerous" for modern women,[11] and perhaps even a "poison" (attributed to all great fiction) that spurs readers to reevaluate their own lives.[12] The second view, with its allusion to a range of texts and cultural traditions, brings the discussion full circle to *Nezame*'s unconventional aspects—arguably the key to its reception of *Genji* and its theme in general.

Nezame at Night: *A (Very) Brief History*

Unlike the other two tales in this study, *Nezame* lacks even plausible links to a particular author. Fujiwara Teika credits the text, like *Hamamatsu*, to the Sarashina diarist, but most scholars today doubt the attribution. No credible candidate has emerged to take the diarist's place. Intriguingly, however, the association with Go-Reizei's court persists: another candidate, also a dark horse, worked for Princess Yūshi.[13] *Nezame* does share its cohorts' textual problems. Like *Hamamatsu*, the tale is missing substantial sections of the narrative, including an eight-year stretch in the middle and an indeterminate number of books at its end. As noted earlier, the loss makes it unusually difficult to discuss common topics like narrative structure and character development. Nor are there any competing textual lines, as with *Sagoromo*, to provide supplementary details. Only eight, nearly equally damaged manuscripts remain extant—although one of these, as noted in the introduction, is a gold-flecked affair now considered a national treasure.

In part because of this damage, which seems to have occurred fairly early in the text's history, *Nezame* does not enjoy many direct literary or critical tributes—save perhaps the aforementioned manuscript that might very well count for both. It is difficult to imagine someone commissioning such an expensive work without a firm sense of the narrative's worth. The short list of more detailed responses includes a cheerful, early medieval revision called *The Tale of Nezame* (*Nezame monogatari*), a Noh play called "Lady Nezame" (Nezame no ue), and an Edo-period synopsis. A damaged picture scroll, focused on the missing sections, completes the premodern list. The major modern tributes, alluded to earlier, belong to Tsushima Yūko, a writer known for her interest in Heian texts. Tsushima frames her novel *On the Banks of the River of Fire* (*Hi no kawa no hotori de*, 1983) around her own heroine's reading of *Nezame*. It is this character, contemplating another romantic relationship, who calls the tale dangerous.

Despite their scarcity, these tributes do shed some light on *Nezame*'s theme. Nearly all of them refocus our attention on the heroine, confirming the importance of the one atypical detail of her profile: her allegedly extreme suffering. It is the medieval *Tale of Nezame*, however, that gives us the most insight into this aspect of the text. As noted, the *Tale* lends *Nezame* a more cheerful outline, a revision also found in the "Sagoromo stories" discussed earlier. The *Tale* writer does this, in part, by omitting descriptions of Nezame's suffering, just as we saw with the "Sagoromo" version of Asukai and her wet nurse. More importantly, the *Tale* writer transforms many of the allusions that support the original story line. Both the original and revised texts open with the same lines of verse: the epigraph to this chapter. In this poem, Nezame complains that the mysterious music teacher mentioned earlier has not returned, even though the full moon of the eighth month (the normal harbinger of these visits) has come and gone. The verse reflects more than the heroine's artistic disappointment. During one of the earlier visits, the teacher promises that if Nezame memorizes these melodies, "she will one day even share them with the Emperor,"[14] presumably by becoming an imperial consort. As many critics observe, this scene relies on the "musical transmission story" (*ongaku denshōdan*), a plot convention best known from *The Tale of Utsuho* but also popular with Murasaki and other Heian writers. In these sequences, a hero or heroine achieves glory through imperial or divine recognition of his or her musical talent, often after an impromptu concert. Nezame's reference to the closed pathway to "heaven," like the clouds a conventional hyperbole for the palace, announces the failure of this plot convention as well as the teacher's prophecy. So, too, does Nezame's emphasis that "even" someone from the moon will not come, much less an envoy from the actual capital. In the view of some scholars, the *Nezame* author's decision not to complete the "musical transmission" sequence reflects the rise of literary realism in tale fiction.[15] More immediately, however, it announces the writer's resolve to tell her own story, realistic or not. The grammar with which Nezame describes the barring of the pathway confirms this. Not only does she use a suffix, appropriately enough, in the "story-telling past."[16] The main verb, translated as "closed" (*tozu*), can be either transitive or intransitive, raising the question of who shut the door in the first place.

The Tale of Nezame keeps Nezame's poem, perhaps to attract fans of the original story.[17] However, it also ignores the poem's message and completes the "musical transmission" sequence, explaining how Nezame's talents eventually gain her and her family a happy ending.[18] Moreover, as various scholars have pointed out, the *Tale* introduces several additional plot conventions into the narrative, including the "bullied stepchild story."[19] Nezame's sister, for instance, becomes her stepsister, which is the better to explain the women's rivalry over Gonchūnagon. Kannon, meanwhile, the bodhisattva associated with Ishiyama Temple, where Nezame gives birth to her first child in the original story—and where Murasaki supposedly wrote *Genji*—appears on the scene to ensure the happy ending, a self-explanatory example of the "miraculous intervention story" (*reikendan*). These changes, which deliberately restructure the *Tale* around generic formulas, explain the revision's more traditional title. They may even reflect a return to male authorship, since medieval poets, the presumed authors of such revisions, often experimented with allusion in their own verse.[20] In so doing, they seem to support the argument that convention is unimportant to the original plot. The *Nezame* picture scroll, which seems to neglect Nezame's own story in favor of more traditional subplots like her son's courtship of a princess, makes the same point.[21]

The Tale of Nezame also, however, makes a second set of revisions to *Nezame at Night,* alerting us to the original text's more complex relationship to tradition. Once again, the changes involve the opening verse. In addition to the "musical transmission" convention, Nezame's poem evokes the key formula of the tale genre: the "noble in exile" convention, in which the hero or heroine must wander strange lands in order to attain glory and atone for past mischief. This pattern surfaces as early as the *Record of Ancient Matters* (*Kojiki,* ca. 712), Japan's oldest extant fictional text.[22] Nezame's reference to the moon (*tsuki no miyako;* literally, "the moon capital") draws directly on the most famous example of this convention: *The Tale of the Bamboo Cutter,* whose heroine, Kaguyahime, spends years on earth for her "crimes" on her lunar home. At first, the effect of the allusion seems to be another rejection of tale convention. Unlike Kaguyahime—who returns to the moon at the end of *The Bamboo Cutter*—Nezame admits that she is trapped on earth (and outside of the palace) forever. Based on the revisions just mentioned, one would expect the writer of the original *Nezame* to drop the convention here, while the *Tale* author should complete it. Instead, the reverse is true. Throughout *Nezame,* the writer reiterates the association between her text and *The Bamboo Cutter,* as when Gonchūnagon states that "Kaguyahime lived in the house of the old bamboo cutter, after all,"[23] when he first sees Nezame by moonlight. Moreover, while Nezame generally stays in her comfortable home in the capital, the writer deliberately mimics the exile convention by setting the lovers' first meeting in a different residence, where the heroine has been sent to avoid a taboo. When Gonchūnagon discovers her there, Nezame herself alludes to *The Bamboo Cutter* by calling their meeting both the result of a karmic bond and a crime, evoking Kaguyahime's own competing explanations for her exile. In short, the *Nezame* writer repeatedly evokes Kaguyahime's suffering to underscore her own theme. The writer even links the moon, which usually presages positive developments in *The Bamboo Cutter,* to Nezame's sufferings, adding an ironic edge to her "exile" on earth.[24]

The author of *The Tale of Nezame* keeps some of the original references to *The Bamboo Cutter*, such as Gonchūnagon's comparison of Nezame and Kaguyahime. The vast majority of these allusions, however, disappear from the new tale. The few new citations, meanwhile, refer to Kaguyahime's triumphant return home, subverting the *Nezame* writer's own use of the intertext. Taken alone, these changes might seem just part of the medieval trend toward happy endings. The *Tale* writer also, however, deliberately drops a second set of "conventional" allusions from *Nezame*, this time to *Genji*'s Ukifune. Again, this is not a small change; Ukifune surfaces dozens of times, in both prose and poetry, in the original *Nezame*. Significantly, Ukifune is also closely linked to Kaguyahime. Not only does Murasaki, in her "The Picture Contest" (E awase) chapter, call *The Bamboo Cutter* "the forefather of tales,"[25] identifying it as the source of the genre and one of her own inspirations. Ukifune enjoys a special reputation among modern critics as Kaguyahime's best "niece."[26] By removing Ukifune, the *Tale* writer excludes *Nezame*'s two extended nods to the exile convention and *Genji* itself. Like the revisions to Asukai's wet nurse and the controversy over *Hamamatsu*'s reincarnations, this decision highlights a point crucial to the original *Nezame*: in this case, the redefinition of the exile plot.

Genji *and* The Bamboo Cutter

Before discussing *Nezame*, it will be helpful to make a longer review of the "noble in exile" convention. As noted above, this pattern first appears in *The Tale of the Bamboo Cutter*, which takes its title from the old man who finds Kaguyahime (literally, the "Shining Princess") in a glowing stalk of bamboo. It is not clear why the heroine has been sent to earth; some passages point to a "crime," as noted earlier, while Kaguyahime calls it a matter of "fate." Later, the heroine's father (apparently the emperor of the moon) claims that he sent her to earth to reward the bamboo cutter's hard work.[27] The narrator focuses instead on what happens once the bamboo cutter finds the girl. Like other "divine children" (*kami no sazukego*) in Japanese folklore,

Kaguyahime brings the woodcutter and his wife good fortune. After bringing her home, the old man harvests a number of gold-filled trees from the same grove, allowing him and his wife to retire in comfort. Moreover, once Kaguyahime grows up (in the miraculous span of a few months), her beauty attracts the interest of five powerful nobles and even the emperor, all of whom want her for a wife. This development seems to promise the old couple still greater fortune in the form of a politically profitable alliance, but the heroine rejects her suitors, first by setting them impossible tasks, then, when the Emperor surrounds her house with his soldiers, by escaping to the moon with a supernatural escort. At the end of the tale, Kaguyahime has forgotten her exile entirely; the magical cape she pulls on to ascend to the heavens erases the experience.

Like *Genji, The Bamboo Cutter* and its use of the exile convention profoundly influenced later tale fiction. *The Tale of Utsuho,* for example, sends hero Toshikage on a decades' long voyage across Asia before bringing him home to triumph with his music lessons (gleaned from other celestial figures in China and Persia). *The Tale of Hamamatsu* also alludes to the exile story, as Chūnagon's use of his trip to escape Lord Taishō and the various "crimes" of the Consort's ancestors suggest. No writer, however, makes more of *The Bamboo Cutter* than Murasaki. In addition to calling the tale the source of all fiction, Murasaki repeatedly draws on it for her own story. She flags Genji and Fujitsubo, her two most important characters, with allusions to Kaguyahime: people call Fujitsubo the "Shining Sun Princess"[28] and Genji himself the shining prince, the latter sobriquet, as noted earlier in the study, ultimately attributed to a Korean physiognomist. Kaguyahime's "nieces," meanwhile, populate even the tale's secondary subplots, as the stories of Yūgao and Tamakazura attest. Murasaki's structural debt to *The Bamboo Cutter* is still more important. Like Kaguyahime, Genji endures a humble exile away from his glittering capital to atone for his crimes: in this case, the seductions of Fujitsubo and Oborozukiyo. Like Kaguyahime, Genji ultimately returns home in glory, becoming both a regent and (nominally) a retired emperor, symbolically regaining his lost rank. In short, Genji is in one sense a male Kaguyahime, exiled from his own moon capital: the imperial court.

As readers quickly recognize, however, Genji's story also departs from that of Kaguyahime on at least two major points. Despite the sharper emphasis on his crimes, Genji does not truly suffer in exile. His home in Suma is comfortable and "beautifully constructed,"[29] as Tō no Chūjō also observes when he visits there; retainers even deepen a stream to improve the looks of the garden. Genji's days, meanwhile, are spent not suffering but "pasting sheets of colored paper together for poetry practice and sketching pictures on patterned Chinese silk."[30] In short, Genji behaves as if on holiday, only interrupting his amusements (which the narrator justifies as the hero's attempts to console his men) to protest his innocence. Even when these brazen claims provoke the one true terror of his exile, the storm and lightning strike on his lodgings at Suma, Genji ultimately escapes unrepentant to a still more luxurious life at Akashi, this time financed by the Akashi Priest. Kaguyahime, by contrast, loses the untold splendors of the moon capital to suffer in comparative squalor on earth. When the heavenly escort comes for her, its members repeatedly call the bamboo cutter's beautiful mansion and earth itself a "dirty" or "impure" place.[31]

Second, and conversely, while Genji does return home in glory, as convention requires, his success eventually unravels. His new wife, the Third Princess, betrays him with Kashiwagi and conceives a bastard son, the mirror image of Genji's own crime. Worse still, this marriage, which Genji undertook thinking of the princess's aunt Fujitsubo, sends his lover Murasaki into a fatal decline, ruining his most important relationship. Shortly after the heroine's death, Genji retreats from public life, and then from the tale itself. In a sense, while Genji has ample public glory at the end of his life, private misery keeps him from enjoying it. Moreover, Genji's crimes stem from the same source, since it is his obsessive longing for his mother and perhaps his lost rank that send him chasing Fujitsubo in the first place. It is no coincidence that he chooses to go to Suma, if only to forestall an official punishment. Genji's real exile is ultimately an emotional one, only incidentally related to gender or politics. Kaguyahime, by contrast, has no choice in her exile—and she stops feeling completely once she dons her cloak and ends it.

Murasaki repeats her examination of internal and self-chosen exile throughout *Genji*. Yūgao, named for her moonlike "evening faces" flowers, chooses to wander from lover Tō no Chūjō when she receives a threatening letter from his wife. Tamakazura, their daughter, chooses to remain in hiding once nurse Ukon brings her back from the provinces, afraid that Tō no Chūjō will laugh at her rustic manners. Both "crimes" seem to be internal, reflecting a lack of faith in both others and oneself. Because Yūgao does not trust Tō no Chūjō to protect her, she exposes herself to Genji's courtship and Rokujō's spirit attack. Tamakazura, who takes refuge with the hero, suffers a similar result. Nor is either woman wrong to mistrust, as the failed court career of the Ōmi Lady (Tō no Chūjō's truly comical daughter) and the death of Yūgao in their different ways illustrate. The story of Ukifune, *Genji*'s darkest iteration of the exile pattern, makes the same point. Ukifune, the so-called "drifting boat," spends years moving between the provinces and Uji and affairs with Niou and Kaoru. At first, her status seems to be the problem; since she is the unrecognized child of a prince, and unloved even by her low-ranking stepfather, neither Kaoru nor Niou feels compelled to treat her with respect. At the end of the tale, however, it becomes clear that something else is the problem. Despite her nun's robes and feigned amnesia—allusions to Kaguyahime's magical garment—Ukifune again finds herself surrounded by suitors. For this heroine, there is no release, even through death or, as in Tamakazura's case, an unwanted but stable marriage. For this reason, some scholars argue that Ukifune is a kind of Heian everywoman, with her crime and so her exile essentially reducible to her gender.[32] Here again, the situation is more complex. Murasaki deliberately places part of the blame on

Ukifune's own passion for Niou, which both encourages the courtier and incites at least one of Ukifune's attendants to become his accomplice.

Murasaki's changes to the exile plot of *The Bamboo Cutter* reflect her growing interest in the consequences of inner turmoil, something she also explores in her stories about romantic substitutes. The *Genji* writer is clearly also, however, developing a point raised by *The Bamboo Cutter* itself. Not only is Kaguyahime's suffering, as suggested earlier, linked explicitly to her time on earth, it is more particularly tied to her experience of courtship. Kaguyahime rejects her five suitors before she even meets them, protesting that "not only are they ugly, but I don't know how serious they are. If I marry one of them now, he might very well betray me, and then I'll regret it."[33] In deference to the bamboo cutter, however, she eventually agrees to wed whichever of the men fulfills the task she sets for him. Since the tasks are by definition impossible—to find the historical Buddha's begging bowl, for example, or the skin of the fire rat, a legendary creature impervious to flame—Kaguyahime feels safe. In fact, she laughs with delight when the men present her with counterfeits, confirming her original instincts. These reactions contrast sharply with Kaguyahime's affectionate relationships with both her adoptive parents and (less intimately) the emperor, all of whom she is crushed to leave at the end—at least until she dons that uncanny cloak.[34] In short, Kaguyahime's sufferings while in exile, as Murasaki's own tributes to the convention reflect, stem from romantic disillusionment. *The Bamboo Cutter*'s conclusion reiterates this point. Before Kaguyahime leaves earth, she sends the emperor a letter and some elixir of immortality to help ease his grief. Instead of rejoicing, however, the devastated ruler has a servant take both gifts to the top of Mount Fuji and burn them, announcing his loss to the heavens. Life means nothing to the emperor without Kaguyahime, at least beyond the naturally allotted span. The name of the mountain, by contrast, and the sorrow it reflects, means "timeless" or eternal—just like the grief found in "Song of Unending Sorrow," *Genji*'s other great source.[35]

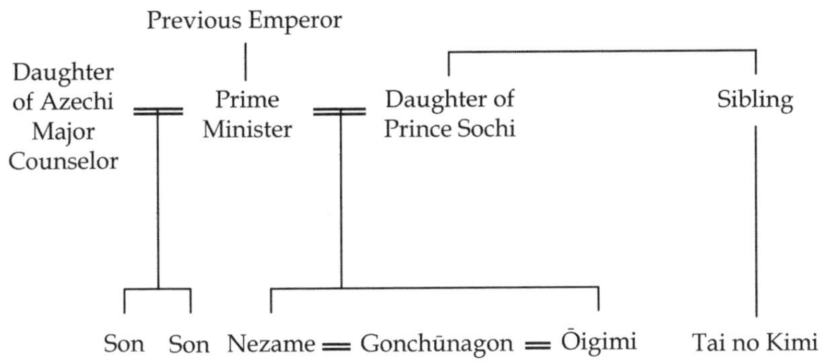

Fig. 4 Simplified genealogy for *Nezame at Night*
═ marital or romantic relationship | parent-child relationship

Nezame in Exile

Nezame, too, focuses on emotional suffering, as the different titles illustrate. In fact, this is the only major form of exile the text features, since Nezame spends so much of her time at home. The first meeting with Gonchūnagon, like those with the lute teacher, is atypical in this sense; most of the lovers' subsequent meetings take place in Nezame's home, during Gonchūnagon's visits to Ōigimi. Some critics also speak of temporal exile in *Nezame*, since the heroine retreats to thoughts of happier days after each meeting with Gonchūnagon and other troubling events.[36] A close reading of the beginning of the affair also suggests, however, that Nezame's "exile" is far from metaphorical. Like those of Genji and Ukifune, it is essentially existential in nature. Nezame suffers because she lives, not for the sake of a generic heroic penance. While the text's many gaps make definitive statements impossible, an analysis of the beginning of *Nezame* shows that the author deliberately casts Nezame's adventures as inevitable in Heian society—and not just for a person of her rank and gender. In this sense, calling *Nezame* a "woman's tale" is not enough.[37] This text, unlike *Sagoromo, Hamamatsu*, and even *Genji*, is about everyone—or at least all aristocrats and their (blue-blooded) servants, who, in Heian court tales, are the only people who count.

Introductions

As noted earlier, *Nezame* begins with a spectacular statement of its theme. "Of all the relationships I have heard of, none brought more heartache than that of this sleepless pair, despite the depth of their commitment."[38] The lines promise an unusually difficult love story and thus (following *The Bamboo Cutter*) an unusually painful exile for the heroine. Since most couples in tale fiction blame their troubles on mutual shallowness, the assertion that even Nezame's "deep" bond leads to suffering seems to underscore its special nature. So, too, does the music teacher's second prophecy, several pages later, that Nezame is "fated to torment [herself] with too much lonely thought" (48; Richard, 56).

It is important to recognize, however, that the narrator immediately begins to undermine this claim by introducing other, more serious examples of suffering. "When I asked about the roots of this," she continues,

> I found that the Prime Minister at the time was a brother of the retired Emperor Suzaku who had become a Genji. Although he was a skilled performer on both the *koto* and the flute, and a talented student of Chinese letters, he had been born to a mere consort and so lacked any real backing at court. It seems that his brother had therefore decided to have him serve the realm as a commoner. Thanks to this careful planning, the minister enjoyed widespread acclaim and his career flourished. (45; Richard, 52)[39]

Like many characters in tale fiction, the Prime Minister (*dajō daijin*)—Nezame's father—suffers the same fate as Genji: although he was born a prince, and has many suitable talents, he is forced to become a commoner for lack of political support. In fact, this is one of the defining traits of post-*Genji* fathers, making all later heroes essentially second-generation exiles. There are, of course, variations on this point. *Hamamatsu*'s hero, as noted earlier, descends from Prince Shikibukyō, a man who retained his rank. Sagoromo's father, meanwhile, is charged with committing some "crime" and so earning his demotion to commoner status. In the case of Nezame's father, the problem is simply his mother's backing at court, a setting familiar from

Genji itself. Critics generally read this introduction as a formulaic segue from *Nezame*'s thematic prologue to the story of the two lovers. As with the stories of the Consort's lineage in *Hamamatsu,* however, this history also refers to the heroine. The Prime Minister's experience, as the narrator observes, is the "root" of Nezame's own story. In effect, this story, and the sequels that follow, explain why the heroine is doomed to the suffering outlined in the opening line. Although her father succeeds beautifully as a commoner, she literally inherits his earlier misfortune, the explosive combination of talent and frustration that defines the "noble in exile" plot's protagonist.

The balance of this family portrait makes Nezame seem not just heroic (in generic terms) but paradoxically typical. After introducing the Prime Minister, the narrator continues to discuss the man's family life.

> One of the Prime Minister's main wives, the daughter of the Azechi Major Counselor, had given him two sons. The daughter of Prince Sochi, meanwhile, had borne two daughters. When these women raced to their deaths, with no thought for these keepsakes, the Prime Minister grew completely disillusioned with the world and, building a large, wonderful residence, moved there by himself and summoned all of the children. With no heart for the normal course of things [i.e., remarrying], he took them under his wing and brooded over their educations himself. (45; Richard, 52)[40]

Like *Sagoromo*'s Horikawa Chancellor, the Prime Minister has multiple "main wives," a clear recipe for conflict. Heian aristocrats typically chose one main wife from the more (or most) powerful set of in-laws. In this case, however, apparently no such balance has been established, probably because the two fathers-in-law are nearly equally matched. Both "Azechi" and "Sochi" are honorary offices reserved for the elite, although the major counselor technically holds the junior fourth grade, while a prince granted the title of Sochi (as seen earlier, often given to at least nominal exiles) ranks junior third. As a result, the narrator uses honorific language for the Prince's daughter and granddaughters, Nezame and her sister. However, the Prince's own failure to become emperor and his specific title of Sochi, prefaced by the Prime Minister's story, suggest that he is politically vulnerable. As a result, his daughter cannot eclipse her less elite rival and the women continue to wrangle, without a thought for their children and ultimately, as the text literally puts it, "competing to death."

The women's fates may seem predictable if tragic, given the circumstances; in *Genji*, a parade of female characters die from the emotional toll of rivalry, from the hero's mother to heroine Murasaki. The narrator's bald description of the women's hostility, however, as well as the Prime Minister's dramatic reaction to it, present an unusually shocking depiction of these hostilities. Not only do the Prime Minister's wives lose their own lives to jealousy, but they are apparently so hostile to each other that even the proverbially deep love for their children does not move either one to quit the contest. This line further darkens our view of the women, since, as Murasaki often reminds us, parents courted the "darkness" of attachment, in Buddhist terms, by loving their children too much.[41] The Prime Minister's shocked response to the deaths of his wives reinforces this point. "Completely disillusioned," he builds a new house and resolves not to remarry. Moreover, he designs this "wonderful" building (discussed below) to accommodate all four children, who would normally have been left with their maternal relatives. Finally, he resolves to personally educate even his politically valuable daughters, a task that Genji himself leaves to the heroine. The narrator highlights the eccentricity of the Prime Minister's actions by describing them in words normally associated with birds, or, we might say, mother hens: he shelters the children "under his wing" (*mihane no shita*) and "brood[s] over [them]" (*hagukumi*).

This is not to say that the Prime Minister shuns all companionship; not long after the death of Nezame's mother, he begins an affair with the woman's young cousin, Tai no Kimi. Once again, however, jealousy reasserts itself. The Prime Minister's behavior offends the older daughter's wet nurse, "a very wellborn woman . . . whom the minister had previously called on whenever he felt lonely" (51; Richard, 59). Tai no

Kimi, who dislikes the Prime Minister's attentions in any case, soon finds herself the object of considerable hostility. The wet nurse even mocks her as the "*new* main wife," reminding both the reader and presumably the Prime Minister of the old competition. At least to the reader's knowledge, the Minister takes no further lovers for the duration of the book.

The narrator's opening claims notwithstanding, nothing in Nezame's own story compares to this. She does not die from jealousy, unlike her mother and her mother's rival, and even after years of persistence during which Gonchūnagon wins her love, she still refuses to display any sign of jealousy. For example, when Gonchūnagon marries a princess, frustrated that Nezame refuses to make their relationship public, his mother-in-law the Dowager Empress has to make up charges that Nezame is mounting spirit attacks on the princess to gain sympathy at court. By contrast, Nezame's sister Ōigimi (Gonchūnagon's first wife) dies from jealousy of the same woman and shows considerable hostility—along with her attendants and favorite brother—to Nezame herself. Nezame's patience, while reinforcing her ideal quality, again makes her suffering seem less exceptional. If she were truly more upset than the average Heian woman, she would presumably lose control like Rokujō and act out.

The final segment of the Prime Minister's family history, which introduces Nezame and her siblings, recapitulates the heroine's paradoxical normalcy. As noted, the Prime Minister retreats from the world after his wives die, moving with his children to his "large, wonderful" house. In one sense, this residence—called "wonderful" in the sense of both "strange" and "appealing"—suggests Genji's Rokujō mansion and the estate of Sagoromo's father: all three buildings symbolize the owners' rejection of their world and a related attempt to found a kind of private empire. While Genji and the Horikawa Chancellor create shadow palaces, however, the Prime Minister initially seems to reject the imperial enterprise. Not only does he abandon all formal wives or "consorts," the Minister even takes the tonsure once Ōigimi marries Gonchūnagon, symbolically renouncing his political ambitions. For this reason, he is often compared to Uji's Eighth Prince.[42] Unlike that character, however, who loses his chance to become crown prince and thus emperor when Genji returns in glory from his exile, the Prime Minister decides to raise his children for success. As the narrator continues, concluding the family portrait,

> The Prime Minister taught the boys the flute and Chinese letters, and as the girls grew into gifted young women, he taught the older sister the lute and the younger one the thirteen-stringed zither. Each played her instrument beautifully. The younger sister was especially talented, and by thirteen, when she might still have been indulging in childish games, she had outstripped her teacher. She could play any piece perfectly on sight. The Prime Minister sadly concluded that this gift had come to her from a previous life. (45–46; Richard, 53)

As the narrator points out, the Prime Minister takes pains to educate his children in the arts necessary to prosper in court society: music and (for the boys) "Chinese letters," that is, the Chinese classics and poetry. These are, of course, the same talents that failed the Minister himself as a prince, a fact that immediately casts a pall on the children's fates. No matter how gifted they are, there will be a limit to their success; this, too, is part of the family inheritance. After suggesting this, the narrator immediately describes the exceptional talents of the younger sister, Nezame. This portrait again highlights Nezame's role as a noble in exile. With her uncanny gift for music, Nezame—a commoner—is doomed to outshine her surroundings, a fact that inevitably causes her father grief. The passage is equally remarkable, however, for what it leaves out. Unlike similar introductions in *Genji*, *Sagoromo*, and earlier tales (*Hamamatsu*'s first book, as noted, is not extant), there is no attempt to describe the heroine beyond her musical talents and the general assertion that she, like her sister, is a "gifted young woman." We get no sense of her thoughts or her personality. More unusually, we hear nothing about her looks, not even a conventional reference to her beauty. This silence persists into the next scene, where the narrator finally spares a thought for the "lovely features" and "elegance" of Ōigimi (46; Richard, 53).

It bears mentioning that the narrator provides no physical descriptions of any of the characters to this point in the tale, including the Prime Minister himself. For quite some time, the only detailed description is reserved for the heavenly music teacher, who appears in Nezame's dreams looking "like a person from a Chinese painting" with her "striking" good looks and formal (upswept) hairstyle (46–47; Richard, 54). Moreover, the writer eventually describes Nezame through her father's eyes, once he sets a wedding date for Ōigimi. The Prime Minister's fear that Nezame is "of such superior looks and quality that she might not be long for this world" is fairly typical of heroic portraits in Heian fiction, including *Genji* (50; Richard, 58). Nonetheless, the writer's refusal to describe the heroine's looks in the tale's introduction, the normal place for such portraits, also serves a purpose. It reproduces in prose the featureless anonymity of the "slash-eyed hook-nosed" aristocrats of Heian art (as one critic asserts for the first part of *Nezame* in general).[43]

This blank introduction to Nezame serves several purposes. On one level, it forces the reader to focus on the heroine's talents, key to both the interrupted "musical transmission" and "noble in exile" conventions and such subsequent developments as Nezame's arrangement of successful marriages for her own stepdaughters. It might also, perhaps less plausibly, allow for more readers to identify with her. Given the obvious repetition of Nezame's supposedly unique suffering in the lives of other characters, however, the omission of even a general reference to the hero's appearance may also underscore her role as a kind of generic hero. Every heroine discussed in this study, at least, has a family like Nezame's—and, as the narrator points out, it is the family that is her story's "root."

The Marriage

After describing Nezame's music lessons, the narrator begins her tale in earnest, with the first installment of the promised romance. Significantly, the chain of events which produces Nezame's meeting with Gonchūnagon turns on the question of marriage, another routine but complex consideration in

Heian life. Ōigimi, now 20, has reached a suitable age, and the Prime Minister is worrying about finding her a husband. His deliberations on the matter confirm that, withdrawn from the world or not, he and his children remain very much within the imaginative constraints of court life.

Right now, at the palace, there's the daughter of the Minister of the Left and Chancellor [the same man holds both posts], whom the Emperor shows every courtesy; she's both the mother of the Crown Prince and has the rank of empress. In private, meanwhile, the Emperor lavishes his affections on the Shōkyōden Consort, the daughter of his brother Prince Shikibukyō. There's no point in sending Ōigimi to him now, and the Crown Prince is only a child. What should I do with her? (49; Richard, 57)[44]

As this passage reveals, the Prime Minister's first instinct is to send Ōigimi to the palace, either as a consort for his brother the Emperor or as the bride of the Crown Prince. Unfortunately, neither action seems feasible. The Emperor already has several wives and his son is too young to marry. Moreover, the Prime Minister sees that even the Emperor's "private" affections for the Shōkyōden Consort—daughter of yet another Prince Shikibukyō, a name familiar from *Hamamatsu*—cannot displace the current empress, daughter of the most powerful noble at court. The Prime Minister literally calls the Consort a "private thing" (*watakushi mono*), the same phrase used in *Genji* to describe the Kiritsubo Emperor's delight in the young hero.[45] There, too, these affections mean little in the public realm, since Genji is made a commoner, while Kokiden's son is named the crown prince. In *Nezame*, the Prime Minister observes that the Emperor himself literally thinks of his "private" lover "with pain" or pity, as if acknowledging her family's weakness.[46] Evidently a practical man as well as a loving father, the Prime Minister—who has personally witnessed the cruelties of competition—quickly abandons his hopes for Ōigimi. Once again, Nezame's father—the "root" of her suffering, according to the narrator—turns out to be unusual. As a result, her later suffering again seems conventional, making her exile a function of ordinary experience.

The Prime Minister's ultimate decision to marry Ōigimi to another man also illustrates Nezame's atypically ordinary exile. Casting about for suitable bridegrooms, the Minister suddenly thinks of Gonchūnagon, not quite 20 and—like Nezame—"so handsome, noble and talented that he is almost too good for this world" (49; Richard, 57). In fact, the young noble seems practically imperial, "revered in public and private alike as the light of the world" and, by the typical pun, the cynosure of the court. This introduction clearly marks Gonchūnagon as the tale's male protagonist and Nezame's fated lover. However, for the anxious Prime Minister, it also makes him the ideal match for Ōigimi. With his looks, lineage, and promising rank—technically, Gonchūnagon is both a middle captain and a (provisional) middle counselor—the young man is the perfect son-in-law. As before, however, the Prime Minister also considers the potential bridegroom's emotional qualifications. "He's the Chancellor's favorite child, the Empress's brother, and the Crown Prince's uncle," the Prime Minister marvels. "He'll never want for anything, and yet even so, with the world at his feet, he never shows the least bit of pride or mistreats people. What a fine young man he is! Any woman who can't be an empress or give birth to a prince would be lucky to marry someone like him" (49; Richard, 57).[47] In short, the Prime Minister seems less impressed with Gonchūnagon's political prominence than the courtier's kind heart. This sensitivity to Ōigimi's future happiness reinforces the Minister's ideal quality (and perhaps, humorously, his eccentricity), but it also paints both daughter's sufferings as something that anyone might experience. Most Heian fathers, after all—at least in tale fiction—do not take their children's emotions so much into account. Gonchūnagon's father, the Minister of the Left, betrays as much in his own consent to the marriage. "Why not? Ōigimi is the best possible match for my son, other than one of the princesses. They will make a very suitable couple" (50; Richard, 57–58). This is all that Ōigimi's father-in-law has to say on the subject.

Of course, the real interest of Ōigimi's marriage lies in the frame it provides for Nezame's own affair with Gonchūnagon.

After concluding the marriage negotiations, the Prime Minister reflects that "it's really my younger daughter who would look best with Gonchūnagon," but the Minister cannot bring himself to shame Ōigimi by marrying Nezame off first, even though the heroine is his favorite (50; Richard, 58). That the Prime Minister gives Ōigimi to Gonchūnagon, against his will and better judgment, once again shows his empathy for his daughter: not only does he not wish to embarrass Ōigimi, but he realizes that he should arrange a marriage for her while her charms are at their peak. In a sense, this subplot provides yet another practical explanation for Nezame's supposedly unprecedented suffer ing. It is not that the lovers' bond was "shallow," or that her father was cruel. Even the best-intentioned decisions, at least those that honor precedent, can cause pain. Gonchūnagon's father's claim that Ōigimi is "the best possible match" for his son (other than a princess) again underscores the point. Not only is Ōigimi clearly unworthy of Gonchūnagon, as the Prime Minister recognizes; their match will be anything but "suitable," contrary to her father-in-law's hopes. Ultimately, as noted earlier, Gonchūnagon will actually marry a princess—and still prefer Nezame. In short, both fathers' judgments, whether offhand or considered, lead inexorably to the suffering of the prologue, both for the lovers and Gonchūnagon's supposedly happier wives. Once again, Nezame's emotional exile, while more intense than those of the other characters, is nonetheless fairly typical—in sharp contrast to the "mismatch" the Korean physiognomist proposes between Genji's qualities and his fate.

The Lovers' Meeting

Before long, the romantic cataclysm comes to pass. Frightened by some "threatening omens" on the first day of the seventh month, the Prime Minister interrupts the preparations for Ōigimi's wedding to sponsor a series of protective rites for Nezame, now 16 (50; Richard, 58). The digression creates discord between the sisters, already divided by the younger girl's mastery of the lute (originally Ōigimi's instrument) and some subtler tensions. Tai no Kimi, formerly companion to both of the girls, has taken the place of Nezame's dead wet nurse, and Ōigimi resents it. Ōigimi's nurse, meanwhile, remains jealous of Tai no Kimi's involvement with the Prime Minister and loses no opportunity to slander either the attendant or the heroine. Even these prosaic stresses take their toll on the heroine. Nezame and Tai no Kimi spend their time not laughing and gossiping, as one might expect of such fortunate women, but "consoling each other for all the griefs and difficulties" in their lives (51; Richard, 60).

When a serious directional taboo sends Nezame to the house of Tai no Kimi's brother, things get even worse. One of Tai no Kimi's nieces, the daughter of the Governor of Tajima, is also staying at the house, and the women soon get in the habit of gathering on the veranda, sensing security in numbers and perhaps their residence. (It is, after all, the house of a bishop). Unfortunately, on the last night of Nezame's stay—either the sixteenth or eighteenth of the same month[48] and thus just after the full moon—Gonchūnagon arrives next door to visit his ailing wet nurse and overhears one of the women's impromptu concerts. Urged on by his retainer Yukiyori, who has been spying on the women, the courtier slips through the bamboo grove separating the two houses for a closer look. The sight of Nezame, now reclining against her instrument and gazing up at the moon, sets his pulse racing. Feeling as if he has glimpsed "the clear light of the full moon through the clouds," Gonchūnagon waits until the women have retired for the evening, then steals in to Nezame and has his way with her (55; Richard, 63). The sufferings prophesied by the narrator, the music teacher, and the "threatening omens" have begun for Nezame—neatly flanked by a reminder of *The Bamboo Cutter*'s quite distinct exile plot.

As noted earlier, this encounter, and the affair it precipitates, ruin Nezame's relationship with her sister, introducing a new source of anguish into the tale: alienation from one's family. Once Ōigimi discovers the truth, she lies awake, listening for Gonchūnagon's attempts to contact Nezame in the next bedroom. Nezame does the same, horrified by her sister's wrath and her own, unmistakable pregnancy, which further binds her to Gonchūnagon. As a result, many critics see the affair as an indictment of Heian's polygamous marriage practices and the "male egoism" that supported it.[49] Nezame, unlike Ukifune or even Kaguyahime, is completely innocent. She and her attendants are cold to Gonchūnagon when he appears and continue to rebuff him for nearly the duration of the text, again stressing the inevitability of her suffering. Gonchūnagon's retainer Yukiyori, the son of the noble's wet nurse, also contributes to this impression. Not only does the retainer fan Gonchūnagon's passions, literally opening a path through the bamboo for him. He also mistakenly identifies Nezame as Tajima's third daughter, even if he does call her "the genuine article [and] just extraordinary" even compared to her pretty "sisters" (53; Richard, 62).

This association between Nezame and Tajima's daughter (like Yukiyori, a midranks figure) does more than simply underscore the heroine's lack of distinguishing visual features, the first indicator of her representative status. Once again, it imbeds her in a plot about suffering. This particular daughter of the Governor, as it happens, has a scandalous reputation. According to Yukiyori, Tajima's third daughter is supposed to marry a minor captain, the son of a Genji major counselor, but unbeknownst to her parents, she already has a lover: a middle captain born to Prince Shikibukyō, Nezame's uncle. However, even when the Governor learns of the affair, he refuses to break off the engagement. The story simultaneously recalls the plight of the Shōkyōden Consort, Prince Shikibukyō's other child, and foreshadows Nezame's impending difficulties. While responsibility for the affairs differs, all three women—and all six lovers—find themselves in relationships filled with heartache and, inevitably, duplicity. The Emperor, the narrator implies earlier, maintains order by showing his empress "every courtesy," even if his deepest affections lie with the Consort. Tajima's daughter apparently does the same in her marriage, as Gonchūnagon immediately intuits. As he laughingly remarks to Yukiyori, "Well, she can't be very happy about that, can she?

The woman clearly has excellent taste. She's probably still longing for the captain" (53; Richard, 62).[50] The couple may even still be meeting, presumably causing additional suffering for the Governor's new son-in-law. As we have seen, the same will be true for Ōigimi as well, although the narrator does not reveal the inner feelings of the empress. The episode also indicates the inevitability of Gonchūnagon's own actions. A noble who acknowledges the wishes of a governor's daughter, even when they defy her parents' wishes and social convention, is unlikely to honor his own marriage, particularly when the affair also seems to be "fated." Gonchūnagon, it turns out, is no revolutionary. By assuming that Tajima's daughter has "excellent taste"—something he infers from both her music and her choice of the nobler-born lover—he implicitly distinguishes her from the governor class, justifying his own interest. As he reflects after seeing Nezame, "She must be the most beautiful girl of that rank. Why else would I find someone like her so dazzling?" (55; Richard, 63–64).[51] That Gonchūnagon, whom the Prime Minister had earlier praised for his modesty and self-restraint, even thinks of the social hierarchy shows how much he himself remains caught in it. Before slipping into the house and seducing Nezame, the courtier—"despite his rare self-discipline"—considers her supposedly lower rank and decides he can overlook her predictable resistance (55; Richard, 64). In Heian fiction, it turns out that even perfect son-in-laws have this failing, but then so do perfect fathers. The *Nezame* author makes the same point on status only pages before in the story of the Prime Minister and Tai no Kimi. However, this—unlike *Sagoromo*'s Asukai plot—is no midranks romance. As the tale's various formal marriages also show, everyone in *Nezame* goes into "exile" in court relationships. The heroine just signals the new plot.

Conclusions

In the end, Gonchūnagon, too, must defer to convention. Once he realizes that Nezame (whom he still believes to be the Governor's child) has not had a lover, he attempts to pass himself off as the middle captain, believing that she must have been corresponding with the man to give rise to rumors of an affair. This subterfuge, he reasons, will make the seduction less of a shock. The kindness, however, is also self-serving. According to the narrator, Gonchūnagon, too, is concerned about rumors, and "[does] not want to identify [him]self too quickly in such lowly company" (57; Richard, 66). This concern with rumor surfaces throughout Heian fiction, leading many heroes to counterfeit. As discussed earlier in this study, Sagoromo hides his identity from Asukai in order to keep the affair from Princess Genji. Genji misleads Yūgao, meanwhile, arguably because he already has a reputation, as the narrator of the "Broom Tree" chapter suggests.

In Gonchūnagon's case, however, there seems to be no reason for the fear besides a general concern with social opinion. Even if, as he reflects, "her common parents and siblings" would be aghast at their social gap and forbid her to see him—exactly as they had with the middle captain—these people have no claim on someone of his background (59–60; Richard, 69). He has already admitted that he can treat someone as "far inferior . . . to him in rank" as she is exactly as he likes. All of the other references to consequences are deliberately oblique, such as Gonchūnagon's worries that "the gossip would be miserable" or that "the rumors could be terribly inconvenient" (59, 60; Richard, 68, 69). Even Gonchūnagon's solution revolves around this concern.

> Even if I think that I'll die if I can't see her soon, it would be smarter to wait for a while and ask the Empress to invite her to become an attendant; then I could see her at court. If I could just get her to leave home like that, I could whisk her away with me whenever I liked and see her secretly, like a private thing. If I could arrange things like that, there would be no reason for people to talk. Was there ever an emperor without his women from the provinces? If I choose to devote my affections to some palace attendant, who can find anything wrong with that? That's the only way this can work. If I leave her as a commoner's daughter and go stealing off to see her in some hovel, I will just make a spectacle of myself." (60; Richard, 69)

Gonchūnagon's thoughts retain an element of snobbery, as his dismissive remark about "women from the provinces" or *uneme* (sometimes translated as "tribute women") reflects. However, his fears about the gossip an affair might cause, particularly when expressed so abstractly, also make a serious point. Like the introduction to Nezame's family and the passages about Ōigimi's marriage, these thoughts confirm that Nezame's worries and the sleepless evenings they cause are neither unusual nor particular to her gender and rank. Even Gonchūnagon, with all of his connections, must worry over his affairs—even an affair with a woman he mistakenly assumes to be the willing daughter of a subordinate. This conclusion returns us to *Nezame*'s thematic prologue, the statement that "of all the relationships I have heard of, none brought more heartache than that of this sleepless pair, despite the depth of their commitment." By the time Gonchūnagon and Nezame begin their affair, the narrator has proven, through numerous subplots and intertexts, that this is simply not true. Everyone in this text suffers, for reasons apparently too obvious—at least for Heian readers—to bother spelling out.

The point about context offers a final hint for re-reading *Nezame*, one that returns us to issues raised in this study's first chapter. Heian writers often use the phrase translated here as "relations between men and women" (*hito no yo*)—a variation on the "world" pun discussed earlier in this study—to denote the realm of human activity more generally, as well as the rarified sphere of imperial rule. No less a source than the preface to *Collection of Ancient and Modern Verse*, the first anthology of Japanese poetry, includes this usage. Both of these worlds figure in *Nezame*'s plot, as the preceding discussion and later scenes with the Empress Dowager suggest. These references to the wider world also, however, carry thematic weight. Heian relationships, particularly in the crucible of the Rear Court, frequently blurred the lines between romance, politics, and what we might even call "business." Even before delving into its supposed subject matter, Gonchunagon and Nezame's mutual unmasking and their subsequent suffering, *Nezame* shows how delicate these calculations could be. In this sense at least, Tsushima was right. *Nezame* is a dangerous book, perhaps because of it lovers' very conventionality. By rewriting romance from its foundations, the *Nezame* writer shows that everyone suffered from these difficulties. In court society, at least, there was no escaping them.

POSTSCRIPT

Murasaki's Fan Fiction?

He did not want to compose another *Don Quixote*—which would be easy—but *the Don Quixote*. It is unnecessary to add that his aim was never to produce a mechanical transcription of the original; he did not propose to copy it. His admirable ambition was to produce pages which would coincide—word for word and line for line—with those of Miguel de Cervantes.

— Jorge Luis Borges, "Pierre Menard, Author of *Don Quixote*"

After reading *Sagoromo, Hamamatsu,* or *Nezame,* it is tempting to return to Murasaki's cryptic obituary for Genji in "The Perfumed Prince": "Once his light vanished, there could hardly be anyone dazzling enough among his heirs to take his place." One wishes to refute the claim, to show how these texts and their heroes both compare to and even surpass Murasaki's: in Sagoromo's spectacular appointment to the throne, for example, or *Nezame*'s increasingly complex interior portraits. These responses, however, misread both the "Prince" narrator's statement and the broader tale genre. As suggested in the introduction to this study, Heian writers expected readers to know their precursors, an assumption probably learned from contemporary poets. Even Murasaki, for example, asks readers to judge her hero against his "forefathers" in the genre, both directly and through explicit allusions to earlier texts. The

"Prince" narrator merely refocuses this impulse within *Genji* itself. In this sense, choosing a successor to Genji and his tale is both wrong and irrelevant. All of these texts, *Genji* included, function best when read with the others. The act of comparison itself is the point.

Considering this argument, as well as *Genji*'s own special place in the tale genre, several of my own students over the years have asked whether it might be useful to read late Heian texts in particular as "fan fiction," a genre best known in the field of Anglo-American science fiction. These stories, usually published in amateur magazines but also appearing as novels, feature favorite characters from films and television series like *Star Trek* in fresh but generically consistent narratives. For instance, a novel may feature *Star Trek*'s Captain Kirk and the crew of his starship Enterprise visiting yet another strange planet in their quest to explore the universe. Alternatively, a writer may introduce a new character into the existing story line. "Mary Sue" stories, for example, follow a newly introduced Enterprise crewmember—often "the youngest smartest person ever to graduate from the academy and ever get a commission at such a tender age"—as she interacts with the heroes of the series. In these narratives, Mary Sue typically "saves the day by her wit and ability, and, if we are lucky, has the good grace to die at the end, being grieved by the entire ship."[1]

As this last comment suggests, fan fiction has its own subgenres and constituencies, not all of whom agree on what a legitimate addition to the fictional pool looks like. In many cases, these offerings are meant primarily if not exclusively to entertain their authors themselves, an effort which will always leave someone in the audience out. As critics have argued, however, fan fiction (which also includes series devoted to figures like Sherlock Holmes and Jane Austen as well as the heroes of graphic novels) frequently serves an additional function. Fan texts may also seek to discuss their models, particularly when formal critics refuse to do so. This is a well-established point in the history of science fiction fan works.

Since, as one researcher observes, the genre was "not truly 'scientific,' yet neither . . . considered serious 'fiction'"[2] when it emerged in the 1930s, academics and professional critics refused to touch it. Frustrated readers leapt into the breach, creating magazines and conferences that attempted to "critically examin[e] [the genre] and the ideas it presented."[3] In short, fan work—at first, limited to traditional analyses—sought to fill a perceived critical gap. This writing continued even when science fiction and other popular genres found a home in the academy, usually through studies of reception rather than textual criticism per se.[4] In science fiction author Samuel Delany's view, fan fiction is simply more useful than formal scholarship, because rather than attempting to place the genre in social or literary history, it tells particular writers what does and doesn't "work."[5] These comments carry considerable weight, given the intimacy between author and audience that the critical disdain for the genre created. "If the demands are thoughtful and sensible," Delany remarks, "there's always some SF writer somewhere who will find the suggestion interesting enough to give it a try. And if—as happens on occasion—the readership responds? Well, then, you've changed the genre."[6] Perhaps for this reason, he admits to writing much of his own criticism in the form of novels, making the fictional and critical circle complete.

Many of the points raised about modern fan genres clearly apply to late Heian fiction. As the *Sagoromo* patron's tale contest and the Sarashina diarist in their different ways suggest, contemporary readers were eager to discuss tale fiction, a subject that formal critics—male poets—refused to take up until the medieval era. Moreover, as argued throughout this study, late Heian texts clearly present counterpoints to *Genji* in particular, highlighting areas that need "work," at least in the view of the late Heian audience. *Hamamatsu*, for example, redirects readers to the family roots of "romantic" obsessions, while *Sagoromo* highlights the social implications of midranks relationships. In a sense, these concerns became the subgenres of court fiction and, as Delany predicts, they changed it. While the "Kaoru-type" hero and other *Genji* elements resurface throughout later tales, *Nezame* and its fellows also leave their mark, ranging from novel female protagonists to a renewed interest in foreign settings and fantastic elements. In a sense, *The Untitled Book* is the culmination of this process, creating a "space" to discuss not just tale fiction, but the fictional conversations already in progress within the genre itself.[7]

The problem with the fan fiction label, however—at least with late Heian tales—is that it tends to imply an artificial distinction between *Genji* and its successors or, more broadly, between Murasaki and her compatriots. Critics are perhaps correct to distinguish between professional authors and people publishing in fanzines or circulating amateur sketches at anime conventions, although even here, the lines are blurry. Delany, as noted, considers his own novels a critical response to the science fiction genre, while Rumiko Takahashi (author of a graphic novel set in the Heian era) was herself once a "fan" artist. People and texts can always shift categories, depending upon their reception—a process itself driven both by popularity and excellence. Senji and the author(s) of *Hamamatsu* and *Nezame*, however, lived and worked in the same world as Murasaki. Their texts were almost certainly produced for the same mixture of personal and professional ends. Most importantly, Murasaki herself responded to earlier writers, as even my abbreviated discussions of her allusions to *The Tale of the Bamboo Cutter* and "Song of Unending Sorrow" suggest. We cannot fairly call late Heian works fan texts—or for that matter, epigones—without doing the same to *Genji*, and few readers can have serious interest in that. Actual Heian fan fiction, as inventive biographies like *The Tale of Murasaki* and erotic stories of "pillow boys"[8] in their own ways suggest, is a different creature entirely.

The comparison to fan fiction does, however, remind us to exercise our imaginations when we read Heian court tales, including *The Tale of Genji*. This means reading widely in tales and other contemporary genres so that we can recognize textual echoes when they are present. It also means considering what these echoes mean, that is, "what enables [them] to make sense" to the later audience.[9] As I have argued throughout this study, this often means exploring apparent misreadings or rejections of earlier themes and characters rather than dismissing them as interpretive mistakes. Once again, Murasaki herself is our best guide, at least in method. Both in "The Picture Contest" and her famous defense of tales in "Fireflies" (Hotaru) the writer depicts characters discussing court fiction, arguing as to which texts are more moving or whether the genre itself should be considered "lies" or truth. One does not have to take sides to appreciate both the quality and intensity of both discussions. Murasaki clearly thought tales were worth fighting over, even in fiction—and her readers were listening.

APPENDIX

Plot Summaries

The following plot summaries are primarily intended to help readers place my arguments about *Sagoromo*, *Hamamatsu*, and *Nezame* in context. This is especially important since *Sagoromo* and *Nezame* are currently unavailable in complete published translations. For readers interested in the tales' academic reception, however, I have based these synopses on those found in standard scholarly references. As a result, readers can also use these synopses to deduce what plot points the academy has focused on. I enclose in parentheses details not covered in the summaries but important for my own arguments.

The Tale of Sagoromo

Book One

Sagoromo opens with a handsome youth bringing flowers to Princess Genji, the beautiful girl who shares his family's home.[1] The following scene reveals that the young man is the hero, the son of the Horikawa Chancellor and nephew to the current and retired emperors. He is 17 or 18 years of age. He and Princess Genji share the compound with the Horikawa Chancellor and his three wives: Lady Horikawa, a former shrine priestess and sister to another retired emperor; Lady

Dōin, the daughter of the current prime minister; and Lady Bōmon, daughter of the late Prince Shikibukyō and mother to Horikawa's only daughter, the current empress and mother to the first-born prince. Lady Horikawa has raised Princess Genji since the latter was a small child, and she and Sagoromo are like brother and sister.

The action really begins after these introductions, with Sagoromo on his way home from court one evening early in the fifth month. He exchanges poems with one woman en route, then, the next day, has similar exchanges with two more, one of the consorts of the crown prince and the daughter of a retired emperor (later reintroduced as the First Princess). That evening, he returns to court and participates in an impromptu concert. When the Emperor forces him to perform a flute solo afterwards, a heavenly prince moved by the performance descends to take Sagoromo to a more suitable home with his own kind. The Emperor manages to stay the hero's departure. To console the youth he hints that he will allow him to marry the Second Princess, his favorite daughter, but Sagoromo privately remains committed to Princess Genji, for whom he nurtures a secret passion. The following month he visits her and inadvertently confesses his love. She recoils from the non-fraternal declaration, but Sagoromo continues to stall the imperial marriage.

One evening returning home from the palace, Sagoromo saves a woman being abducted by a renegade priest. Sagoromo takes her home, but he also ends up falling in love with her himself. Over the course of their affair, Asukai, as she is known, conceives a child, but before she can alert him to the fact, her nurse—desperate to make ends meet—arranges for her to marry a noble headed for the provinces, who, as it happens, is Michinari, the son of Sagoromo's wet nurse. Since the hero never revealed his identity to Asukai, the nurse does not consider him a reliable source of support. She tricks the heroine into boarding a carriage and eventually a boat for the southern province of Tsukushi. When Asukai sees Michinari's fan, a parting gift from Sagoromo, she realizes her lover's identity and resolves to throw herself into the sea.

Book Two

With Princess Genji still aloof and Asukai missing, Sagoromo suddenly learns from Michinari's younger brother that his new sister-in-law was Asukai—and that she has drowned herself. Meanwhile, the Horikawa Chancellor continues to push Sagoromo to accept the offer of marriage to the Second Princess. Even the date has been set. However, before then the hero sleeps with the princess in secret, an informal visit that horrifies her mother, to whom the heroine does not reveal the intruder's identity. As it becomes clear that the Second Princess is with child, her mother falls ill from worry. The older woman masks her own illness as pregnancy and retreats with her daughter to a residence outside of the capital. When the child is born, a boy the image of Sagoromo, the princess's resentful mother succumbs to her illness and soon dies. The princess herself becomes a nun, and while Sagoromo, now enamored of the woman, tries repeatedly to visit her again, she strongly rebuffs him.

The following year, the Emperor steps down from the throne, taking the Second Princess to a hermitage outside of the capital. The new emperor summons Princess Genji to the Rear Court, but the death of his father postpones the marriage. Finally, a dream oracle convinces the Horikawa Chancellor that she cannot go to the emperor at all. She must serve as the Kamo Shrine Priestess, by special request of the god himself. The Second Princess's sister, whom the retired emperor had hoped to marry to Sagoromo in her stead, is named Ise Shrine Priestess. Sagoromo visits Princess Genji as she begins her Kamo preparations, but she remains resolute in her rejection of him. The hero responds by sneaking off to Kokawa, a Buddhist temple and pilgrimage site, to take the tonsure. Before he can do so, however, he encounters Asukai's brother, now a mountain priest, who informs Sagoromo that she is safe: he rescued her from her attempted suicide. Sagoromo learns that the siblings are actually the children of a deceased first-generation commoner (making Asukai's lineage considerably nobler than he had thought). The priest promises to reveal her whereabouts the next morning.

Book Three

The following morning, when Sagoromo seeks out the priest, he learns that the man has left to attend to Asukai, apparently gravely ill. Still ignorant of her location, the hero returns to the capital. He begins visiting his son by the Second Princess, now living with another of her sisters. (The retired emperor still believes the boy to be his son.) Sagoromo tries to contact the Second Princess herself, but she continues to ignore his advances. Meanwhile the childless Lady Dōin adopts Imahime and then attempts to send her to the Rear Court (in other words, to marry her to the emperor). When Horikawa refuses to assist her, Dōin appeals to her sister, the emperor's mother, who tentatively arranges things. She then asks Sagoromo to help the girl with her musical skills. The hero is stunned by the girl's ignorance but he does learn some useful information from her "mother-substitute." Apparently Imahime's deceased mother was Asukai's aunt, and another common relative, the Tokiwa Nun, was until recently caring for Asukai outside of the capital. Unfortunately Asukai is now dead, but the governess also informs him that the First Princess has taken in his daughter by Asukai. As for Imahime, two days before her imperial marriage, Lady Dōin's brother sneaks into her rooms. The uproar caused by the governess when she discovers the interloper makes the girl a laughingstock, and the Rear Court plans dissolve.

Sagoromo decides to visit his daughter secretly at the First Princess's court residence, but another noble sees him there and his gossip results in a forced marriage between the hero and the First Princess herself. As Sagoromo still continues to woo the Second Princess, his new bride soon realizes that he only visited her to see the child, and the relationship degenerates. Sagoromo also becomes his son's guardian, although under the pretense of serving the retired emperor, and begins spending much of his time with the boy at the father's residence. Horikawa's lectures about his responsibility to the First Princess merely drive him to Princess Genji's chambers at the shrine, where he is kept at a polite distance. At the end of the year, the hero sponsors a large memorial service for Asukai at Tokiwa.

The following year Princess Genji moves officially to the Kamo Shrine. Both Sagoromo and the current emperor, who had hoped to bring her to the Rear Court eventually, are sad to see her move so decisively out of reach, but the hero arranges to send one of the Second Princess's sisters to court in her stead, so the emperor at least is happy. The new consort even bears him a sorely needed crown prince. Sagoromo, however, remains desolate, and when an attempted visit to the Second Princess ends badly, he resolves to take the tonsure in earnest. In preparation, he tells his mother the truth about his daughter with Asukai. The night before he plans to leave the capital, he visits Princess Genji at the shrine and offers her a final *koto* performance. A violent storm arises, and the shrine building itself thunders three times, while a mysterious fragrance fills the air. While everyone else present is amazed and frightened, Sagoromo proceeds with his plans, taking his farewells from parents and children under the guise of leaving to visit the First Princess's ailing mother.

Book Four

That night the Kamo god comes to the Horikawa Chancellor in a dream and informs him of Sagoromo's true plans, thus preventing them. Sagoromo grows still more melancholy at this turn of events, but one day, unexpectedly, he glimpses the beautiful widow of a former prince and, his interest piqued, urges the woman's son, a middle captain in the Inner Palace Guards and royal advisor, to introduce him to a sister. When Sagoromo finally glimpses Saishō's sister, as she is known, he is stunned to discover a striking resemblance to Princess

Genji, and after a series of reversals (her mother's death, her brother's own marriage and subsequent inability to care for her), the pair begin an affair. He moves her to his father's residence, where he effectively treats her as his wife, despite paying official deference to the higher-ranking First Princess. The latter for her part grows increasingly cold to her foster daughter, Sagoromo's child.

The following year illness devastates the capital, and the Emperor, himself plagued by ominous dreams, resolves to retire. Since there is no other available candidate for crown prince (the author seems to forget Horikawa's grandson by Bōmon's daughter here), he appoints Sagoromo's son, still believed to be the retired emperor's child, to the office. Just before the Emperor's retirement the Ise Shrine Priestess receives an oracle from imperial deity Amaterasu that Sagoromo himself be named to the throne. Sagoromo mourns this final blow to a possible relationship with Princess Genji (as emperor, his affairs will be under strict scrutiny), and the pair exchange farewell poems. When the hero becomes emperor, both of his parents receive honorary imperial ranks. Since the First Princess refuses to join him as empress, he brings Saishō's sister to court and, upon the birth of a prince and the First Princess's own rapid tonsure and death, grants her the office. All three of Sagoromo's children receive lavish ceremonies appropriate to their ages. Asukai's daughter is even named a ranking princess.

When the Tokiwa Nun dies, Asukai's daughter inherits her mother's remaining possessions, including a picture diary of her last days. Sagoromo, newly remorseful, destroys it as part of the offerings in an elaborate memorial for Asukai. Later the new emperor makes a formal procession to the hermitage of the Second Princess and her father, where, after consoling the ailing retired sovereign, he has a final fruitless meeting with the nun. The tale closes with his gloomy reflections on their failed relationship as he gazes out on the late autumn garden.

The Tale of the Hamamatsu Middle Counselor

Missing book (reconstructed)

Chūnagon's late father was known as Prince Shikibukyō. When Chūnagon learns through dreams and other sources that his father has been reborn as the Chinese Emperor's Third Prince, he requests three years of leave from the Japanese court in order to visit him.[2] Chūnagon's mother, the late prince's wife, is remarried to a major captain of the Inner Palace Guards, Left Division (hereafter known as Lord Taishō). Lord Taishō cannot accept Chūnagon's love for his oldest daughter, Taishō no Kimi (also known as Ōigimi), both because of their "sibling" relationship and because of his own plans to send her to court and make her empress. Nonetheless, Chūnagon succeeds in consummating the relationship, and to her father's great anger, Taishō no Kimi is soon with child. Alternatively, Lord Taishō may have discovered the pregnancy after the hero's departure for China. In any case, the child, a daughter, is born during Chūnagon's absence.

Lord Taishō has no choice but to abandon his plans to wed Taishō no Kimi to the (new) Prince Shikibukyō, the future crown prince. Instead, he gives the prince Taishō no Kimi's younger sister. Since Chūnagon's mother deeply loves her son, the tale probably also depicted how she suffers from Chūnagon's and Lord Taishō's strained relationship. Just before Chūnagon leaves for China, he visits the crown prince for an exchange of poetic farewells. Chūnagon also recites several more verses en route to the final port of departure (in Tsukushi). Taishō no Kimi, left alone with her suffering, recites several sad poems of her own and eventually takes the tonsure.

Book One

Here the emphasis shifts from Chūnagon's failed relationship with Taishō no Kimi to his adventures in China, specifically, to his affair with the Heyang Consort (*Kōyōken no kisaki*), also known as *Kara no kisaki* or the Chinese Consort. The sobriquet derives from her residence in Heyang District outside of the capital. (Hereafter, I will refer to this heroine simply as the Consort.) In the first part of the book, Chūnagon is reunited with his father, the young Third Prince, who lives with his mother the Consort. When Chūnagon catches a glimpse of the Consort, the Chinese Emperor's favorite and thus the object of considerable ill will from the other palace women, her beauty mesmerizes him. For her part, the Consort, impressed (along with the rest of the Chinese court) by the hero's looks and talents, already mourns his inevitable departure. The Consort's mixed lineage—her father is a Chinese prince and her mother a Japanese prince's daughter—strengthens her sense of attachment to Chūnagon. She sees in him a link to her mother (left behind in Japan when the Consort was only five). The stage is thus set for their love affair long before the actual meeting itself. In fact, Chūnagon is so taken with this elusive beauty that he refuses the affections of Wu Jun (*Go no Kimi*), the favorite daughter of China's most powerful minister. Meanwhile, disturbed by various omens, the Consort retreats to a house in the mountains. Chūnagon unwittingly makes a pilgrimage to the same area to pray for their union, and a dream message assures him that this will occur.

In the next part of the book the fated encounter with the Consort takes place. Drawn to a nearby house by the sound of a Chinese zither, Chūnagon spies a woman who looks exactly like the Consort. Unaware that the resemblance is more than coincidence, he slips into the stranger's rooms and consummates his "new" interest. The Consort and her attendants, only too aware of Chūnagon's identity, let him believe that she will continue the affair and, pretending to defer to a taboo, send him on his way. When he returns to the house a few days later, she has vanished. She is, however, already with child. Chūnagon spends the rest of his time in China pining for the missing woman, even as he continues to visit the Third Prince and Consort, who has returned to Heyang.

Only a short time before the hero's departure, when the Emperor asks the Consort to perform for him in the guise of an attendant, does Chūnagon see his mystery woman again. He remains ignorant, however, of her true identity.

The conclusion to this book relates Chūnagon's gradual discovery of the truth through the Consort's sympathetic relative and attendant Nü Wang (*Joō no Kimi*). Realizing that the relationship cannot continue, and also troubled by dreams of his anxious mother in Japan, the hero resolves to return home. During their farewell meeting, the Consort entrusts Chūnagon with a wooden box to take to her mother. She also gives the hero their son, sho she has learned in a dream will rise to great heights in Japan.

Book Two

The action returns to Japan. The first section takes place in Tsukushi, the hero's first stop in his journey home. Chūnagon sends for his old wet nurse from the capital to care for his son by the Consort, and through her learns for the first time of Taishō no Kimi's tonsure. He also narrowly avoids an affair with the daughter of the assistant senior governor-general of Dazaifu (an official known as *daini*), whose father arranges for the pair to pass a night together. (To the father's frustration, Chūnagon does not consummate the relationship with the woman, hereafter known as Daini's daughter.) The second section of the book relates the hero's reunion with his stepfather, Lord Taishō, and the rest of the family. Noting Chūnagon's ever more striking good looks, Lord Taishō begins to regret Taishō no Kimi's tonsure. Chūnagon for his part can still not believe the unfortunate turn of affairs and, after meeting the daughter born of their relationship, drives Taishō no Kimi to tears with his complaints. He then makes his formal return to court. The balance of this section recounts the lovers' gradual transition to an amicable, religious lifestyle in Chūnagon's home (where Taishō no Kimi has been living with Chūnagon's mother since the scandal erupted). Eventually, however, the hero grows nostalgic for the Consort. The conclusion of the book describes him reading the Consort's letter to her mother (enclosed in the box she handed him before he left for Japan) and resolved to set out for the mountains of Yoshino, where the mother, now a nun, is said to be living.

Book Three

This book opens with Chūnagon's arrival in Yoshino. The hero first meets the priest who, according to the Consort's letter, first brought her news of her mother during a trip to China. Chūnagon hears repeatedly of the Consort's family history, first from the priest, then from her mother (now a devout Buddhist practitioner known as the Yoshino Nun). He also learns of the Consort's half-sister, Yoshinohime, but despite his deep curiosity returns to the capital without having met her.

Here the narrative temporarily reverts to the story of Daini's daughter, who has come to the capital with her mother in search of Chūnagon. Learning that the hero is living, apparently quite contentedly, with the nun Taishō no Kimi, the mother arranges for the girl to marry Chūnagon's uncle, a captain in the Outer Palace Guards (*emon no kami*). This man, interestingly, is already married to a half-sister of Yoshinohime. After the wedding, Chūnagon finally consummates his own relationship with the woman (much to her chagrin). Later, he is forced to consider a marriage to the Emperor's favorite daughter, the child of the Shōkyōden Consort. But Chūnagon cannot forget the Heyang Consort, and in the conclusion of this book, he again travels to Yoshino, hoping to find a substitute for her in Yoshinohime. The Yoshino Nun, now ailing, entrusts the girl to his care, and the episode ends with Chūnagon beginning to visit Yoshinohime in person.

Book Four

This book also proceeds without plot interruption. The time for the proposed marriage to the princess has drawn near, but Chūnagon manages to decline the offer with the help of the head of the Office of Palace Attendants. When he sees the

Yoshino Nun in numerous dreams, he returns to the mountain retreat. The Nun, on her deathbed, soon attains salvation in the Buddhist Pure Land (symbolized by the marvelous fragrance and purple clouds that mark her passing). Chūnagon remains with the grieving Yoshinohime for some time, during which period the pair grows increasingly close. He eventually brings her back to the capital to live with his wet nurse and his son by the Consort. However, unresolved feelings for the Consort—and the priest's warning that Yoshinohime must not risk pregnancy for three more years—prevent him from consummating his growing affections. He continues to live with Taishō no Kimi. (During this period, he also dreams repeatedly of the Consort, finally hearing a loud voice proclaim her rebirth in one of the Buddhist heavens.) Meanwhile, Prince Shikibukyō, Taishō no Kimi's former suitor, learns of Yoshinohime and determines to steal her away for himself.

Book Five

The final book opens with Chūnagon bewailing the disappearance of Yoshinohime. She has been spirited away by Prince Shikibukyō during a retreat at Kiyomizu Temple. Chūnagon is of course beside himself with worry, but in spite of his best efforts he cannot find her. In an attempt to dispel his gloom the hero visits his uncle's wife, Daini's daughter. (She is now expecting Chūnagon's child.) While there, he also steals a glimpse of his uncle's first wife, Yoshinohime's half-sister and the daughter of another prince. To Chūnagon's disappointment, the woman looks nothing like his missing love. Later, he sees the Consort herself in a dream, announcing to him that because of the strength of their shared passion she will be reborn again in Yoshinohime's womb.

The narrative then turns to Yoshinohime, still in Prince Shikibukyō's care and grown grievously ill from emotional distress and her ill-fated pregnancy. The Prince can no longer bring himself to refuse her repeated requests for Chūnagon. Yoshinohime is in any case now the Prince's wife, since to save face Chūnagon pretends that she is his half-sister and therefore cannot challenge the relationship. The Prince, for his part, believes Yoshinohime to be the sister of Chūnagon's rumored Yoshino lover. (Chūnagon takes in Yoshinohime and cares for her, although the Prince continues to visit.) At the tale's end, Chūnagon learns that the Consort has in fact died, confirming his dream oracle in the previous book. Wu Jun, pining for Chūnagon, has taken the tonsure. (In the same letter, delivered by an acquaintance visiting from China, the hero also learns that the Consort's death has prompted the Chinese Emperor to take the tonsure and that the Third Prince, Chūnagon's father, is now the crown prince.)

Nezame at Night

Part One

Nezame begins with a Genji prime minister who, widowed by both of his wives, has taken in his children to raise alone.[3] The daughter of Prince Sochi leaves him two girls, Ōigimi (literally, the older sister) and Nezame (literally, Naka no Kimi or the middle or younger sister). The daughter of the Azechi Major Counselor, meanwhile, has left him two sons, known by their captain-level posts in the Outer Palace Guards, Left Division (*saemon no kami*) and the Inner Palace Guards, Right Division (*uzaishō chūjō*). The Prime Minister teaches all of the children music and the other courtly arts, but Nezame, a talented *koto* player and great beauty, is his favorite.

The year that Nezame turns 13, on the fifteenth night of the eighth month, a heavenly figure (dressed like a Chinese woman) appears in her dreams. The figure praises Nezame's musical talent, teaches her five secret melodies for the *biwa* lute, and then vanishes. The following year the figure appears again. After teaching the girl five more melodies, she prophecies that the heroine "is fated to torment [herself] with too much lonely thought."[4] Nezame waits for the figure to reappear the following year, but she never returns.

Meanwhile, the eldest son of the Chancellor and Minister of the Left, a promising youth at the rank of middle counselor (hereafter referred to as Gonchūnagon to avoid confusion with the *Hamamatsu* hero), becomes engaged to Ōigimi. When he spots Nezame during a visit to his ailing wet nurse—the former is waiting out a directional taboo next door—he is overwhelmed by her beauty and sleeps with her, mistaking her for the daughter of a provincial governor. He also lies about his own identity. Only after the marriage to Ōigimi takes place does the pair realize the truth. Nezame, expecting Gonchūnagon's child, grows ill with worry. This causes her father, ignorant of the affair, to grow sick himself, and he retreats to the outskirts of the capital in Hirosawa. Nezame, for her part, goes secretly to Ishiyama Temple and gives birth to a daughter (known for this reason as Ishiyama Himegimi). Gonchūnagon gives the child to his parents to raise, hiding the mother's identity. Unfortunately, Ōigimi discovers the affair and withdraws in anger from both of them. Their father, still unsuspecting, has taken the tonsure, and so, as his sons choose sides (the elder with Ōigimi, the younger with the heroine), the family begins to fall apart. Undaunted, Gonchūnagon continues to pursue Nezame, who remains miserable. She is now 18.

Part Two (reconstructed)

This section, which seems to have covered about eight years, relates the heroine's marriage to an old major captain in the palace guard, also known posthumously by his later title of Chancellor-Minister of the Left (or simply as the Old Chancellor, by which I will refer to him hereafter to avoid confusion with the father of the *Sagoromo* hero). The Old Chancellor already has three daughters by his late wife. At first Nezame shrinks from her husband, but she gradually comes to appreciate his unqualified love for her (epitomized by his taking in her second child with Gonchūnagon—a son, Masago, born after the marriage—as his own). Gonchūnagon, reacting to the marriage, agrees to marry the daughter of the retired emperor.

Ōigimi does not take the news of Gonchūnagon's new wife well. She grows ill from grief and dies after giving birth to his daughter. Nezame takes in the child. Soon, her aged husband dies. The Emperor, long captivated by reports of the heroine's beauty, tries to use the opportunity to summon her to court as head of the Palace Attendants' Office (in practice an additional consort), but the heroine manages to send her oldest stepdaughter instead. The other two girls marry a middle captain of the Inner Palace Guards, the son of a prince, and a major counselor (Gonchūnagon's brother), respectively. Nezame now heads a household of six.

Part Three

Gonchūnagon continues to try to visit Nezame, but at the mature age of 28, she is no longer so pliable, and she refuses to have anything to do with him. Instead, she concentrates on managing the affairs of her eldest stepdaughter, still serving the Emperor at court. The heroine even goes to the palace to oversee things personally. Unfortunately, the Emperor takes advantage of her presence to try to get close to her. In this he is abetted by his mother, the Dowager Empress, who resents Gonchūnagon's continued pursuit of the heroine at the expense of his wife, her daughter. She contrives to lead the Emperor to Nezame, who spends a tense night keeping him at bay. Finally the heroine manages to slip away, horrified at what the court rumor mill will make of the incident and at how Gonchūnagon might react.

The experience reveals to Nezame that, in spite of herself, she continues to care for Gonchūnagon. She even directly relies on him for help in leaving the palace, where the frustrated Emperor is determined to keep her. But once she regains her calm, she again distances herself from Gonchūnagon, causing him great frustration as well. At this juncture, a spirit identifying itself as the heroine's takes possession of Gonchūnagon's wife (the tale's famous "living spirit incident" or *ikisudama jiken*). The spirit curses the princess and vows to have Gonchūnagon for herself. Here, again, Nezame is forced to confront the strength of her repressed emotions. When the spirit appears a second time, the heartsick heroine retreats to her father's house in Hirosawa and resolves to take the tonsure.

Gonchūnagon is naturally horrified by this news. Gathering together their two children, he rushes to Hirosawa and confesses everything to the heroine's father, now a priest. The stunned former minister is mortified by his own ignorance. It also becomes clear that Nezame is once again with child. To her great disappointment, she is forced to abandon her religious plans. She returns to the capital, where an overjoyed Gonchūnagon makes their relationship public. Nezame, however, can neither forget her disappointment nor completely trust her lover, who continues to visit his wife, the princess, as well. Even after the heroine and her stepdaughter give birth amid great fanfare to sons, Nezame continues to long for the next world and (as the narrator puts it) her nights of wakeful worry continue.

Part Four (reconstructed)

Nezame's daughter with Gonchūnagon, Ishiyama Himegimi, becomes the consort of the Crown Prince. When the Emperor, still yearning for the heroine, quits the throne, the Crown Prince accedes and the girl becomes empress. Her nephew, son of the head of the Palace Attendants' Office, becomes the new crown prince. All of Nezame's children are in their glory. Masago, whom the Emperor had once kept with him at court in the heroine's stead, is now middle captain of the third rank (a high rank for the position and sign of imperial favor). The young noble falls in love with the retired sovereign's favorite daughter, the Third Princess and daughter of the Shōkyōden Consort, but when her father learns of their affair, he strips Masago of his title and bars the pair from meeting.

At this time, if not before Masago's punishment, the heroine fakes her own death (the so-called "fake-death incident" or *nisejini jiken*) perhaps in order to escape the Emperor's zealous courtship or the Dowager Empress's schemes. Alternatively, she may actually die, then come back to life. In either case, Masago believes the rumors of her passing and goes into mourning outside of the capital. The former emperor, distraught, takes the tonsure. But Nezame, moved by her son's predicament, sends a letter to her former suitor asking him to restore Masago's rank. Everyone is stunned and delighted to learn that she is still alive. The former emperor not only restores Masago to his former position, he promotes him and allows his daughter to resume the affair publicly. Nezame, having at some point at last achieved her wish to become a nun, finally dies, to the general distress of the court.

Reference Matter

Notes

Introduction

EPIGRAPH: *Genji monogatari*, vol. 5, p. 17; Tyler, *Tale of Genji*, p. 785.

1. I borrow the conventional translations of the two characters' names, also used by Tyler.

2. For a fuller discussion of the relationship between radiance and imperial power in *Genji*, see Kawazoe, *Genji monogatari hyōgen shi*, pp. 249–59. The book also contains a lengthy survey of the metaphor's more general role in court tales, which Kawazoe associates with a kind of liminality again tied to imperial lineage. See, for example, pp. 192–203.

3. The famous Heian expression of this truth occurs in Poem 139 of the *Kokinshū*: "When I breathe the scent / of the orange blossoms that await / the fifth month / I recall the fragrance on / sleeves of lovers from the past."

4. I borrow Ivan Morris's translation of *hikaru kimi*, made famous in Morris's *World of the Shining Prince*.

5. *Genji monogatari*, vol. 2, p. 106; Tyler, *Tale of Genji*, p. 202.

6. Kanda, *Monogatari bungaku, sono kaitai*, pp. 13–63.

7. I borrow this term from Mitani Kuniaki, who admonishes readers of *Genji* to stay alert to the connections that Murasaki Shikibu establishes between different characters and subplots. See, for example, *Nyūmon Genji monogatari*, pp. 9–13.

8. *Genji monogatari*, vol. 5, p. 21; Tyler, *Tale of Genji*, p. 786.

9. Watson, *Lotus Sutra*, p. 20. The original can be found in *Genji monogatari*, vol. 5, p. 512. My translation of the *Genji* passage slightly distorts the allusion, which literally says that there is no time when

people do not grieve (*nageki*, also "fallen trees" or firewood) for the hero. There is also an untranslated pun on light and ashes.

10. *Genji monogatari*, vol. 1, p. 25; Tyler, *Tale of Genji*, p. 6. The reaction comes from the Emperor's attendants, who scorned Kiritsubo in life only to recognize her worth too late.

11. *Sarashina nikki*, p. 302; I. Morris, *As I Crossed a Bridge of Dreams*, p. 47.

12. *Genji monogatari*, vol. 1, p. 17; Tyler, *Tale of Genji*, p. 3.

13. See Mitani Kuniaki, *Nyūmon Genji monogatari*, pp. 13–25, for further discussion of this point.

14. *Genji monogatari*, vol. 1, p. 40; Tyler, *Tale of Genji*, p. 13.

15. *Genji monogatari*, vol. 1, p. 53; Tyler, *Tale of Genji*, p. 21.

16. The remark appears in the *Poetry Contest in Six Hundred Rounds* (*Roppakyuban uta awase*, 1193); the original is quoted in Sorensen, "Contest and Context," p. 15.

17. The text, "The Story of a Memorial Service for Genji" (Genji kuyō sōshi, fourteenth century), is briefly summarized in Brazell, *Twelve Plays*, p. 220.

18. See Goff, *Noh Drama and* The Tale of Genji, for translations and a broader discussion of this subject.

19. For a discussion of the scene's religious significance, see McCormick, "*Genji* Goes West," pp. 75–76. McCormick also discusses the album in which the illustration appears, part of Harvard University's museum collection. A color reproduction of the scene appears in another discussion of the album in Kitagawa, "Behind the Scenes," p. 33. For a broader survey of artistic depictions of *Genji*, including a translation of an artist's handbook to the tale, see Murase, *Iconography of* The Tale of Genji.

20. Rohlich, "In Search of Critical Space," p. 180.

21. Written by Yura and Yoshimura, respectively; see works cited.

22. Osamu Hashimoto, quoted in Abel, "Translation as Community." My favorite example of these allegedly hostile appropriations of *Genji* is an artistic tribute by Amano Yoshitaka, illustrator of the popular serial *Vampire Hunter D* and one of the original character designers for the *Final Fantasy* video games. Needless to say, this collection of illustrations—published in Japan in 2002 and English in 2006—differs considerably from earlier *Genji* artwork in its aesthetic.

23. Shūkan Hikaru Genji Henshūbu; see works cited.

24. Ury, "Tales."

25. For a fuller discussion of this argument, and the meaning of *yōen*, see the introduction to Lammers, *The Tale of Matsura*, pp. 27–52. The study also includes a complete translation.

26. Lammers discusses Teika's changes to earlier tale poems and scenes in many of the notes to his translation. In general, the point of these revisions seems to be to introduce a magical quality to the earlier scene or heighten its sense of mystery, both consistent with the notion of *yōen*. See, e.g., *Tale of Matsura*, pp. 20–21, 45–46, and p. 94 n. 87. These pages also show Teika's use of *Hamamatsu* and *Sagoromo*.

27. Lammers, *Tale of Matsura*, p. 20. As Lammers notes, Teika draws explicit allusions to *Genji* when convenient, but there is enough difference between his use of this tale and the others to warrant the statement, which is also consistent with Teika's warnings about avoiding trite references in verse.

28. *Mumyōzōshi*, p. 98; Marra, "*Mumyōzōshi*, Part 3," p. 418. For a complete translation of the *Mumyōzōshi*, see also Marra's "*Mumyōzōshi*, Introduction and Translation" and "*Mumyōzōshi*, Part 2." Shunzei's Daughter's separate discussions of the three late Heian tales appear in "*Mumyōzōshi*, Part 2," pp. 292–305.

29. *Sagoromo monogatari*, p. 29. The line refers to a poem in "Spring Shoots I" (Wakana jo), where Genji reflects on his affair with Oborozukiyo. See *Genji monogatari*, vol. 4, p. 84; Tyler, *Tale of Genji*, p. 599. There is also a related allusion to the "Butterflies" (Kochō) chapter.

30. The remark appears in Teika's *Exemplary Poems of Recent Times* (*Kindai shūka*, 1209); cited in Huey, *Making of Shinkokinshū*, p. 21.

31. Fujioka, *Kokubungaku zenshi*.

32. Bloom, *Anxiety of Influence*.

33. Inui, "*Yoru no nezame*: 'mohō' to 'kaisaku' no aida," p. 16.

34. The poem, recorded in *Shōyūki*—the diary of Michinaga's cousin Fujiwara Sanesuke (957–1046)—is quoted and translated in H. McCullough, *Great Mirror*, p. 40. I have used my own translation of the relevant lines here.

35. *Eiga monogatari*, vol. 3, p. 183; W. and H. McCullough, *Flowering Fortunes*, p. 775.

36. *Eiga monogatari*, vol. 3, p. 183 note 14.

37. The contest, discussed at greater length in the next chapter, is reprinted in Hagitani, *Heianchō uta awase taisei*, pp. 1094–1123.

38. W. and H. McCullough, *Flowering Fortunes*, p. 42.

39. W. and H. McCullough, *Flowering Fortunes*, p. 42 note 78.

40. E.g., "The Tale of Genji in Japan and the World: Social Imaginary, Media, and Cultural Production," March 25–26, 2005, Columbia University; Harper and Shirane, eds., *The Genji Reader* (forthcoming).

41. E.g., "Centers and Peripheries in Heian Japan," June 11–13, 2002, Harvard University; Adolphson, *Gates of Power*.

Chapter One

EPIGRAPH: Woolf, "THE TALE OF GENJI," p. 53.

1. *Kokin wakashū*, p. 49; Rodd, *Kokinshū*, p. 35.

2. Woolf, "THE TALE OF GENJI," p. 53.

3. Tsunoda, "Kōkyū no rekishi," pp. 77–78.

4. The first part of each woman's sobriquet reflects an alternate pronunciation of the Chinese characters used to write her family name. "Sei" can be pronounced "Kiyo," suggesting "Kiyowara," while the "Fuji" of "Fujiwara" is also read as "Tō."

5. *Genji monogatari*, vol. 3, p. 212; Tyler, *Tale of Genji*, p. 461.

6. *Makura no sōshi*, p. 91; I. Morris, *Pillow Book*, p. 39.

7. I borrow Ivan Morris's wonderful titles for these lists.

8. E.g., Takahashi, *Monogatari to e no enkinhō*, p. 26.

9. Bowring, *Diary of Lady Murasaki*, p. xv.

10. Yamanaka, "Kōkyū: sono naimen," pp. 14, 23.

11. Mitamura, "Joseitachi no saron," pp. 63–64. Shrine priestesses normally retired from their posts with the death of the emperor who appointed them or the death of a family member; the relative or sponsor's passing was thought to contaminate the women and risk offending the gods they served on the court's behalf.

12. Akiyama, "Bungaku no naka no kōkyū," pp. 27–34.

13. Tsunoda, "Nihon bunka to kōkyū," p. 6.

14. Totman, *Japan before Perry*, p. 48.

15. Tsunoda, "Nihon bunka to kōkyū," p. 10.

16. I. Morris, *Shining Prince*, p. 206.

17. Totman, *Japan before Perry*, p. 54.

18. Shirane, *The Bridge of Dreams*, p. 30.

19. Field; see works cited. See also Murofushi, "Monogatari bungaku."

20. Mitani Eiichi, "Kōkyū, naishinnō saron no bungaku." The word "salon," which I have italicized in translation, here and elsewhere appears in *katakana* (the Japanese syllabary used for loan words and for special emphasis), sharply distinguishing it from the rest of the text.

21. Gibson, *Women in Seventeenth-Century France*, pp. 330, 175–81.

22. Clergue, *Salon*, p. 14.

23. E. and J. de Goncourt, *The Woman of the Eighteenth Century*, pp. 31–32.

24. Clergue, *Salon*, p. 23.

25. Clergue, *Salon*, pp. 14, 23. The initial reference is to the Hôtel de Rambouillet.

26. Clergue, *Salon*, p. 7.

27. Tyler, "Lady Murasaki's Erotic Entertainment"; M. Morris, "Desire and the Prince."

28. Quennelle, *Genius in the Drawing Room*, p. 11.

29. *Genius in the Drawing Room* was simultaneously published under this name by a different press.

30. Gibson, *Women in Seventeenth-Century France*, p. 175.

31. Clergue, *Salon*, p. 42.

32. Gibson, *Women in Seventeenth-Century France*, p. 176.

33. Gibson, *Women in Seventeenth-Century France*, p. 175.

34. Gibson, *Women in Seventeenth-Century France*, p. 175.

35. Marotti, *John Donne*, p. 30.

36. Quoted in Gibson, *Women in Seventeenth-Century France*, p. 180.

37. Marra, *Representations of Power* and *Aesthetics of Discontent*; Smits, "Poets."

38. Marra, *Aesthetics of Discontent*, pp. 101–26.

39. The quotation is from Sarra, *Fictions of Femininity*, p. 89. See Bargen, *A Woman's Weapon*, for a sustained discussion on spirit possession in *Genji* and Heian culture at large.

40. Gibson, *Women in Seventeenth-Century France*, p. 176.

41. Wet nurses, usually drawn from the ranks of family attendants, retained their title when nursing ended; see Yoshikai, *Heianchō no menototachi*, pp. 137–48.

42. Kanō, "Nyōbō," pp. 114–15; Suda, *Heian jidai kōkyū*, pp. 307–8.

43. Fukumori, "A Re-Visionary History," pp. 11–12. See also Mitamura, *Hyōgen no ronri*.

44. Yamanaka, "Nichijō," pp. 99–104.

45. Kanō, "Nyōbō," p. 120.

46. Kanō, "Nyōbō," p. 116.

47. See Kanō, "Sei."

48. While the French affairs may also have been coercive, such activity seems to have been less widespread in the salon, or at least systematic, than in the Rear Court, and in any case involved far less complicated relationships. See Gibson, *Women in Seventeenth-Century France*, pp. 177–78.

49. Yoshikai, *Heianchō no menototachi*, p. 363 and p. 9, respectively.

50. Shirane, *Bridge of Dreams*, p. 220.

51. Okada, *Figures of Resistance*, p. 116.

52. The following overview relies heavily on Mitani and Sekine, "Kaisetsu." Additional biographical information comes from *Heian jidaishi jiten* and other sources as noted.

53. *Princeton Companion*, p. 219.

54. *Mumyōzōshi,* pp. 79–80; Marra, "*Mumyōzōshi,* Part 3," p. 409. Unfortunately, the rest of the tale is lost, except for another fragment that Shunzei's Daughter quotes.

55. Komachiya, "Rokujō saiin no senji ron," p. 464.

56. Mitani and Sekine, "Kaisetsu," p. 9. See also *Heian jidaishi jiten.*

57. W. and H. McCullough, *Flowering Fortunes,* p. 136.

58. Komachiya, "Rokujō saiin no senji ron," pp. 456–57.

59. The tale appears in *Tales of the Tsutsumi Middle Counselor* (*Tsutsumi chūnagon monogatari,* ca. 1055); see Backus, *The Riverside Counselor's Stories,* for a translation.

60. Kuge Haruyasu, *Heian kōki monogatari no kenkyū,* p. 78.

61. Hinata, "Janru no seiritsu," pp. 61, 67.

62. Kuge, *Heian kōki,* pp. 76–77. Kuge's assumptions about the rules are debatable. Some scholars conjecture that entire texts may have been read aloud for judgment, while others speculate that the completed manuscripts were submitted in advance. See Hinata, "Janru no seiritsu," pp. 65–66, and Hagitani, *Heianchō uta awase,* p. 1107, respectively.

63. *Eiga monogatari,* vol. 3, p. 402.

64. Tokoro, "Saiin Baishi naishinnō no jiseki," pp. 699–701.

65. See Horiguchi, "Saiin kōtaisei to Heianchō kōki bungei sakuhin."

66. Sakamoto Shōzō, *Fujiwara Yorimichi no jidai,* pp. 59–61.

67. Quoted in Tokoro, "Saiin Baishi naishinnō no jiseki," p. 696.

68. Hagitani, *Heianchō uta awase,* pp. 941–42.

69. Hinata, "Janru no seiritsu," p. 66.

70. Tokoro, "Saiin Baishi naishinnō no jiseki," p. 699.

71. Sakamoto Shōzō, *Fujiwara Yorimichi no jidai,* pp. 40–42, 75.

72. Katayama, "Minamoto Morofusa josetsu," p. 675.

73. Katayama, "Minamoto Morofusa josetsu," pp. 678–79, 682–84.

74. Katayama, "Minamoto Morofusa josetsu," pp. 679, 670; Sakamoto Shōzō, *Fujiwara Yorimichi no jidai,* pp. 34–35, 69–70.

75. Sakamoto Shōzō, *Fujiwara Yorimichi no jidai,* pp. 66–70.

76. Kuge Hirotoshi, *Sagoromo monogatari jinbutsu to hōhō,* p. 247.

77. E.g., Mitani and Sekine, "Kaisetsu," pp. 17–18; Katayama, "Minamoto Morofusa josetsu," p. 680.

78. E.g., Hagitani, *Heianchō uta awase,* pp. 1289–90; Tokoro, "Saiin Baishi naishinnō no jiseki," p. 717; Mitani and Sekine, "Kaisetsu," pp. 14, 18.

79. Katayama, "Minamoto Morofusa josetsu," p. 680.

80. Hagitani, *Heianchō uta awase,* p. 943.

81. Katayama, "Minamoto Morofusa josetsu," p. 681.
82. Hagitani, *Heianchō uta awase*, p. 1080.
83. Sakamoto Shōzō, *Fujiwara Yorimichi no jidai*, pp. 102–140.
84. Mitani and Sekine, "Kaisetsu," p. 4.
85. Kuge Haruyasu, "Sagoromo sakusha," p. 44.
86. Mitani and Sekine, "Kaisetsu," pp. 7–8; Kuge Haruyasu, "Sagoromo sakusha," pp. 44–46.
87. *Heian jidaishi jiten*. I borrow the translation of the term from Ury, "Chinese Learning and Intellectual Life."
88. This may have been true of all of the Six Poets; see Katayama, "Minamoto Morofusa josetsu," p. 678.
89. *Heian jidaishi jiten*.
90. Tokoro, "Saiin Baishi naishinnō no jiseki," p. 706.
91. Kuge Haruyasu, "Sagoromo sakusha," p. 50.
92. Kuge Haruyasu, "Sagoromo sakusha," p. 46.
93. Mitani and Sekine, "Kaisetsu," p. 8.
94. Tokoro, "Saiin Baishi naishinnō no jiseki," p. 718.
95. Kuge Haruyasu, "Sagoromo sakusha," p. 49.
96. Yoshikai, *Heianchō no menototachi*, pp. 179–87.

Chapter Two

EPIGRAPH: *Genji monogatari*, vol. 1, p. 58; Tyler, *Tale of Genji*, p. 23.

1. *Genji monogatari*, vol. 1, p. 81; Tyler, *Tale of Genji*, p. 31.
2. Shunzei's Daughter makes the first claim in *The Untitled Book*; one version of Teika's diary *A Record of the Clear Moon* (*Meigetsuki*, 1180–1235) includes the second.
3. *Mumyōzōshi*, p. 61; Marra, "*Mumyōzōshi*, Part 2," p. 294. Marra refers to Asukai by another sobriquet, Michishiba.
4. Three of these stories, broadly representative of the cycle's numerous variants, appear in *Muromachi jidai monogatari taisei*.
5. Mitani Eiichi makes the argument for equating divergences among the tale's extant manuscripts with heightened audience interest. According to him, the Asukai affair displays the most variation across the tale's three textual lineages; see *Ihon bungakuron hen*, especially pp. 107–30.
6. The actual reference is to a folksong or *saibara* that runs: "Let us lodge at Asukai, the shadows are cool, the water is cold, the rushes are soft." Both Sagoromo and Asukai repeatedly return to this image; indeed, the hero thinks of the song even before she does; see *Sagoromo monogatari*, p. 67. Subsequent references to *Sagoromo* appear in parentheses in the text.

7. Some versions of the tale immediately narrate Asukai's rescue by her long-lost brother, a one-eyed priest, but the cliffhanger ending in the manuscript adopted in the version used here is considered to be the older form. In both cases, long after the heroine vanishes, the subplot continues to unfold through other characters' accounts of her. According to them, Asukai gives birth to a daughter and takes the tonsure before dying of a broken heart. Sagoromo eventually finds this child, along with Asukai's diary and several poems, and she herself reappears briefly in a dream near the end of the tale.

8. As Mitani Eiichi points out, nurses in Heian fiction generally aid and abet lovers (*Ihon bungakuron hen,* p. 189). Even *Records of Marvelous Happenings in Japan* (*Nihon ryōiki,* 822) enshrines the stereotype, describing both Kichijō Tennyo (a goddess of fortune) and the Bodhisattva Kannon as taking the form of wet nurses to help worthy believers. The character assumes a darker profile in the *Genji,* cf. Horton, "They also serve." *Sagoromo*'s medieval readers, however, seem to have expected the conventional figure.

9. The house itself may also belong to the wet nurse, further underscoring her generosity; see Kurata, *Sagoromo no koi,* p. 72.

10. In some versions of the tale, generally grouped with the text used here, Michinari later describes the nurse crying when Asukai seems to have drowned; see Mitani Eiichi, *Ihon bungakuron hen,* p. 111.

11. Mitani Eiichi, *Ihon bungakuron hen,* pp. 185–259, details these and other differences across four textual lines.

12. *Sagoromo no shitahimo,* p. 442. Jōha gives no explanation for the statement, although there are certainly other Heian examples of nurses colluding with priests; see Morishita, "Kohon Sumiyoshi monogatari," p. 128. Regardless, the *Sagoromo* writer clearly contradicts it by describing the nurse's shocked response to the kidnapping (*Sagoromo monogatari,* p. 72).

13. Mitani Eiichi, *Ihon bungakuron hen,* pp. 187–89; 191–259. Others add comparisons to *Genji* heroine Suetsumuhana's vindictive aunt and the wicked stepmother in *Sumiyoshi*; see Kurata, "Sagoromo to iu hito," p. 62, and Morishita, "Kohon Sumiyoshi monogatari," p. 127.

14. Mitani Eiichi, *Ihon bungakuron hen,* pp. 190, 193, 217–18. The claim works only if we share his cynical view of even the nurse's sympathetic moments.

15. Mitani Eiichi relates the trend in the variants and Muromachi stories to the influence of *setsuwa* or Buddhist parable fiction and an accompanying shift to male authorship; see *Ihon bungakuron hen,* pp. 120, 212–14.

16. See *Mumyōzōshi,* p. 61.

17. Kuge Haruyasu, *Heian kōki monogatari,* p. 154, also notes the substitution of the parents, relating it to a more general shift in readership. It is interesting to note that even these versions of the subplot do not completely vilify the parents; they are described as genuinely anxious to see Asukai settled before they die. They do, however, angrily disinherit her brother when he tells them that he has saved Asukai from suicide, displaying the simpler stock characterization typical of the genre in general.

18. Kuge Haruyasu, *Heian kōki monogatari,* p. 153.

19. Saiki, "Sagoromo monogatari ni okeru menoto no yakuwari," pp. 202–205.

20. Saiki, "Sagoromo monogatari ni okeru menoto no yakuwari," p. 206. See also Kuge Haruyasu, *Heian kōki monogatari,* pp. 150–52. Yoshikai notes that *Sagoromo* contains more references to nurses and nurse-like characters than any Heian text but *Genji* (see *Heianchō no menototachi,* p. 38).

21. Mitani Eiichi, *Ihon bungakuron hen,* pp. 190–91.

22. Michinari also fusses over Asukai herself, anxiously telling the hysterical heroine that "I hear that people in your condition always feel sick like this. . . . But if you stop eating now, it will only make it worse. You have to be careful" (*Sagoromo monogatari,* p. 108). While he misreads the situation (she refuses to eat because she is upset by the kidnapping), his concern does him credit, again softening our view of both him and his accomplice.

23. Kuge Haruyasu takes the very different position that Michinari's kind treatment of Asukai, notably his unwillingness to force sexual relations with her, underscores the nurse's cruelty, although he does not elaborate on the point. See *Heian kōki monogatari,* p. 154.

24. The women's names refer to streets bordering their respective sections of the shared estate, located between Nijō ōji and Sanjō bōmon.

25. Mitani and Sekine foreground this motive in their annotation, glossing the phrase "the daughter of someone who might be suitable" as referring specifically to her husband's child.

26. "As long as the parents and so forth are there, looking after her, and she's safely tucked away with all her future before her, it's easy to see how someone could catch wind of a talent or two and take an interest. . . . Everyone around her glosses over her failings and praises the charms that she ought to have anyway, until it would never occur to you think any different. Have a look for yourself, though, and you are bound to find a less attractive picture" (*Genji monogatari,* vol. 1, p. 57; Tyler, *Tale of Genji,* p. 22).

27. It is not clear what the substitute would need to lie about, given the obvious appeal of Dōin's household. The line is probably meant to underscore the woman's dishonesty and the poor judgment of anyone who would agree to work with or hire her.

28. The brother is a *saishō chūjō,* an imperial advisor and captain in the Inner Palace Guards.

29. There is an implicit comparison here with the staff of *Sagoromo*'s Second Princess, who manage not only to hide the woman's pregnancy (the result of Sagoromo's impetuous visit in spite of his refusal to marry her) but to pass off the child as the princess's brother. The princess's mother, who later dies from frustration with Sagoromo, takes a leading role in the deceit, but she could clearly never have managed it without a dedicated and competent group of attendants.

30. The text refers to the *kado no osa,* a low-ranking courtier responsible for policing the capital.

31. See D'Etcheverry, "Rethinking Late Heian," pp. 87–98.

32. I am indebted to *Genji* critic Mitani Kuniaki (Mitani Eiichi's son) for encouraging me to consider *Sagoromo*'s subversions of the *Genji* model. I do not use his preferred term for the technique, parody (*hanpuku*), because in my opinion Senji is parodying the midranks convention itself, not Murasaki's more thoughtful reflections on it.

33. Hoshiyama also comments on the author's midranks interest, which he says gave her literary wings; see "Yūgao monogatari kara Asukai Onnagimi monogatari e," p. 35.

34. *Genji monogatari,* vol. 1, p. 81; Tyler, *Tale of Genji,* p. 31. I borrow Tyler's rendition of *shiremono no monogatari* as "fool's tale," discussed below.

35. Genji famously calls down the wrath of the wellborn Rokujō by reflecting that she could use some of Yūgao's humility. See *Genji monogatari,* vol. 1, p. 163; Tyler, *Tale of Genji,* p. 66.

36. See Kurata, *Sagoromo no koi,* pp. 68, 69–78. Kurata argues that Asukai's sense of inferiority keeps her from telling Sagoromo her troubles and thus contributes to the tragedy. This sense of status, however, only makes her identify more fully with the romantic ideal. As she quietly reflects, pondering the nurse's plan to marry and move them to the provinces, "Won't he [Sagoromo] be surprised when I disappear, like a character in an old tale?" (*Sagoromo monogatari,* p. 100). Her refusal (or perhaps inability, as a midranks heroine) to consider any other option contrasts sharply with the nurse's more pragmatic behavior and views.

37. *Genji monogatari,* vol. 1, p. 82; Tyler, *Tale of Genji,* p. 32.

38. *Genji monogatari*, vol. 1, p. 164; Tyler, *Tale of Genji*, p. 67.

39. *Genji monogatari*, vol. 1, p. 82; Tyler, *Tale of Genji*, p. 32.

40. *Genji monogatari*, vol. 1, p. 167; Tyler, *Tale of Genji*, p. 68.

41. *Genji monogatari*, vol. 1, p. 194; Tyler, *Tale of Genji*, p. 79. Although it is not a midranks affair, Genji also blames jealousy (rather than wounded pride) later in the tale when he recognizes Rokujō's spirit possessing his main wife Aoi.

42. Mitani Eiichi, *Ihon bungakuron hen*, p. 189; Kuge Haruyasu, *Heian kōki monogatari*, p. 154.

43. The *Kazueryō*, part of the *Minbushō* (Ministry of Popular Affairs), was responsible for managing provincial taxes as well as various government expenditures. In a sense, the nurse was married to the provincial governor of provincial governors, a connection that further underscores both her midranks identity and her material concerns.

44. Mitani Eiichi, *Ihon bungakuron hen*, pp. 189–90.

45. Ukifune's mother, a former attendant and lover to a prince but now married to a provincial governor, concludes from her own experience that elite lovers are not to be trusted—although, as discussed below, she later changes her mind. Although the wedding ultimately falls through, the mother had earlier set aside all of the best things in her husband's household for Ukifune's marriage to a midranks official. Apparently there are ranks even within the midranks, and the bridegroom decides instead to marry Ukifune's stepsister, her rich father's favorite.

46. The pair also compete, in the public eye, as potential bridegrooms for elite women and, privately, for the affection of Niou's wife. Some critics also assert that they are, in a sense, philosophical rivals, with Kaoru allegedly representing the more rational approach to love and Niou, the libidinal; see Pekarik, "Rivals in Love," pp. 217–30. The men do not differ at all, however, in their elite status or their sense of the gulf that separates them from Ukifune; both remain the self-conscious heroes of the romance.

47. Kanda, *Monogatari bungaku, sono kaitai*, pp. 18–27. He acknowledges a debt here to the psychoanalytic arguments of literary critic Renée Girard.

48. *Genji monogatari*, vol. 6, p. 36; Tyler, *Tale of Genji*, p. 981.

49. See Shirane, "The Uji Chapters and the Denial of the Romance," pp. 113–38. In addition to characterizing in these terms Ukifune and Ōigimi, Ukifune's half-sister who starves herself rather than accept Kaoru, Shirane also includes under this rubric the supposedly successful story of Ōigimi's sister Naka no Kimi. As he

points out, once Naka no Kimi is safely established in Niou's household as the mother of a likely future crown prince, she loses her husband's romantic interest.

50. Mitani and Sekine, "Kaisetsu."

51. It is evident, of course, that the Akashi Lady of Winter (the least favorite season with Heian poets) ranks lowest in this company. Since spring and autumn vie for precedence in the literary imagination, however, the residents of these quarters are symbolically equal, although their actual relationships to Genji differ.

52. Kuge Haruyasu, *Heian kōki monogatari*, pp. 160–61.

Chapter Three

EPIGRAPH: *Hamamatsu chūnagon monogatari*, p. 291; Rohlich, *Tale*, p. 149. The last line of the poem literally refers to the balls of thread used to spin a kind of patterned cloth.

1. Bynner, "A Song of Unending Sorrow," p. 269. In principle, I employ the pinyin system of transliterating Chinese names. However, since Rohlich's translation of *Hamamatsu* uses the Wade-Giles system, I have also given the Wade-Giles version in parentheses at the first occurrence of names from the tale to avoid confusion.

2. Bynner, "A Song of Unending Sorrow," p. 269.

3. *Genji monogatari*, vol. 1, p. 18; Tyler, *Tale of Genji*, p. 3.

4. Pollack, *Fracture of Meaning*, p. 61.

5. Mitani Kuniaki, *Nyūmon Genji monogatari*, pp. 53–54. Mitani confines his remarks here to the influence of the "Song" on Kiritsubo, but given how her own story serves as a model for subsequent events in the tale at large, the general point holds.

6. Hibbett, *Seven Japanese Tales*, p. 144.

7. *Ise monogatari*, pp. 162–63; H. McCullough, *Tales of Ise*, p. 93.

8. *Mumyōzōshi*, p. 74; Marra, "*Mumyōzōshi*, Part 2," p. 302. Shunzei's daughter refers to the tale as *Mitsu no Hamamatsu*.

9. The alternate title appears in Teika's colophon to *The Sarashina Diary*, which he also rescued from potential obscurity.

10. See *Mumyōzōshi*, p. 74; Marra, "*Mumyōzōshi*, Part 2," pp. 303–4.

11. Mishima, *Haru no yuki*, p. 369. Mishima may also have modeled the series on *Sagoromo*; see Suzuki Yasue, "*Sagoromo monogatari* to kinki."

12. Kanda, *Monogatari bungaku, sono kaitai*, pp. 164–66, 171–78.

13. Kanda, *Monogatari bungaku, sono kaitai*, pp. 171–78.

14. *Hamamatsu chūnagon monogatari*, p. 294; Rohlich, *Tale*, p. 152.

15. *Hamamatsu chūnagon monogatari*, p. 301; Rohlich, *Tale*, p. 156.

16. *Genji monogatari*, vol. 1, p. 30; Tyler, *Tale of Genji*, p. 9.

17. *Genji monogatari*, vol. 4, p. 306; Tyler, *Tale of Genji*, p. 680.

18. *Genji monogatari*, vol. 4, p. 289; Tyler, *Tale of Genji*, p. 675.

19. E.g., *Genji monogatari*, vol. 4, p. 310; Tyler, *Tale of Genji*, p. 882.

20. Rohlich, *Tale*, pp. 69–70; *Hamamatsu chūnagon monogatari*, pp. 170–71.

21. *Hamamatsu chūnagon monogatari*, p. 153; Rohlich, *Tale*, p. 55. I essentially borrow Rohlich's translation here, since the line is so short and his version adept. Subsequent references to *Hamamatsu* appear in parentheses in the text, with the page numbers of the original and translated versions.

22. Field, *Splendor of Longing*, p. 24.

23. Field, *Splendor of Longing*, p. 21.

24. See Borgen, *Sugawara no Michizane*, pp. 240–50. Borgen thinks this last point unlikely, but the rarity of such embassies by this period is beyond dispute.

25. Suzuki Hiromichi, *Nezame monogatari no kisoteki kenkyū*, pp. 15–16.

26. Kanda, *Monogatari bungaku, sono kaitai*, pp. 171–78.

27. There are differences between the collections on this point. According to one critic, *Miraculous Tales* pessimistically focuses on the future effects of our own behaviors, while *Marvelous Happenings* seeks to entertain us by showing the same errors in the past lives of others. Dykstra, *Miraculous Tales*, pp. 7–8.

28. Kanda, *Monogatari bungaku, sono kaitai*, pp.156–62.

29. Kanda, *Monogatari bungaku, sono kaitai*, p. 160.

30. Kanda, *Monogatari bungaku, sono kaitai*, pp. 186–87 note 13.

31. There is some debate about this line, due to an apparent transcription error in the earliest manuscript. Some textual lineages credit the Prince's "company" with reassuring Chūnagon, while others refer to the boy's "heart." Either way, the point about his success as a substitute stands.

32. Once again, the original language is obscure here. My translation, like Rohlich's, reflects the consensus, although I have followed the annotator and reversed the comparison. Rohlich has the people saying that the Third Prince resembles Chūnagon, but the less honorific language and the onlookers' longer acquaintance with the boy suggest the reverse.

33. Unfortunately, the passage repeats the obscure phrasing of the first reference. *Genji* readers will recall the Kiritsubo Emperor's

comment to Genji about the infant Reizei: "I had a number of children, but you were the only one I spent as much time with as I do now with him. . . . That must be why he reminds me so much of you." *Genji monogatari*, vol. 1, p. 329; Tyler, *Tale of Genji*, p. 142.

34. Kanda also makes this point; see *Monogatari bungaku, sono kaitai*, p. 182. This may be one reason the authors of the "Sagoromo stories" discussed earlier literally resurrect Asukai, rather than make the hero await her rebirth.

35. *Genji monogatari*, vol. 1, p. 201; Tyler, *Tale of Genji*, p. 84.

36. *Genji monogatari*, vol. 1, p. 206; Tyler, *Tale of Genji*, p. 86.

37. *Genji monogatari*, vol. 1, p. 207; Tyler, *Tale of Genji*, p. 87.

38. As the writer informs us just before this passage, Heyang was the residence of Pan Yue (J. Hangaku, 247–300), a gifted poet and administrator. She makes double use of the information by placing it in the mouths of Chinese nobles, who are stunned to discover that Chūnagon outdoes even this exemplar. Pan lived as a recluse for eight years or so, although by the time he took up residence in Heyang he had regained an official position. He was apparently better known for his good looks, an association that also flatters Chūnagon; see *Indiana Companion*, p. 648. My thanks to William Nienhauser, Jr. for pointing this out.

39. I borrow the translation from Shirane, *Bridge of Dreams*, p. 155. Okada, *Figures of Resistance*, p. 258, refers to them more precisely as "affinitive links." Shirane's *The Bridge of Dreams* and Field's *Splendor of Longing* also include expanded discussions of the motif. The first person to fill this role is actually the young brother of Utsusemi, the first woman Genji pursues as a result of the "rainy night's discussion." The boy, who spends the night with Genji after Utsusemi herself escapes him, is also noteworthy because Genji "acts like a father to him" while currying favor with the woman, anticipating his adoption of Murasaki. See *Genji monogatari*, vol. 1, p. 108; Tyler, *Tale of Genji*, p. 43.

40. *Genji monogatari*, vol. 5, p. 356; e.g., Tyler, *Tale of Genji*, p. 921.

41. *Genji monogatari*, vol. 1, p. 43; Tyler, *Tale of Genji*, p. 14.

42. *Genji monogatari*, vol. 1, p. 209; Tyler, *Tale of Genji*, p. 87.

43. Kanda observes that the Third Prince fades from view once Chūnagon meets him, proving that the hero is really looking for something else. *Monogatari bungaku, sono kaitai*, p. 174

44. *Genji monogatari*, vol. 5, p. 59; Tyler, *Tale of Genji*, p. 805.

45. Reizei's marriage to Tamakazura's daughter also reprises the Kiritsubo story, since his earlier consorts, including the daughter of

the jealous Rokujō, resent the newcomer despite earlier promises not to. Unlike in the earlier subplot, however, the emperor himself is not strongly committed to the girl, depriving the affair of tragic stature.

46. Kanda, *Monogatari bungaku, sono kaitai*, p. 172 note 11.

47. There are numerous problems with this passage. For instance, the phrase I translate as "crystal jade" may instead refer to an as yet unidentified Chinese lady known for her beauty. The description of the Consort's "charm" and the reference to "this world" have also been understood differently. In all cases but those discussed above, I follow the annotator's (and Rohlich's) interpretation.

48. I. Morris, *World of the Shining Prince*, p. 90. The palace to which Morris refers is Temmu's Yoshino residence.

49. On Yoshino's role in Temmu's career—and the early Japanese imagination in general—see Ebersole, *Ritual Poetry and the Politics of Death*, esp. pp. 30–37.

50. See *Hamamatsu*, p. 470 note 391. Rohlich follows this reading in his translation of the verse.

51. Shortly into the extant tale, the narrator states that Chūnagon "seems to shine," another qualified comparison to Genji (*Hamamatsu chūnagon monogatari*, p. 154; Rohlich, *Tale*, p. 56). This time, amusingly, the writer feels compelled to explain Chūnagon's brilliance, prefacing the comment by noting that the hero has "really prepared himself" for his first encounter with Chinese officials.

52. Ebersole, *Ritual Poetry and the Politics of Death*, p. 39. Ebersole defines the term *katami* (which he leaves in the original) as "a site or object associated with a deceased individual," a significantly broader usage than that found in tale fiction.

53. Tanabata, the seventh night of the seventh month of the lunar calendar, celebrates the annual meeting of the stars Altair and Vega. The Chinese, and then Japanese, likened the stars to celestial lovers kept apart by the gods for the rest of the year so the man (an oxherder) and the woman (a weaver) will do their work.

54. I particularly like Rohlich's translation of this phrase: "she did not consider it an inviolate trust."

55. Perhaps to remind the reader of Chūnagon's illegitimate son with the Consort, the narrator deliberately compares the mansion where the concert takes place to the Reizei palace.

56. I borrow the last line of Rohlich's translation of the verse.

57. There is some disagreement about the phrase I have translated as "becomes pregnant" (*ninjitamawaba*), since no other examples

of this usage exist. I follow the annotator, who suggests that this may be a special verb used by priests, since it is a priest who relays the prophecy to Chūnagon. In any case, the priest also states that "if [Yoshinohime] should be made aware of the world [a common description of sexual relations] before age twenty" she will come to grief, confirming the general taboo on intercourse.

58. Chūnagon notes the line before delivering the Consort's letter (*Hamamatsu chūnagon monogatari*, p. 260; Rohlich, *Tale*, p. 130), then repeats it to himself twice (both on *Hamamatsu chūnagon monogatari*, p. 260; Rohlich, *Tale*, p. 131).

59. The narrator repeats this claim on the next page (*Hamamatsu chūnagon monogatari*, p.320; Rohlich, *Tale*, p. 167).

60. The annotator takes Chūnagon's comment as referring more generally to the heroine's wasted life as a nun.

61. The word translated here as "roots" (*hontai*) also appears in the initial discussion of the Consort's mother (*Hamamatsu chūnagon monogatari*, p. 266; Rohlich, *Tale*, p. 134).

62. *Sarashina nikki*, p. 317; I. Morris, *As I Crossed a Bridge of Dreams*, p. 64.

63. Sarra, *Fictions of Femininity*, p. 85.

Chapter Four

EPIGRAPH: *Yoru no nezame*, p. 49; Richard, "Developments," p. 56. For a competing translation of the third part of the tale, based on a slightly different manuscript, see Hochstedler, *Tale of Nezame*. This translation should not to be confused with the medieval revision of *Nezame* discussed below.

1. *Princeton Companion*, p. 260. The editors of the *Companion*, while noting the alleged condition of the manuscript, are less concerned with the effect on *Nezame* scholarship proper than with the loss to readers and what the editors consider the relatively light influence of the tale on later texts.

2. I am indebted to *Genji* scholar Midorikawa Masako for alerting me to the connotation of the *Yowa no nezame* label (at least among modern scholars) as somewhat outmoded, which I had been using for its poetic resonance.

3. *Sagoromo monogatari*, p. 52.

4. See Sakakura, "'Yoru no nezame' to 'Yowa no nezame'" and Sekine Yoshiko, "*Nezame* daigo kō."

5. *Yoru no nezame*, p. 45; Richard, "Developments," p. 52.

6. *Mumyōzōshi*, p.63; Marra, "*Mumyōzōshi*, Part 2," p. 295.
7. *Mumyōzōshi*, p. 63; Marra, "*Mumyōzōshi*, Part 2," p. 295.
8. Karajima, "Monogatarishi 'Genji igo' danshō," p. 295.
9. Noguchi, "*Yoru no nezame* no shudai," p. 261.
10. Suzuki Kazuo, "Nezame no Ue no miryoku." On Nezame's influence on later heroines, see Karajima, "Monogatarishi 'Genji igo' danshō" and Matsumoto, "*Yoru no nezame* no *Towazugatari* e no eikyō."
11. Tsushima, *Hi no kawa no hotori de*, p. 418.
12. Nakamura, "*Yowa no nezame* to gendai," pp. 2–3.
13. Nomura, "*Yoru no nezame* to Dewa no Ben."
14. *Yoru no nezame*, p. 47; Richard, "Developments," p. 52.
15. Kawazoe, "*Yoru no nezame* to wakei."
16. The heroine uses the verbal suffix *keri*, which also connotes the sudden realization of a truth or condition. Here, both senses of the suffix are in evidence. On the distinction between this and other "past" tenses, see Okada, *Figures of Resistance*, pp. 35–42.
17. Inui, "*Yoru no nezame* to kaisakubon," p. 303.
18. In the missing conclusion, the heroine's daughter marries the emperor, completing the pattern. Some critics claim that *Genji*'s Akashi plot (another example of the "musical transmission story") is the immediate source of this part of the tale. See Sakamoto Nobumichi, "Ongaku denshōdan no keifu," p. 38.
19. Kawazoe, "*Yoru no nezame* to wakei," p. 4.
20. See Inui, "*Yoru no nezame* to kaisakubon *Nezame monogatari*," p. 299.
21. Nagai, *Nezame monogatari no kenkyū*, pp. 25–30. Nagai speculates that unenthusiastic response to the tale's psychological sections forced this reversion to conventional elements.
22. I refer here to the *Kojiki*'s portraits of heroes, beginning with the Amaterasu's brother Susanoo, who are forced to leave their communities and find fame and fortune in the process.
23. *Yoru no nezame*, p. 55; Richard, "Developments," p. 64.
24. Amamiya, " *Yoru no nezame* no kōsō."
25. *Genji monogatari*, vol. 2, p. 380; Tyler, *Tale of Genji*, p. 325.
26. Inui, "*Yoru no nezame*: 'mohō' to 'kaisaku' no aida," pp. 14–17. The description of Ukifune as Kaguyahime's literary niece is from Sekine Kenji, *Monogatari bungakuron*.
27. *Taketori monogatari*, p. 103; Keene, *Tale of the Bamboo Cutter*, p. 135.
28. *Genji monogatari*, vol. 1, p. 44; Tyler, *Tale of Genji*, p. 15.
29. *Genji monogatari*, vol. 2, p. 188; Tyler, *Tale of Genji*, p. 239.
30. *Genji monogatari*, vol. 2, p. 200; Tyler, *Tale of Genji*, p. 244.

31. *Taketori monogatari*, pp. 103–4, 105; Keene, *Tale of the Bamboo Cutter*, pp. 135, 137.

32. See Kojima, "Ukifune to 'onna no tsumi.'"

33. *Taketori monogatari*, p. 56; Keene, *Tale of the Bamboo Cutter*, p. 23.

34. *Taketori monogatari*, p. 97; Keene, *Tale of the Bamboo Cutter*, p. 121.

35. *Taketori monogatari*, p. 108; Keene, *Tale of the Bamboo Cutter*, p. 145. The pun comes from writing "Fuji" with alternate characters meaning "not / no" and "time," as seen in some classical texts.

36. Kawazoe, "*Yoru no nezame* to wakei."

37. I take the phrase "woman's tale" from Yokoi, "*Nezame* ron."

38. *Yoru no nezame*, p. 45; Richard, "Developments," p. 52. Subsequent references to *Nezame*, both the original and the Richard translation, appear in parentheses in the text.

39. Richard assigns the Prime Minister slightly different instruments, presumably based on differences in his text.

40. Richard translates the passage as saying that the minister has one main wife, the daughter of the Azechi Major Counselor.

41. The most famous expression of this sentiment, frequently cited by Murasaki, is Fujiwara Kanesuke's verse (#1103) in the *Later Anthology of Poetry* (*Gosen wakashū*, ca. 951): "The heart of a parent is not darkness, but still I have lost myself in thoughts of my child."

42. Matsumura, "*Yowa no nezame* no kōsō ni tsuite."

43. Nunomura, "*Yoru no nezame* no shudai," p. 26. Nunomura refers to the relatively limited descriptions of Nezame's thoughts in this part of the text.

44. Richard makes the Shōkyōden Consort the special favorite of the Prime Minister, not the emperor. My version reflects the annotator's interpretation.

45. *Genji monogatari*, vol. 1, p. 19; Tyler, *Tale of Genji*, p. 3.

46. This pity-inducing state of affairs may well explain the Consort's attraction for the emperor. See Childs, "The Value of Vulnerability." Childs refers specifically to a woman's physical vulnerability as exciting affection, but the political point seems relevant. A woman with strong backing (one thinks of Genji's wife Aoi) would presumably not find herself in such a situation in the first place.

47. My translation, while staying closer to the original than Richard's by emphasizing the Minister's respect for Chūnagon rather than his disappointment for Nezame, follows Richard's decision to reassign the narrator's description of Chūnagon to the minister's thoughts.

48. The NKBT text reads the eighteenth, which matches the narrator's description of this as their seventeenth day in seclusion. How-

ever, other manuscripts describe the night as the sixteenth. Either way, the writer presumably wishes to set the scene near the full moon of the fifteenth. The narrator may also wish to imply that it is a month before the famous full moon of the fifteenth of the eighth month, when Nezame's music teacher used to visit.

49. Nunomura, "*Yoru no nezame* no shudai," p. 28.

50. My translation differs considerably from Richard's, who gives the line to Yukiyori and has Tajima's daughter stubbornly continuing to see her first lover in secret.

51. This is a difficult passage; as the annotator notes, one may also interpret the second statement as simply reflecting Chūnagon's shock at Nezame's beauty, with no regard for her rank. Richard follows this view in his translation. Since Chūnagon clearly thinks of rank initially, however, I favor the explicitly classist reading.

Postscript

EPIGRAPH: Jorge Luis Borges, "Pierre Menard, Author of *Don Quixote*," pp. 48–49.

1. Byrd, "Star Trek Lives," p. 58.

2. Southard, "Language of Science-Fiction," p. 19.

3. Southard, "Language of Science-Fiction," p. 20.

4. See, e.g., Radway, *Reading the Romance*; Harris and Alexander, *Theorizing Fandom*.

5. Delany and Tatsumi, "Interview," p. 28.

6. Delany and Tatsumi, "Interview," p. 28.

7. Rohlich, "In Search of Critical Space."

8. Fell, *The Pillow Boy of the Lady Onogoro*. This novel, which features Murasaki Shikibu, Sei Shōnagon, and other Heian luminaries, has apparently succeeded in crossing over into the mainstream market. Three years after specialty press Serpent's Tale published it, the novel was reissued by a division of Harcourt Brace and met with very strong reviews in the popular press.

9. Delany and Tatsumi, "Interview," p. 28.

Appendix

1. Summary based on Mitani Eiichi, "*Sagoromo monogatari*."

2. Summary based on Morioka, "*Hamamatsu chūnagon monogatari* no kenkyū," pp. 161–72. I could not rely on the same reference work as for the other two tales because its entry focuses on the missing book. It would be unfair to call this approach emblematic of modern

criticism of the tale and, in any case, it is useless as a basic introduction to the text.

3. Summary based on Nagai, "*Yoru no nezame* monogatari." I have adjusted the order in which some information is given, although the conventional critical divisions of the texts (referring to "parts" instead of "books") are retained.

4. *Yoru no nezame*, p. 45; Richard, "Developments," p. 52.

Works Cited

Unless otherwise specified, the place of publication for all Japanese works except journals is Tokyo. The following abbreviations are used for series and frequently cited anthologies:

HM IV	*Heianchō monogatari IV* (Heian court tales IV). Ed. Nihon bungaku kenkyū shiryō kankōkai. Yūseidō, 1980.
KS	*Kōkyū no subete* (Everything about the Rear Court). *Kokubungaku: kaishaku to kyōzai no kenkyū* 25, no. 13 (Oct. 1980).
NKBT	*Nihon koten bungaku taikei*. 102 vols. Iwanami shoten, 1957–68.
NKBZ	*Nihon koten bungaku zenshū*. 51 vols. Shōgakukan, 1970–78.
SNKBZ	*Shinpen Nihon koten bungaku zenshū*. 88 vols. Shōgakukan, 1994–.
SNKS	*Shinchō Nihon koten shūsei*. 85 vols. Shinchōsha, 1976–89.

Abel, Jonathan. "Translation as Community: The Opacity of Modernizations of *Genji monogatari*." In *Nation, Language, and the Ethics of Translation*, ed. Sandra Bermann and Michael Wood, pp. 146–58. Princeton, NJ: Princeton University Press, 2005.

Adolphson, Mikael S. *The Gates of Power: Monks, Courtiers, and Warriors in Premodern Japan*. Honolulu, HI: University of Hawai'i Press, 2000.

Akiyama Ken. "Bungaku no naka no kōkyū: *Genji monogatari* no sekai kara" (The Rear Court in literature: The world of *The Tale of Genji*). *KS*, pp. 27–34.

Amamiya Takao. "'*Yoru no nezame*' no kōsō to sakusha ni tsuite: 'tsuki no miyako' no tennin kōka no settei igi o megutte" (The author and structure of *Nezame at Night*: the meaning of the heavenly visitor from 'the moon capital'). *HM IV*, pp. 263–76.

Backus, Robert L., trans. *The Riverside Counselor's Stories: Vernacular Fiction of Late Heian Japan*. Stanford, CA: Stanford University Press, 1985.

Bargen, Doris G. *A Woman's Weapon: Spirit Possession in the Tale of Genji*. Honolulu, HI: University of Hawai'i Press, 1997.

Bloom, Harold. *The Anxiety of Influence: A Theory of Poetry*. New York: Oxford University Press, 1997.

Borgen, Robert. *Sugawara no Michizane and the Early Heian Court*. Honolulu, HI: University of Hawai'i Press, 1994.

Borges, Jorge Luis. "Pierre Menard, Author of *Don Quixote*." 1941. Trans. Anthony Bonner. In *Ficciones*, pp. 45–55. New York: Grove Press, 1962.

Bowring, Richard, trans. *The Diary of Lady Murasaki*. New York: Penguin Books, 1996.

Brazell, Karen, ed. *Twelve Plays of the Noh and Kyōgen Theaters*. Ithaca, NY: East Asia Program, Cornell University, 1990.

Bynner, Witter. "A Song of Unending Sorrow." In *Anthology of Chinese Literature: From Early Times to the Fourteenth Century*, ed. Cyril Birch, pp. 266–69. New York: Grove Press, 1965.

Byrd, Patricia. "Star Trek Lives: Trekker Slang." *American Speech* 53, no. 1 (Spring 1978): 52–58.

Childs, Margaret H. "The Value of Vulnerability: Sexual Coercion and the Nature of Love in Japanese Court Literature." *Journal of Asian Studies* 58, no. 4 (Nov. 1999): 1059–79.

Clergue, Helen. *The Salon: A Study of French Society and Personalities in the Eighteenth Century*. New York: Burt Franklin, 1971.

Dalby, Liza. *The Tale of Murasaki*. New York: Nan A. Talese, 2000.

de Goncourt, Edmond and Jules. *The Woman of the Eighteenth Century: Her Life, from birth to death, her Love and her Philosophy in the worlds of Salon, Shop and Street*. Trans. Jacques Le Clercq and Ralph Roeder. New York: Minton, Balch, and Company, 1927.

Delany, Samuel R. and Takayuki Tatsumi. "Interview: Samuel R. Delany." *Diacritics* 16.3 (Autumn 1986): 26–45.

D'Etcheverry, Charo. "Cannibalizing Memory: Teika, Sanetaka, and Fujioka's *Sagoromo*." In *Issues of Canonicity and Canon Formation in Japanese Literary Studies*, ed. Stephen D. Miller, pp. 259–68. Proceedings of the Association for Japanese Literary Studies, 2000.

——. "Rethinking Late Heian: *Sagoromo, Nezame, Hamamatsu,* and the Rear Court." Ph.D. diss., Princeton University, 2000.

Dykstra, Yoshiko K., trans. *Miraculous Tales of the Lotus Sutra from Ancient Japan.* Hirakata City, Japan: Intercultural Research Institute, Kansai University of Foreign Studies, 1983.

Ebersole, Gary L. *Ritual Poetry and the Politics of Death in Early Japan.* 1989. Princeton, NJ: Princeton University Press, 1992.

Eiga monogatari (A Tale of Flowering Fortunes). Ed. Yamanaka Yutaka et al. *SNKBZ,* vols. 31–33.

Fell, Alison. *The Pillow Boy of the Lady Onogoro.* London: Serpent's Tail, 1994; New York: Harvest Books, 1997.

Field, Norma. *The Splendor of Longing in the Tale of Genji.* Princeton, NJ: Princeton University Press, 1987.

Fujioka Sakutarō. *Kokubungaku zenshi: Heianchō hen* (A complete history of Japanese literature: the Heian court). Ed. Akiyama Ken et al. Heibonsha, 1974.

Fukumori, Naomi. "Sei Shonagon's *Makura no soshi*: A Re-Visionary History." *Journal of the Association of Teachers of Japanese* 31, no. 1 (April 1997): 1–44.

Genji monogatari (The Tale of Genji). Ed. Akiyama Akio et al. *SNKBZ,* vols. 20–25.

Gibson, Wendy. *Women in Seventeenth-Century France.* London: Macmillan Press, 1989.

Goff, Janet. *Noh Drama and* The Tale of Genji. Princeton, NJ: Princeton University Press, 1991.

Hagitani Boku. *Heianchō uta awase taisei zōho shintei* (Revised and expanded compendium of Heian court poetry contests). Vols. 2 and 3. Kyoto: Dōhōsha, 1995–96.

Hamamatsu chūnagon monogatari (The Tale of the Hamamatsu Middle Counselor). In *Takamura monogatari, Heichū monogatari, Hamamatsu chūnagon monogatari,* ed. Endō Yoshimoto and Matsuo Satoshi, pp. 153–440. *NKBT,* vol. 77. Iwanami shoten, 1964.

Harper, Thomas, and Haruo Shirane, eds. *The Genji Reader.* New York: Columbia University Press, forthcoming.

Harris, Cheryl and Alison Alexander. *Theorizing Fandom: Fans, Subculture, and Identity.* Cresskill, NJ: Hampton Press, 1998.

Heian jidaishi jiten (A dictionary of Heian period history). Ed. Kodaigaku kyōkai. 3 vols. Kadokawa shoten, 1994.

Hibbett, Howard, trans. *Seven Japanese Tales.* New York: Perigee, 1981.

Hinata Kazumasa. "Janru no seiritsu: monogatari bungaku" (The rise of a genre: tale literature). In *11–12 seiki no bungaku*, ed. Kubota Jun et al., pp. 61–90. Iwanami shoten, 1996.

Hochstedler, Carol, trans. *The Tale of Nezame: Part Three of "Yowa no Nezame Monogatari."* Ithaca, NY: China-Japan Program, Cornell University, 1979.

Horiguchi Satoru. "Saiin kōtaisei to Heianchō kōki bungei sakuhin: *Sagoromo monogatari* o chūshin to shite" (The Kamo priestess rotation system and late Heian court literary works: *The Tale of Sagoromo*). *Kodai bunka* 31, no. 10 (Oct. 1979): 22–45.

Horton, H. Mack. "They Also Serve: Ladies-in-Waiting in *The Tale of Genji*." In *Approaches to Teaching Murasaki Shikibu's* The Tale of Genji, ed. Edward Kamens, pp. 95–107. New York: Modern Language Assocation, 1993.

Hoshiyama Ken. "Yūgao monogatari kara Asukai Onnagimi monogatari e: *Sagoromo monogatari* ni okeru jinbutsu zōkei no hito hōhō" (From the tale of Yūgao to the tale of Asukai: one method of characterization in *The Tale of Sagoromo*). *Chūko bungaku* 56 (Nov. 1995): 27–36.

Huey, Robert. *The Making of Shinkokinshū*. Cambridge, MA: Harvard University Asia Center, 2002.

The Indiana Companion to Traditional Chinese Literature. Ed. William Nienhauser, Jr. Bloomington, IN: Indiana University Press, 1986.

Inui Sumiko. "*Yoru no nezame*: 'mohō' to 'kaisaku' no aida" (*Nezame at Night*: between imitation and revision). *Nihon bungaku* 47, no. 1 (Jan. 1998): 10–17.

———. "*Yoru no nezame* to kaisakubon *Nezame monogatari*: 'uki' onna kara 'ukinitaetaru' onna e" (*Nezame at Night* and its revision *The Tale of Nezame*: from a 'gloomy' woman to a woman 'who endured grief'). In *Monogatari: sono tensei to saisei*, ed. Monogatari kenkyūkai, pp. 296–308. Yūseidō, 1994.

Ise monogatari (Tales of Ise). In *Taketori monogatari, Ise monogatari, Yamato monogatari, Heichū monogatari*, ed. Katagiri Yōichi et al., pp. 111–244. *NKBZ*, vol. 8.

Kanda Tatsumi. *Monogatari bungaku sono kaitai: "Genji monogatari" Uji jūjō ikō* (The dissolution of tale literature: after *The Tale of Genji*'s Uji chapters). Yūseidō, 1992.

Kanō Shigefumi. "Nyōbō" (Attendants). In *KS*, pp. 114–20.

———. "Sei" (Sex). In *KS*, pp. 121–25.

Karajima Masao, "Monogatarishi 'Genji igo' danshō: *Yoru no nezame, Ima torikaebaya* kara *Wagami ni tadoru himegimi* e" (Postscript on the history of tales 'after Genji': from *Nezame at Night* and *Ima Torikaebaya* to *Wagami ni Tadoru Himegimi*). In *"Genji monogatari" to sono shūhen*, ed. Imai Gen'ei, pp. 119–37. Osaka: Izumi shoin, 1989.

Katayama Takeshi. "Minamoto Morofusa josetsu: kōki sekkan jidai no hensō" (An introduction to Minamoto Morofusa: changes in the late age of marriage politics). In *Kōki sekkan jidaishi no kenkyū*, ed. Kodaigaku kyōkai, pp. 665–90. Yoshikawa kōbunkan, 1990.

Kawazoe Fusae. *"Genji monogatari" hyōgen shi: yu to ōken no isō* (A history of expressions in *The Tale of Genji*: the topology of metaphor and kingship). Kanrin shobō, 1998.

——. "*Yoru no nezame* to wakei: kishu ryūri no yukue" (*Nezame at Night* and tale plots: the trajectory of the noble in exile). *Nihon bungaku* 35.5 (May 1986): 1–13.

Keene, Donald, trans. *The Tale of the Bamboo Cutter*. New York: Kodansha International, 1998.

Kitagawa, Anne Rose. "Behind the scenes of Harvard's *Tale of Genji* Album." *Apollo* 154, no. 477 (Nov. 2001): 28–35.

Kojima Naoko. "Ukifune to 'onna no tsumi'" (Ukifune and 'the woman's crime'). *"Genji monogatari" hihyō* (Criticism on *The Tale of Genji*). Yūseidō, 1995.

Kokin wakashū (Collection of Ancient and Modern Verse). Ed. Ozawa Masao. *NKBZ*, vol. 7.

Komachiya Teruhiko. "Rokujō Saiin Senji ron: *Sagoromo monogatari* no sakusha" (On the Senji of the Sixth Street Kamo priestess's household: the author of *The Tale of Sagoromo*). In *Heian jidai no sakka to sakuhin*, ed. Ishikawa Tōru, pp. 439–64. Musashino shoin, 1992.

Kuge Haruyasu [Hirotoshi]. *Heian kōki monogatari no kenkyū: Sagoromo, Hamamatsu* (Research on late Heian tales: *Sagoromo* and *Hamamatsu*). Shintensha, 1984.

——. "*Sagoromo* sakusha Rokujō Saiin Senji ryakuden kō" (Some thoughts on the biographical sketch of *Sagoromo* author Senji of the Sixth Street Kamo priestess's household). *Kodai bunka* 32, no. 9 (Sept. 1980): 41–52.

Kuge Hirotoshi [Haruyasu]. "*Sagoromo monogatari* no ibun to juyō to no aida" (The gap between *The Tale of Sagoromo*'s reception and its variants). In *"Sagoromo monogatari" no shikai*, ed. Ōchō monogatari kenkyūkai, pp. 355–95. Shintensha, 1994.

———. *"Sagoromo monogatari" no jinbutsu to hōhō* (Characters and techniques of *The Tale of Sagoromo*). Shintensha, 1993.

Kurata, Minoru. *Sagoromo no koi* (Sagoromo's love affairs). Kanrin shobō, 1999.

———. "Sagoromo to iu hito: *Sagoromo monogatari* no hito hyōgen" (A person called Sagoromo: the use of "person" in *The Tale of Sagoromo*). *Kodai bungaku kenkyū: dai niji* 6 (Oct. 1997): 57–75.

Lammers, Wayne P., trans. *The Tale of Matsura: Fujiwara Teika's Experiment in Fiction*. Ann Arbor, MI: Center for Japanese Studies, University of Michigan, 1992.

Makura no sōshi (The Pillow Book). Ed. Matsuo Satoshi and Nagai Kazuko. *NKBZ*, vol. 11.

Marotti, Arthur F. *John Donne, Coterie Poet*. Madison, WI: University of Wisconsin Press, 1986.

Marra, Michele. *The Aesthetics of Discontent: Politics and Reclusion in Medieval Japanese Literature*. Honolulu, HI: University of Hawai'i Press, 1991.

———, trans. "*Mumyōzōshi*, Introduction and Translation." *Monumenta Nipponica* 39. 2 (Summer 1984): 115–45.

———, trans. "*Mumyōzōshi*, Part 2." *Monumenta Nipponica* 39. 3 (Autumn 1984): 281–305.

———, trans. "*Mumyōzōshi*, Part 3." *Monumenta Nipponica* 39. 4 (Winter 1984): 409–34.

———. *Representations of Power: The Literary Politics of Medieval Japan*. Honolulu, HI: University of Hawai'i Press, 1993.

Matsumoto Yasushi. "*Yoru no nezame* no *Towazugatari* e no eikyō" (*Nezame at Night*'s influence on *Towazugatari*). *Kodai bunka* 32, no. 11 (Nov. 1980): 45–51.

Matsumura Takeo. "*Yowa no nezame* no kōsō ni tsuite" (On the structure of *Nezame at Midnight*). In *Oka Kazuo hakushi shōju kinen ronshū: Heianchō bungaku kenkyū sakka to sakuhin*, ed. Waseda Daigaku Heianchō bungaku kenkyūkai, pp. 374–89. Yūseidō, 1971.

McCormick, Melissa. "*Genji* Goes West: The 1510 *Genji* Album and the Visualization of Court and Capital." *Art Bulletin* 85, no. 1 (Mar. 2003): 54–85.

McCullough, Helen Craig, trans. *Ōkagami, The Great Mirror: Fujiwara Michinaga (966–1027) and His Times*. Ann Arbor, MI: Center for Japanese Studies, University of Michigan, 1991.

———, trans. *Tales of Ise: Lyrical Episodes from Tenth-Century Japan*. Stanford, CA: Stanford University Press, 1968.

McCullough, William H. and Helen Craig, trans. *A Tale of Flowering Fortunes: Annals of Japanese Aristocratic Life in the Heian Period.* 2 vols. Stanford, CA: Stanford University Press, 1980.

Mishima Yukio. *Haru no yuki* (Spring Snow). Shinchōsha, 1968.

Mitamura Masako. "Joseitachi no saron: Daisaiin saron o chūshin ni" (Women's salons: the salon of the Great Kamo priestess). *Kokubungaku: kaishaku to kyōzai no kenkyū* 34, no. 10 (Aug. 1989): 63–67.

——. *"Makura no sōshi": hyōgen no ronri*. Yūseidō, 1995.

Mitani Eiichi. "Kōkyū, naishinnō saron no bungaku" (Literature in the salons of the Rear Court and imperial princesses). In *Heianchō monogatari III*, ed. Nihon bungaku kenkyū shiryō kankōkai, pp. 262–75. Yūseidō, 1979.

——. *"Sagoromo monogatari"* (The Tale of Sagoromo). In *Monogatari bungaku no keifu I: Heian monogatari.* Vol. 3 of *Taikei monogatari bungakushi*, ed. Mitani Eiichi, pp. 348–55. Yūseidō, 1983.

——. *"Sagoromo monogatari" no kenkyū: denbon keitōron hen* (Research on *The Tale of Sagoromo*: manuscript lineages). Kasama shoin, 2000.

——. *"Sagoromo monogatari" no kenkyū: ihon bungakuron hen* (Research on *The Tale of Sagoromo*: variants). Kasama shoin, 2002.

——, and Sekine Yoshiko. "Kaisetsu." In *Sagoromo monogatari*, pp. 3–22.

Mitani Kuniaki. *Nyūmon "Genji monogatari"* (An introduction to *The Tale of Genji*). Chikuma shobō, 1997.

Morioka Tsuneo. "*Hamamatsu chūnagon monogatari* no kenkyū" (Research on *The Tale of the Hamamatsu Middle Counselor*). In *HM IV*, pp. 159–80.

Morishita Sumiaki. "Kohon *Sumiyoshi monogatari* to *Sagoromo monogatari*: Asukai no monogatari to no kankei" (The early version of *The Tale of Sumiyoshi* and *The Tale of Sagoromo*: the link to the tale of Asukai). In *"Sagoromo monogatari" no shikai*, ed. Ōchō monogatari kenkyūkai, pp. 126–43. Shintensha, 1994.

Morris, Ivan, trans. *As I Crossed a Bridge of Dreams.* New York: Penguin Books, 1975.

——, trans. *The Pillow Book of Sei Shōnagon.* New York: Penguin Books, 1967.

——. *The World of the Shining Prince: Court Life in Ancient Japan.* New York: Knopf, 1969.

Morris, Mark. "Desire and the Prince: New Work on *Genji monogatari*—A Review Article." *Journal of Asian Studies* 49. 2 (May 1990): 291–304.

Mumyōzōshi (The Untitled Book). Ed. Kuwabara Hiroshi. *SNKS*, vol. 34.

Murase, Miyeko. *Iconography of* The Tale of Genji*: Genji Monogatari Ekotoba*. New York: Weatherhill, 1983.

Murofushi Shinsuke. "Monogatari bungaku wa naze ren'ai o tēma to shitsuzuketanoka" (Why did tale literature continue to take love as its theme?). *Kokubungaku: kaishaku to kyōzai no kenkyū* 42, no. 2 (Feb. 1997): 54–60.

Muromachi jidai monogatari taisei (Collection of Muromachi period tales). Ed. Yokoyama Shigeru and Matsumoto Takanobu. Vol. 6. Kadokawa shoten, 1978.

Nagai Kazuko. *"Nezame monogatari" no kenkyū* (Research on *The Tale of Nezame*). Kasama shoin, 1968.

———. "*Yoru no nezame* monogatari" (The Tale of *Nezame at Night*). In *Monogatari bungaku no keifu I: Heian monogatari, Taikei monogatari bungakushi*, ed. Mitani Eiichi, pp. 313–16. Yūseidō, 1983.

Nakamura Shinichirō. "*Yowa no nezame* to gendai" (*Nezame at Midnight* and the present). *Nihon koten bungaku zenshū geppō* 39 (Oct. 1974): 1–3.

Noguchi Motohiro. "*Yoru no nezame* no shudai to kōzō: 'yoru no nezame tayuru yo naku to zo'" (The theme of *Nezame at Night*: 'they say the sleepless nights never ended'). In *HM IV*, pp. 243–62.

Nomura Kazumi. "*Yoru no Nezame* to Dewa no Ben" (*Nezame at Night* and Ben of Dewa). *Heian bungaku kenkyū* 46.6 (June 1971): 117–25.

Nunomura Hiroshi. "*Yoru no nezame* no shudai: genjitsu kyohi no ronri" (The theme of *Nezame at Night*: the logic of rejecting reality). In *Tezaki Masao kyōju taikan kinen ronshū*, ed. Tezaki Masao kyōju taikan kinen jigyō iinkai, pp. 18–32. Toyama: Toyama Daigaku jinbun gakubu, 1980.

Okada, H. Richard. *Figures of Resistance: Language, Poetry, and Narrating in* The Tale of Genji *and Other Mid-Heian Texts*. Durham, NC: Duke University Press, 1991.

Ōkagami (The Great Mirror). Ed. Tachibana Kenji. *NKBZ*, vol. 20.

Pekarik, Andrew. "Rivals in Love." In *Ukifune: Love in The Tale of Genji*, ed. Andrew Pekarik, pp. 217–30. New York: Columbia University Press, 1982.

Pollack, David. *The Fracture of Meaning: Japan's Synthesis of China from the Eighth through the Eighteenth Centuries*. Princeton, NJ: Princeton University Press, 1986.

The Princeton Companion to Classical Japanese Literature. Ed. Earl Miner, Hiroko Odagiri, and Robert E. Morrell. Princeton, NJ: Princeton University Press, 1985.

Quennell, Peter, ed. *Genius in the Drawing Room: The Literary Salon in the Nineteenth and Twentieth Centuries*. London: Weidenfeld and Nicolson, 1980.

Radway, Janice A. *Reading the Romance: Women, Patriarchy, and Popular Literature*. Chapel Hill, NC: University of North Carolina Press, 1991.

Richard, Kenneth. "Developments in Late Heian Prose Fiction: 'The Tale of Nezame.'" Ph.D. diss., University of Washington, 1973.

Rohlich, Thomas. "In Search of Critical Space: The Path to *Monogatari* Criticism in the *Mumyōzōshi*." *Harvard Journal of Asiatic Studies* 57, no. 1 (Jun. 1997): 179–204.

——, trans. *A Tale of Eleventh-Century Japan: Hamamatsu Chūnagon Monogatari*. Princeton, NJ: Princeton University Press, 1983.

Sagoromo monogatari (The Tale of Sagoromo). Ed. Mitani Eiichi and Sekine Yoshiko. *NKBT*, vol. 79.

Sagoromo no shitahimo (Sagoromo's sash strings). In *"Sagoromo monogatari" kochūshaku taisei*, pp. 427–510. Nihon tosho sentâ, 1979.

Saiki Yasutaka. "*Sagoromo monogatari* ni okeru menoto no yakuwari: Onna Ni no Miya monogatari, Asukai Onnagimi monogatari, Imahimegimi monogatari o chūshin ni" (The role of wet nurses in *The Tale of Sagoromo*: the tales of the Second Princess, Asukai, and Imahimegimi). In *"Sagoromo monogatari" no shikai*, ed. Ōchō monogatari kenkyūkai, pp. 195–208. Shintensha, 1994.

Sakakura Atsuyoshi. "'*Yoru no nezame*' to '*Yowa no nezame*'" ('*Nezame at Night*' and '*Nezame at Midnight*'). In *HM IV*, pp. 236–42.

Sakamoto Nobumichi. "Ongaku denshōdan no keifu: *Genji monogatari* Akashi ichizoku kara *Yoru no nezame* e" (The lineage of the musical transmission story: from *The Tale of Genji*'s Akashi family to *Nezame at Night*). *Bungaku* 56.4 (April 1988): 25–39.

Sakamoto Shōzō. *Fujiwara Yorimichi no jidai: sekkan seiji kara insei e* (The age of Fujiwara Yorimichi: from marriage politics to retired emperor rule). Heibonsha, 1991.

Sarashina nikki (The Sarashina Diary). In *Izumi Shikibu nikki, Murasaki Shikibu nikki, Sarashina nikki, Sanuki no suke nikki*, ed. Fujioka Tadaharu et al, pp. 283–362. *NKBZ*, vol. 18.

Sarra, Edith. *Fictions of Femininity: Literary Inventions of Gender in Japanese Court Women's Memoirs*. Stanford, CA: Stanford University Press, 1999.

Sekine Kenji. *Monogatari bungakuron: "Genji monogatari" zengo* (A theory on tale literature: before and after *The Tale of Genji*). Ōfūsha, 1980.

Sekine Yoshiko. "*Nezame* daigo kō" (Thoughts on *Nezame's* title). In *HM IV*, pp. 213–20.

Shirane, Haruo. *The Bridge of Dreams: A Poetics of "The Tale of Genji."* Stanford, CA: Stanford University Press, 1987.

——. "The Uji Chapters and the Denial of the Romance." In *Ukifune: Love in* The Tale of Genji, ed. Andrew Pekarik, pp. 113–38. New York: Columbia University Press, 1982.

Shūkan Hikaru Genji henshūbu. *Shūkan Hikaru Genji: "Genji monogatari" o josei shūkanshi fū ni yomu* (The Shining Genji weekly: reading *The Tale of Genji* like a women's magazine). Nāpuru, 1998.

Smits, Ivo. "Poets in their Place: Reflections on Poetic Salons in Early Medieval Japan." *The Medieval History Journal* 1, no. 2 (July–Dec. 1998): 291–309.

Sorensen, Joseph Tsuyoshi. "Contest and Context: *Monogatari nihyakuban uta awase* and the Poetry Contest Genre." M.A. thesis, University of California, Berkeley, 1999.

Southard, Bruce. "The Language of Science-Fiction Fan Magazines." *American Speech* 57, no. 1 (Spring 1982): 19–31.

Suda, Haruko. *Heian jidai kōkyū oyobi joshi no kenkyū* (Research on the Heian period Rear Court and female court officials). Chiyoda shobō, 1982.

Suzuki Hiromichi. *"Nezame monogatari" no kisoteki kenkyū* (Basic research on *The Tale of Nezame*). Hanawa shobō, 1965.

Suzuki Kazuo. "Nezame no Ue no miryoku" (The appeal of Lady Nezame). *Nihon koten bungaku zenshū geppō* 39 (Oct. 1974): 6–8.

Suzuki Yasue. "*Sagoromo monogatari* to kinki: *Hōjō no umi* e no tensei o shiya ni irete" (*The Tale of Sagoromo* and the taboo: their rebirth in *The Sea of Fertility*). In *Monogatari: sono tensei to saisei*, ed. Monogatari kenkyūkai, pp. 368–88. Yūseidō, 1994.

Takahashi Rumiko. *The Return of Lum Urusei Yatsura: Feudal Furor.* Adapted by Gerard Jones. San Francisco, CA: Viz Communications, 1997.

Takahashi Tōru. *Monogatari to e no enkinhō* (Tales and artistic perspective). Perikansha, 1991.

Taketori monogatari (The Tale of the Bamboo Cutter). In *Taketori monogatari, Ise monogatari, Yamato monogatari, Heichū monogatari*, ed. Katagiri Yōichi et al., pp. 51–108. *NKBZ*, vol. 8.

Tokoro Kyōko. "Saiin Baishi naishinnō no jiseki" (The achievements of Kamo priestess Princess Baishi). In *Kōki sekkan jidaishi no kenkyū*, ed. Kodaigaku kyōkai, pp. 691–721. Yoshikawa kōbunkan, 1990.

Totman, Conrad. *Japan before Perry: A Short History*. Berkeley, CA: University of California Press, 1981.

Tsunoda Bun'ei. "Kōkyū no rekishi" (History of the Rear Court). In *KS*, pp. 35–78.

———. "Nihon bunka to kōkyū" (Japanese culture and the Rear Court). In *KS*, pp. 6–13.

Tsushima Yūko. *Hi no kawa no hotori de* (On the Banks of the River of Fire). Kōdansha, 1988.

Tyler, Royall. "Lady Murasaki's Erotic Entertainment: The Early Chapters of *The Tale of Genji*." *East Asian History* 12 (Dec. 1996): 65–78.

———, trans. *The Tale of Genji*. New York: Penguin Books, 2001.

Ury, Marian. "Chinese Learning and Intellectual Life." In *Heian Japan*, ed. Donald Shively and William H. McCullough, pp. 341–89. Cambridge, UK: Cambridge University Press, 1999.

———. "Tales of *Genji*." *Harvard Journal of Asiatic Studies* 51, no. 1 (Jun. 1991): 263–308.

Woolf, Virginia. "THE TALE OF GENJI: The First Volume of Mr. Arthur Waley's Translation of a Great Japanese Novel by the Lady Murasaki." *Vogue* (London) 66.2 (Late Jul. 1925): 53, 80.

Yamanaka Yutaka. "Kōkyū: sono naimen" (Inside the Rear Court). In *KS*, pp. 14–26.

———. "Nichijō" (The day-to-day). In *KS*, pp. 99–104.

Yokoi Takashi. "*Nezame* ron: 'onna no monogatari' to shite (josetsu)" (On *Nezame*: considering it as "a woman's tale"). Reprinted in *HM IV*, pp. 277–85.

Yoru no nezame (Nezame at Night). Ed. Sakakura Atsuyoshi. *NKBT*, vol. 78.

Yoshikai Naoto. *Heianchō no menototachi: "Genji monogatari" e no kaitei* (Wet nurses at the Heian court: a guide to *The Tale of Genji*). Kyoto: Sekai shisōsha, 1995.

Yoshimura Junko. *Shinrigaku de yomitoku "Genji monogatari" no onna to otoko* (Reading *The Tale of Genji*'s Men and Women through Psychology). Kanazawa: Hokkoku shinbunsha, 1999.

Yura Yayoi. *"Genji monogatari": nemuranai himetachi* (*The Tale of Genji*: Women Who Don't Sleep). Mikasa shobō, 2000.

Glossary

This list is not meant to be an exhaustive catalogue of Japanese terms used in this study nor are the definitions exceedingly precise. It simply glosses some of the most useful words for discussing late Heian tale fiction, to give students a vocabulary on the subject. I have also included one phrase with no Japanese equivalent ("mid-ranks romance"), since as noted in the Introduction to this study, I find it conceptually helpful for Heian fiction in general.

attendant *nyōbō* 女房	female employee of a household in the Rear Court
attendant literature *nyōbō bungaku* 女房文学	texts written by attendants, particularly tale fiction; notable in part for its depiction of Rear Court culture
epigone *aryū* 亜流	derivative text or figure
expedient means *hōben* 方便	unorthodox, usually pragmatic method achieving a desired end, such as someone's enlightenment
Genji curse *Genji no jubaku* 源氏の呪縛	condition humorously said to afflict "late Heian" fiction, in which critics deride tales as "epigones" of *The Tale of Genji*

Heian (period) *Heian jidai* 平安時代	historical era from roughly 794–1185, when power resided in the imperial capital of Heian (modern Kyoto)
Kaoru-type *Kaoru-gata* 薫型	stock hero popular in post-*Tale of Genji* tale fiction; modeled after *Genji*'s Kaoru and notable for his melancholy and oft-stated (but seldom realized) desire to become a monk
keepsake *katami* 形見	souvenir of a lost lover or relative; in tale fiction, usually another person; see also "substitute" and "link"
late Heian (period) *Heian kōki* 平安後期	historical era from roughly the mid-eleventh century to the transfer of power outside of the imperial capital in 1185
late Heian tales *Heian kōki monogatari* 平安後期物語	court tales written in the late Heian period; in this study, particularly *Sagoromo*, *Hamamatsu*, and *Nezame*
Latter Days of the Law *mappō* 末法	Buddhist millenial period believed to have begun in 1052; associated with spiritual decay and widespread disruptions in the social order
lavender links *murasaki no yukari* 紫の縁	*The Tale of Genji* "link" for Fujitsubo in particular; named for Fujitsubo's niece Murasaki, who shares an additional tie with her aunt due to their common association with purple flowers or roots
link *yukari* 縁	character related to and usually used as a surrogate for a lost lover or relative; see also "keepsake" and "substitute"
main chapters *seihen* 正編	primary part of a narrative; in *The Tale of Genji*, the chapters up to Genji's death
main wife *kita no kata* 北の方	formal wife of an aristocrat; usually from the most powerful family in his (sexual) acquaintance

marriage politics *sekkan seiji* 摂関政治	strategy, perfected by the Fujiwara clan, of marrying daughters to princes and emperors to produce imperial grandsons and future patrons
middle ranks *naka no shina* 中の品	middle levels of the Heian aristocracy, typically the provincial-governor class; said in *The Tale of Genji* to be the source of the most interesting women because families move in and out of this category depending on their political and/or economic success
midranks romance	my term for the love affairs between nobles and middle ranks women
"noble in exile story" *kishu ryūritan* 貴種流離譚	plot convention of the tale genre in which a protagonist of noble birth goes into exile, suffers, and returns in glory to the capital
plot convention *wakei* 話形	sequence of events regularly used to structure a narrative
Rear Court *kōkyū* 後宮	imperial women's quarters, including the households of women intimate with the emperor and princesses
substitute *katashiro* 形代	surrogate for a lost lover or relative; see also "keepsake" and "link"
supplementary chapters *zokuhen* 続編	secondary part of or sequel to a narrative; in *The Tale of Genji*, the chapters after Genji's death

Index

Harvard East Asian Monographs
(*out-of-print)

- *1. Liang Fang-chung, *The Single-Whip Method of Taxation in China*
- *2. Harold C. Hinton, *The Grain Tribute System of China, 1845–1911*
- 3. Ellsworth C. Carlson, *The Kaiping Mines, 1877–1912*
- *4. Chao Kuo-chün, *Agrarian Policies of Mainland China: A Documentary Study, 1949–1956*
- *5. Edgar Snow, *Random Notes on Red China, 1936–1945*
- *6. Edwin George Beal, Jr., *The Origin of Likin, 1835–1864*
- 7. Chao Kuo-chün, *Economic Planning and Organization in Mainland China: A Documentary Study, 1949–1957*
- *8. John K. Fairbank, *Ching Documents: An Introductory Syllabus*
- *9. Helen Yin and Yi-chang Yin, *Economic Statistics of Mainland China, 1949–1957*
- 10. Wolfgang Franke, *The Reform and Abolition of the Traditional Chinese Examination System*
- 11. Albert Feuerwerker and S. Cheng, *Chinese Communist Studies of Modern Chinese History*
- 12. C. John Stanley, *Late Ching Finance: Hu Kuang-yung as an Innovator*
- 13. S. M. Meng, *The Tsungli Yamen: Its Organization and Functions*
- *14. Ssu-yü Teng, *Historiography of the Taiping Rebellion*
- 15. Chun-Jo Liu, *Controversies in Modern Chinese Intellectual History: An Analytic Bibliography of Periodical Articles, Mainly of the May Fourth and Post-May Fourth Era*
- *16. Edward J. M. Rhoads, *The Chinese Red Army, 1927–1963: An Annotated Bibliography*
- *17. Andrew J. Nathan, *A History of the China International Famine Relief Commission*
- *18. Frank H. H. King (ed.) and Prescott Clarke, *A Research Guide to China-Coast Newspapers, 1822–1911*
- *19. Ellis Joffe, *Party and Army: Professionalism and Political Control in the Chinese Officer Corps, 1949–1964*

*20. Toshio G. Tsukahira, *Feudal Control in Tokugawa Japan: The Sankin Kōtai System*
*21. Kwang-Ching Liu, ed., *American Missionaries in China: Papers from Harvard Seminars*
*22. George Moseley, *A Sino-Soviet Cultural Frontier: The Ili Kazakh Autonomous Chou*
23. Carl F. Nathan, *Plague Prevention and Politics in Manchuria, 1910–1931*
*24. Adrian Arthur Bennett, *John Fryer: The Introduction of Western Science and Technology into Nineteenth-Century China*
*25. Donald J. Friedman, *The Road from Isolation: The Campaign of the American Committee for Non-Participation in Japanese Aggression, 1938–1941*
*26. Edward LeFevour, *Western Enterprise in Late Ching China: A Selective Survey of Jardine, Matheson and Company's Operations, 1842–1895*
27. Charles Neuhauser, *Third World Politics: China and the Afro-Asian People's Solidarity Organization, 1957–1967*
*28. Kungtu C. Sun, assisted by Ralph W. Huenemann, *The Economic Development of Manchuria in the First Half of the Twentieth Century*
*29. Shahid Javed Burki, *A Study of Chinese Communes, 1965*
30. John Carter Vincent, *The Extraterritorial System in China: Final Phase*
31. Madeleine Chi, *China Diplomacy, 1914–1918*
*32. Clifton Jackson Phillips, *Protestant America and the Pagan World: The First Half Century of the American Board of Commissioners for Foreign Missions, 1810–1860*
*33. James Pusey, *Wu Han: Attacking the Present Through the Past*
*34. Ying-wan Cheng, *Postal Communication in China and Its Modernization, 1860–1896*
35. Tuvia Blumenthal, *Saving in Postwar Japan*
36. Peter Frost, *The Bakumatsu Currency Crisis*
37. Stephen C. Lockwood, *Augustine Heard and Company, 1858–1862*
38. Robert R. Campbell, *James Duncan Campbell: A Memoir by His Son*
39. Jerome Alan Cohen, ed., *The Dynamics of China's Foreign Relations*
40. V. V. Vishnyakova-Akimova, *Two Years in Revolutionary China, 1925–1927,* trans. Steven L. Levine
41. Meron Medzini, *French Policy in Japan During the Closing Years of the Tokugawa Regime*
42. Ezra Vogel, Margie Sargent, Vivienne B. Shue, Thomas Jay Mathews, and Deborah S. Davis, *The Cultural Revolution in the Provinces*
43. Sidney A. Forsythe, *An American Missionary Community in China, 1895–1905*
*44. Benjamin I. Schwartz, ed., *Reflections on the May Fourth Movement.: A Symposium*
*45. Ching Young Choe, *The Rule of the Taewŏngun, 1864–1873: Restoration in Yi Korea*
46. W. P. J. Hall, *A Bibliographical Guide to Japanese Research on the Chinese Economy, 1958–1970*
47. Jack J. Gerson, *Horatio Nelson Lay and Sino-British Relations, 1854–1864*

48. Paul Richard Bohr, *Famine and the Missionary: Timothy Richard as Relief Administrator and Advocate of National Reform*
49. Endymion Wilkinson, *The History of Imperial China: A Research Guide*
50. Britten Dean, *China and Great Britain: The Diplomacy of Commercial Relations, 1860–1864*
51. Ellsworth C. Carlson, *The Foochow Missionaries, 1847–1880*
52. Yeh-chien Wang, *An Estimate of the Land-Tax Collection in China, 1753 and 1908*
53. Richard M. Pfeffer, *Understanding Business Contracts in China, 1949–1963*
*54. Han-sheng Chuan and Richard Kraus, *Mid-Ching Rice Markets and Trade: An Essay in Price History*
55. Ranbir Vohra, *Lao She and the Chinese Revolution*
56. Liang-lin Hsiao, *China's Foreign Trade Statistics, 1864–1949*
*57. Lee-hsia Hsu Ting, *Government Control of the Press in Modern China, 1900–1949*
*58. Edward W. Wagner, *The Literati Purges: Political Conflict in Early Yi Korea*
*59. Joungwon A. Kim, *Divided Korea: The Politics of Development, 1945–1972*
60. Noriko Kamachi, John K. Fairbank, and Chūzō Ichiko, *Japanese Studies of Modern China Since 1953: A Bibliographical Guide to Historical and Social-Science Research on the Nineteenth and Twentieth Centuries, Supplementary Volume for 1953–1969*
61. Donald A. Gibbs and Yun-chen Li, *A Bibliography of Studies and Translations of Modern Chinese Literature, 1918–1942*
62. Robert H. Silin, *Leadership and Values: The Organization of Large-Scale Taiwanese Enterprises*
63. David Pong, *A Critical Guide to the Kwangtung Provincial Archives Deposited at the Public Record Office of London*
*64. Fred W. Drake, *China Charts the World: Hsu Chi-yü and His Geography of 1848*
*65. William A. Brown and Urgrunge Onon, translators and annotators, *History of the Mongolian People's Republic*
66. Edward L. Farmer, *Early Ming Government: The Evolution of Dual Capitals*
*67. Ralph C. Croizier, *Koxinga and Chinese Nationalism: History, Myth, and the Hero*
*68. William J. Tyler, tr., *The Psychological World of Natsume Sōseki*, by Doi Takeo
69. Eric Widmer, *The Russian Ecclesiastical Mission in Peking During the Eighteenth Century*
*70. Charlton M. Lewis, *Prologue to the Chinese Revolution: The Transformation of Ideas and Institutions in Hunan Province, 1891–1907*
71. Preston Torbert, *The Ching Imperial Household Department: A Study of Its Organization and Principal Functions, 1662–1796*
72. Paul A. Cohen and John E. Schrecker, eds., *Reform in Nineteenth-Century China*
73. Jon Sigurdson, *Rural Industrialism in China*
74. Kang Chao, *The Development of Cotton Textile Production in China*

75. Valentin Rabe, *The Home Base of American China Missions, 1880–1920*
*76. Sarasin Viraphol, *Tribute and Profit: Sino-Siamese Trade, 1652–1853*
77. Ch'i-ch'ing Hsiao, *The Military Establishment of the Yuan Dynasty*
78. Meishi Tsai, *Contemporary Chinese Novels and Short Stories, 1949–1974: An Annotated Bibliography*
*79. Wellington K. K. Chan, *Merchants, Mandarins and Modern Enterprise in Late Ching China*
80. Endymion Wilkinson, *Landlord and Labor in Late Imperial China: Case Studies from Shandong by Jing Su and Luo Lun*
*81. Barry Keenan, *The Dewey Experiment in China: Educational Reform and Political Power in the Early Republic*
*82. George A. Hayden, *Crime and Punishment in Medieval Chinese Drama: Three Judge Pao Plays*
*83. Sang-Chul Suh, *Growth and Structural Changes in the Korean Economy, 1910–1940*
84. J. W. Dower, *Empire and Aftermath: Yoshida Shigeru and the Japanese Experience, 1878–1954*
85. Martin Collcutt, *Five Mountains: The Rinzai Zen Monastic Institution in Medieval Japan*
86. Kwang Suk Kim and Michael Roemer, *Growth and Structural Transformation*
87. Anne O. Krueger, *The Developmental Role of the Foreign Sector and Aid*
*88. Edwin S. Mills and Byung-Nak Song, *Urbanization and Urban Problems*
89. Sung Hwan Ban, Pal Yong Moon, and Dwight H. Perkins, *Rural Development*
*90. Noel F. McGinn, Donald R. Snodgrass, Yung Bong Kim, Shin-Bok Kim, and Quee-Young Kim, *Education and Development in Korea*
*91. Leroy P. Jones and Il SaKong, *Government, Business, and Entrepreneurship in Economic Development: The Korean Case*
92. Edward S. Mason, Dwight H. Perkins, Kwang Suk Kim, David C. Cole, Mahn Je Kim et al., *The Economic and Social Modernization of the Republic of Korea*
93. Robert Repetto, Tai Hwan Kwon, Son-Ung Kim, Dae Young Kim, John E. Sloboda, and Peter J. Donaldson, *Economic Development, Population Policy, and Demographic Transition in the Republic of Korea*
94. Parks M. Coble, Jr., *The Shanghai Capitalists and the Nationalist Government, 1927–1937*
95. Noriko Kamachi, *Reform in China: Huang Tsun-hsien and the Japanese Model*
96. Richard Wich, *Sino-Soviet Crisis Politics: A Study of Political Change and Communication*
97. Lillian M. Li, *China's Silk Trade: Traditional Industry in the Modern World, 1842–1937*
98. R. David Arkush, *Fei Xiaotong and Sociology in Revolutionary China*
*99. Kenneth Alan Grossberg, *Japan's Renaissance: The Politics of the Muromachi Bakufu*
100. James Reeve Pusey, *China and Charles Darwin*

101. Hoyt Cleveland Tillman, *Utilitarian Confucianism: Chen Liang's Challenge to Chu Hsi*
102. Thomas A. Stanley, *Ōsugi Sakae, Anarchist in Taishō Japan: The Creativity of the Ego*
103. Jonathan K. Ocko, *Bureaucratic Reform in Provincial China: Ting Jih-ch'ang in Restoration Kiangsu, 1867–1870*
104. James Reed, *The Missionary Mind and American East Asia Policy, 1911–1915*
105. Neil L. Waters, *Japan's Local Pragmatists: The Transition from Bakumatsu to Meiji in the Kawasaki Region*
106. David C. Cole and Yung Chul Park, *Financial Development in Korea, 1945–1978*
107. Roy Bahl, Chuk Kyo Kim, and Chong Kee Park, *Public Finances During the Korean Modernization Process*
108. William D. Wray, *Mitsubishi and the N.Y.K, 1870–1914: Business Strategy in the Japanese Shipping Industry*
109. Ralph William Huenemann, *The Dragon and the Iron Horse: The Economics of Railroads in China, 1876–1937*
*110. Benjamin A. Elman, *From Philosophy to Philology: Intellectual and Social Aspects of Change in Late Imperial China*
111. Jane Kate Leonard, *Wei Yüan and China's Rediscovery of the Maritime World*
112. Luke S. K. Kwong, *A Mosaic of the Hundred Days:. Personalities, Politics, and Ideas of 1898*
*113. John E. Wills, Jr., *Embassies and Illusions: Dutch and Portuguese Envoys to K'ang-hsi, 1666–1687*
114. Joshua A. Fogel, *Politics and Sinology: The Case of Naitō Konan (1866–1934)*
*115. Jeffrey C. Kinkley, ed., *After Mao: Chinese Literature and Society, 1978–1981*
116. C. Andrew Gerstle, *Circles of Fantasy: Convention in the Plays of Chikamatsu*
117. Andrew Gordon, *The Evolution of Labor Relations in Japan: Heavy Industry, 1853–1955*
*118. Daniel K. Gardner, *Chu Hsi and the "Ta Hsueh": Neo-Confucian Reflection on the Confucian Canon*
119. Christine Guth Kanda, *Shinzō: Hachiman Imagery and Its Development*
*120. Robert Borgen, *Sugawara no Michizane and the Early Heian Court*
121. Chang-tai Hung, *Going to the People: Chinese Intellectual and Folk Literature, 1918–1937*
*122. Michael A. Cusumano, *The Japanese Automobile Industry: Technology and Management at Nissan and Toyota*
123. Richard von Glahn, *The Country of Streams and Grottoes: Expansion, Settlement, and the Civilizing of the Sichuan Frontier in Song Times*
124. Steven D. Carter, *The Road to Komatsubara: A Classical Reading of the Renga Hyakuin*
125. Katherine F. Bruner, John K. Fairbank, and Richard T. Smith, *Entering China's Service: Robert Hart's Journals, 1854–1863*

126. Bob Tadashi Wakabayashi, *Anti-Foreignism and Western Learning in Early-Modern Japan: The "New Theses" of 1825*
127. Atsuko Hirai, *Individualism and Socialism: The Life and Thought of Kawai Eijirō (1891–1944)*
128. Ellen Widmer, *The Margins of Utopia: "Shui-hu hou-chuan" and the Literature of Ming Loyalism*
129. R. Kent Guy, *The Emperor's Four Treasuries: Scholars and the State in the Late Chien-lung Era*
130. Peter C. Perdue, *Exhausting the Earth: State and Peasant in Hunan, 1500–1850*
131. Susan Chan Egan, *A Latterday Confucian: Reminiscences of William Hung (1893–1980)*
132. James T. C. Liu, *China Turning Inward: Intellectual-Political Changes in the Early Twelfth Century*
*133. Paul A. Cohen, *Between Tradition and Modernity: Wang T'ao and Reform in Late Ching China*
134. Kate Wildman Nakai, *Shogunal Politics: Arai Hakuseki and the Premises of Tokugawa Rule*
*135. Parks M. Coble, *Facing Japan: Chinese Politics and Japanese Imperialism, 1931–1937*
136. Jon L. Saari, *Legacies of Childhood: Growing Up Chinese in a Time of Crisis, 1890–1920*
137. Susan Downing Videen, *Tales of Heichū*
138. Heinz Morioka and Miyoko Sasaki, *Rakugo: The Popular Narrative Art of Japan*
139. Joshua A. Fogel, *Nakae Ushikichi in China: The Mourning of Spirit*
140. Alexander Barton Woodside, *Vietnam and the Chinese Model.: A Comparative Study of Vietnamese and Chinese Government in the First Half of the Nineteenth Century*
*141. George Elison, *Deus Destroyed: The Image of Christianity in Early Modern Japan*
142. William D. Wray, ed., *Managing Industrial Enterprise: Cases from Japan's Prewar Experience*
*143. T'ung-tsu Ch'ü, *Local Government in China Under the Ching*
144. Marie Anchordoguy, *Computers, Inc.: Japan's Challenge to IBM*
145. Barbara Molony, *Technology and Investment: The Prewar Japanese Chemical Industry*
146. Mary Elizabeth Berry, *Hideyoshi*
147. Laura E. Hein, *Fueling Growth: The Energy Revolution and Economic Policy in Postwar Japan*
148. Wen-hsin Yeh, *The Alienated Academy: Culture and Politics in Republican China, 1919–1937*
149. Dru C. Gladney, *Muslim Chinese: Ethnic Nationalism in the People's Republic*
150. Merle Goldman and Paul A. Cohen, eds., *Ideas Across Cultures: Essays on Chinese Thought in Honor of Benjamin L Schwartz*
151. James M. Polachek, *The Inner Opium War*
152. Gail Lee Bernstein, *Japanese Marxist: A Portrait of Kawakami Hajime, 1879–1946*

*153. Lloyd E. Eastman, *The Abortive Revolution: China Under Nationalist Rule, 1927–1937*
154. Mark Mason, *American Multinationals and Japan: The Political Economy of Japanese Capital Controls, 1899–1980*
155. Richard J. Smith, John K. Fairbank, and Katherine F. Bruner, *Robert Hart and China's Early Modernization: His Journals, 1863–1866*
156. George J. Tanabe, Jr., *Myōe the Dreamkeeper: Fantasy and Knowledge in Kamakura Buddhism*
157. William Wayne Farris, *Heavenly Warriors: The Evolution of Japan's Military, 500–1300*
158. Yu-ming Shaw, *An American Missionary in China: John Leighton Stuart and Chinese-American Relations*
159. James B. Palais, *Politics and Policy in Traditional Korea*
*160. Douglas Reynolds, *China, 1898–1912: The Xinzheng Revolution and Japan*
161. Roger R. Thompson, *China's Local Councils in the Age of Constitutional Reform, 1898–1911*
162. William Johnston, *The Modern Epidemic: History of Tuberculosis in Japan*
163. Constantine Nomikos Vaporis, *Breaking Barriers: Travel and the State in Early Modern Japan*
164. Irmela Hijiya-Kirschnereit, *Rituals of Self-Revelation: Shishōsetsu as Literary Genre and Socio-Cultural Phenomenon*
165. James C. Baxter, *The Meiji Unification Through the Lens of Ishikawa Prefecture*
166. Thomas R. H. Havens, *Architects of Affluence: The Tsutsumi Family and the Seibu-Saison Enterprises in Twentieth-Century Japan*
167. Anthony Hood Chambers, *The Secret Window: Ideal Worlds in Tanizaki's Fiction*
168. Steven J. Ericson, *The Sound of the Whistle: Railroads and the State in Meiji Japan*
169. Andrew Edmund Goble, *Kenmu: Go-Daigo's Revolution*
170. Denise Potrzeba Lett, *In Pursuit of Status: The Making of South Korea's "New" Urban Middle Class*
171. Mimi Hall Yiengpruksawan, *Hiraizumi: Buddhist Art and Regional Politics in Twelfth-Century Japan*
172. Charles Shirō Inouye, *The Similitude of Blossoms: A Critical Biography of Izumi Kyōka (1873–1939), Japanese Novelist and Playwright*
173. Aviad E. Raz, *Riding the Black Ship: Japan and Tokyo Disneyland*
174. Deborah J. Milly, *Poverty, Equality, and Growth: The Politics of Economic Need in Postwar Japan*
175. See Heng Teow, *Japan's Cultural Policy Toward China, 1918–1931: A Comparative Perspective*
176. Michael A. Fuller, *An Introduction to Literary Chinese*
177. Frederick R. Dickinson, *War and National Reinvention: Japan in the Great War, 1914–1919*

178. John Solt, *Shredding the Tapestry of Meaning: The Poetry and Poetics of Kitasono Katue (1902–1978)*
179. Edward Pratt, *Japan's Protoindustrial Elite: The Economic Foundations of the Gōnō*
180. Atsuko Sakaki, *Recontextualizing Texts: Narrative Performance in Modern Japanese Fiction*
181. Soon-Won Park, *Colonial Industrialization and Labor in Korea: The Onoda Cement Factory*
182. JaHyun Kim Haboush and Martina Deuchler, *Culture and the State in Late Chosŏn Korea*
183. John W. Chaffee, *Branches of Heaven: A History of the Imperial Clan of Sung China*
184. Gi-Wook Shin and Michael Robinson, eds., *Colonial Modernity in Korea*
185. Nam-lin Hur, *Prayer and Play in Late Tokugawa Japan: Asakusa Sensōji and Edo Society*
186. Kristin Stapleton, *Civilizing Chengdu: Chinese Urban Reform, 1895–1937*
187. Hyung Il Pai, *Constructing "Korean" Origins: A Critical Review of Archaeology, Historiography, and Racial Myth in Korean State-Formation Theories*
188. Brian D. Ruppert, *Jewel in the Ashes: Buddha Relics and Power in Early Medieval Japan*
189. Susan Daruvala, *Zhou Zuoren and an Alternative Chinese Response to Modernity*
*190. James Z. Lee, *The Political Economy of a Frontier: Southwest China, 1250–1850*
191. Kerry Smith, *A Time of Crisis: Japan, the Great Depression, and Rural Revitalization*
192. Michael Lewis, *Becoming Apart: National Power and Local Politics in Toyama, 1868–1945*
193. William C. Kirby, Man-houng Lin, James Chin Shih, and David A. Pietz, eds., *State and Economy in Republican China: A Handbook for Scholars*
194. Timothy S. George, *Minamata: Pollution and the Struggle for Democracy in Postwar Japan*
195. Billy K. L. So, *Prosperity, Region, and Institutions in Maritime China: The South Fukien Pattern, 946–1368*
196. Yoshihisa Tak Matsusaka, *The Making of Japanese Manchuria, 1904–1932*
197. Maram Epstein, *Competing Discourses: Orthodoxy, Authenticity, and Engendered Meanings in Late Imperial Chinese Fiction*
198. Curtis J. Milhaupt, J. Mark Ramseyer, and Michael K. Young, eds. and comps., *Japanese Law in Context: Readings in Society, the Economy, and Politics*
199. Haruo Iguchi, *Unfinished Business: Ayukawa Yoshisuke and U.S.-Japan Relations, 1937–1952*
200. Scott Pearce, Audrey Spiro, and Patricia Ebrey, *Culture and Power in the Reconstitution of the Chinese Realm, 200–600*
201. Terry Kawashima, *Writing Margins: The Textual Construction of Gender in Heian and Kamakura Japan*
202. Martin W. Huang, *Desire and Fictional Narrative in Late Imperial China*

203. Robert S. Ross and Jiang Changbin, eds., *Re-examining the Cold War: U.S.-China Diplomacy, 1954–1973*
204. Guanhua Wang, *In Search of Justice: The 1905–1906 Chinese Anti-American Boycott*
205. David Schaberg, *A Patterned Past: Form and Thought in Early Chinese Historiography*
206. Christine Yano, *Tears of Longing: Nostalgia and the Nation in Japanese Popular Song*
207. Milena Doleželová-Velingerová and Oldřich Král, with Graham Sanders, eds., *The Appropriation of Cultural Capital: China's May Fourth Project*
208. Robert N. Huey, *The Making of 'Shinkokinshū'*
209. Lee Butler, *Emperor and Aristocracy in Japan, 1467–1680: Resilience and Renewal*
210. Suzanne Ogden, *Inklings of Democracy in China*
211. Kenneth J. Ruoff, *The People's Emperor: Democracy and the Japanese Monarchy, 1945–1995*
212. Haun Saussy, *Great Walls of Discourse and Other Adventures in Cultural China*
213. Aviad E. Raz, *Emotions at Work: Normative Control, Organizations, and Culture in Japan and America*
214. Rebecca E. Karl and Peter Zarrow, eds., *Rethinking the 1898 Reform Period: Political and Cultural Change in Late Qing China*
215. Kevin O'Rourke, *The Book of Korean Shijo*
216. Ezra F. Vogel, ed., *The Golden Age of the U.S.-China-Japan Triangle, 1972–1989*
217. Thomas A. Wilson, ed., *On Sacred Grounds: Culture, Society, Politics, and the Formation of the Cult of Confucius*
218. Donald S. Sutton, *Steps of Perfection: Exorcistic Performers and Chinese Religion in Twentieth-Century Taiwan*
219. Daqing Yang, *Technology of Empire: Telecommunications and Japanese Expansionism, 1895–1945*
220. Qianshen Bai, *Fu Shan's World: The Transformation of Chinese Calligraphy in the Seventeenth Century*
221. Paul Jakov Smith and Richard von Glahn, eds., *The Song-Yuan-Ming Transition in Chinese History*
222. Rania Huntington, *Alien Kind: Foxes and Late Imperial Chinese Narrative*
223. Jordan Sand, *House and Home in Modern Japan: Architecture, Domestic Space, and Bourgeois Culture, 1880–1930*
224. Karl Gerth, *China Made: Consumer Culture and the Creation of the Nation*
225. Xiaoshan Yang, *Metamorphosis of the Private Sphere: Gardens and Objects in Tang-Song Poetry*
226. Barbara Mittler, *A Newspaper for China? Power, Identity, and Change in Shanghai's News Media, 1872–1912*
227. Joyce A. Madancy, *The Troublesome Legacy of Commissioner Lin: The Opium Trade and Opium Suppression in Fujian Province, 1820s to 1920s*

Harvard East Asian Monographs

228. John Makeham, *Transmitters and Creators: Chinese Commentators and Commentaries on the Analects*
229. Elisabeth Köll, *From Cotton Mill to Business Empire: The Emergence of Regional Enterprises in Modern China*
230. Emma Teng, *Taiwan's Imagined Geography: Chinese Colonial Travel Writing and Pictures, 1683–1895*
231. Wilt Idema and Beata Grant, *The Red Brush: Writing Women of Imperial China*
232. Eric C. Rath, *The Ethos of Noh: Actors and Their Art*
233. Elizabeth Remick, *Building Local States: China During the Republican and Post-Mao Eras*
234. Lynn Struve, ed., *The Qing Formation in World-Historical Time*
235. D. Max Moerman, *Localizing Paradise: Kumano Pilgrimage and the Religious Landscape of Premodern Japan*
236. Antonia Finnane, *Speaking of Yangzhou: A Chinese City, 1550–1850*
237. Brian Platt, *Burning and Building: Schooling and State Formation in Japan, 1750–1890*
238. Gail Bernstein, Andrew Gordon, and Kate Wildman Nakai, eds., *Public Spheres, Private Lives in Modern Japan, 1600–1950: Essays in Honor of Albert Craig*
239. Wu Hung and Katherine R. Tsiang, *Body and Face in Chinese Visual Culture*
240. Stephen Dodd, *Writing Home: Representations of the Native Place in Modern Japanese Literature*
241. David Anthony Bello, *Opium and the Limits of Empire: Drug Prohibition in the Chinese Interior, 1729–1850*
242. Hosea Hirata, *Discourses of Seduction: History, Evil, Desire, and Modern Japanese Literature*
243. Kyung Moon Hwang, *Beyond Birth: Social Status in the Emergence of Modern Korea*
244. Brian R. Dott, *Identity Reflections: Pilgrimages to Mount Tai in Late Imperial China*
245. Mark McNally, *Proving the Way: Conflict and Practice in the History of Japanese Nativism*
246. Yongping Wu, *A Political Explanation of Economic Growth: State Survival, Bureaucratic Politics, and Private Enterprises in the Making of Taiwan's Economy, 1950–1985*
247. Kyu Hyun Kim, *The Age of Visions and Arguments: Parliamentarianism and the National Public Sphere in Early Meiji Japan*
248. Zvi Ben-Dor Benite, *The Dao of Muhammad: A Cultural History of Muslims in Late Imperial China*
249. David Der-wei Wang and Shang Wei, eds., *Dynastic Crisis and Cultural Innovation: From the Late Ming to the Late Qing and Beyond*
250. Wilt L. Idema, Wai-yee Li, and Ellen Widmer, eds., *Trauma and Transcendence in Early Qing Literature*
251. Barbara Molony and Kathleen Uno, eds., *Gendering Modern Japanese History*

252. Hiroshi Aoyagi, *Islands of Eight Million Smiles: Idol Performance and Symbolic Production in Contemporary Japan*
253. Wai-yee Li, *The Readability of the Past in Early Chinese Historiography*
254. William C. Kirby, Robert S. Ross, and Gong Li, eds., *Normalization of U.S.-China Relations: An International History*
255. Ellen Gardner Nakamura, *Practical Pursuits: Takano Chōei, Takahashi Keisaku, and Western Medicine in Nineteenth-Century Japan*
256. Jonathan W. Best, *A History of the Early Korean Kingdom of Paekche, together with an annotated translation of* The Paekche Annals *of the* Samguk sagi
257. Liang Pan, *The United Nations in Japan's Foreign and Security Policymaking, 1945–1992: National Security, Party Politics, and International Status*
258. Richard Belsky, *Localities at the Center: Native Place, Space, and Power in Late Imperial Beijing*
259. Zwia Lipkin, *"Useless to the State": "Social Problems" and Social Engineering in Nationalist Nanjing, 1927–1937*
260. William O. Gardner, *Advertising Tower: Japanese Modernism and Modernity in the 1920s*
261. Stephen Owen, *The Making of Early Chinese Classical Poetry*
262. Martin J. Powers, *Pattern and Person: Ornament, Society, and Self in Classical China*
263. Anna M. Shields, *Crafting a Collection: The Cultural Contexts and Poetic Practice of the* Huajian ji 花間集 *(Collection from Among the Flowers)*
264. Stephen Owen, *The Late Tang: Chinese Poetry of the Mid-Ninth Century (827–860)*
265. Sara L. Friedman, *Intimate Politics: Marriage, the Market, and State Power in Southeastern China*
266. Patricia Buckley Ebrey and Maggie Bickford, *Emperor Huizong and Late Northern Song China: The Politics of Culture and the Culture of Politics*
267. Sophie Volpp, *Worldly Stage: Theatricality in Seventeenth-Century China*
268. Ellen Widmer, *The Beauty and the Book: Women and Fiction in Nineteenth-Century China*
269. Steven B. Miles, *The Sea of Learning: Mobility and Identity in Nineteenth-Century Guangzhou*
270. Lin Man-houng, *China Upside Down: Currency, Society, and Ideologies, 1808–1856*
271. Ronald Egan, *The Problem of Beauty: Aesthetic Thought and Pursuits in Northern Song Dynasty China*
272. Mark Halperin, *Out of the Cloister: Literati Perspectives on Buddhism in Sung China, 960–1279*
273. Helen Dunstan, *State or Merchant? Political Economy and Political Process in 1740s China*
274. Sabina Knight, *The Heart of Time: Moral Agency in Twentieth-Century Chinese Fiction*

275. Timothy J. Van Compernolle, *The Uses of Memory: The Critique of Modernity in the Fiction of Higuchi Ichiyō*
276. Paul Rouzer, *A New Practical Primer of Literary Chinese*
277. Jonathan Zwicker, *Practices of the Sentimental Imagination: Melodrama, the Novel, and the Social Imaginary in Nineteenth-Century Japan*
278. Franziska Seraphim, *War Memory and Social Politics in Japan, 1945–2005*
279. Adam L. Kern, *Manga from the Floating World: Comicbook Culture and the* Kibyōshi *of Edo Japan*
280. Cynthia J. Brokaw, *Commerce in Culture: The Sibao Book Trade in the Qing and Republican Periods*
281. Eugene Y. Park, *Between Dreams and Reality: The Military Examination in Late Chosŏn Korea, 1600–1894*
282. Nam-lin Hur, *Death and Social Order in Tokugawa Japan: Buddhism, Anti-Christianity, and the Danka System*
283. Patricia M. Thornton, *Disciplining the State: Virtue, Violence, and State-Making in Modern China*
284. Vincent Goossaert, *The Taoists of Peking, 1800–1949: A Social History of Urban Clerics*
285. Peter Nickerson, *Taoism, Bureaucracy, and Popular Religion in Early Medieval China*
286. Charo B. D'Etcheverry, *Love After* The Tale of Genji*: Rewriting the World of the Shining Prince*